BROWN UNIVERSITY STUDIES

VOLUME X

Americana Series No. 1

THE JOURNALS OF CHARLES KING NEWCOMB

CHARLES KING NEWCOMB

Reproduced from the *Journals of Ralph Waldo Emerson*, Houghton Mifflin Company, 1912. Original daguerreotype in the possession of Miss Sarah N. Gallagher.

THE JOURNALS OF CHARLES KING NEWCOMB

EDITED, WITH A BIOGRAPHICAL AND CRITICAL
INTRODUCTION

BY

JUDITH KENNEDY JOHNSON, Ph.D.

BROWN UNIVERSITY
PROVIDENCE, RHODE ISLAND
1946

COMPOSED, PRINTED AND BOUND BY
THE GEORGE BANTA PUBLISHING COMPANY, MENASHA, WISCONSIN

PREFACE

To students of New England Transcendentalism Charles King Newcomb has been a source of no little interest and speculation. But they have known little more than that he was a friend of Emerson, a Brook Farmer, a graduate of Brown University, and the writer of voluminous journals.

Newcomb lived from 1820 to 1894. The first fifty years of his life were spent mainly in Providence. It was here that Margaret Fuller became acquainted with the young man. She especially appreciated his "pervasive insight" and his "proud perception almost on equal grounds of Homer and Aeschylus, of Dante and Petrarch." Later, with the help of Emerson, she persuaded him to contribute "The Two Dolons" to *The Dial*. This sketch was the only work of his ever published.

Between 1841 and 1845 he was a boarder at Brook Farm, where most of the members regarded him as a strange genius. A typical impression of him was that formed by George Willis Cooke, who described him as "one of the more brilliant and erratic of those who were connected with the farm." Cooke added regretfully that nothing survived of him save "a few traditions and anecdotes."

The highest praise and most careful consideration of Newcomb is found in the writings of Emerson. He characterized Newcomb's manuscripts as "full of subtle genius." In 1859 he paid him the most amazing tribute of all. After a visit with Caroline Sturgis, Emerson wrote: "I knew that she saw, as I saw, that his mind was far richer than mine, which fact nobody but she and I knew or suspected. . . . And now, sixteen years later, we two alone possess this secret still."

My intention in making selections from the Newcomb *Journals* has been to reproduce the parts which are the most valuable, interesting, and typical. Instead of presenting the material chronologically as it appeared in the diary I have divided it according to its subject-matter. In reading over the *Journals* Newcomb, himself, noticed that the writing tended to run into certain channels. After he had written five volumes he gave his work the title of "Principles of Life, illustrated in thoughts on Nature, Scholarship, Shakspear, Government, the war of the great American Rebellion, & Morals & Man in general." My divisions were suggested by the ones which Newcomb thought of, but I have reduced their number. "Arts and Letters" is the equivalent of "Scholarship" and "Shakspear." "Society and Government" includes both "Government" and "the war of the Great American Rebellion," as well as Newcomb's sketches of life in Philadelphia. "Man and Morals" is a rather miscellaneous section which contains "Morals & Man in general," and also "Action" and "Gymnasty," elements which Newcomb added to the title in Volumes Six and Fourteen.

The misspellings and word-coinages have been preserved. Some of the more common are listed here: *apocylypse, agreable, burley, diletanttism, ecstacy, idiocyncracy, metyphisical, mediocer, normaller, plebianism, personication, ventillated,* and *verisimilearity.* He usually inserted an extra letter in words like *detatch, alledge,* or *priviledge;* he almost always preferred *s* to *z* in words like *hase, blase, Elisabeth;* and he consistently omitted the *e* in compounds beginning with *fore-.* He also coined words by adding unexpected endings to words in ordinary use: *biographised, busybodyism, demagoguism, gradationalism, heroicism, invalidcy, isolately, incidentalism, mythologism, practive, practible, soloquial.* In general he did not use an apostrophe in the possessive case.

I should like to thank Miss Sarah N. Gallagher and Mrs. R. Edwards Annin, owners of the Newcomb manuscripts, for permission to edit the *Journals* and for their kindness in sharing with me information and anecdotes about the Newcomb family, and the Houghton Library of Harvard University for permission to quote from the Margaret Fuller manuscripts. Mrs. E. E. Built and Mr. J. S. Jackson of the Special Collections Division of Brown University Library have been extremely helpful in making the Newcomb manuscripts more easily accessible. I am especially grateful to Professor Randall Stewart, who first suggested that I might write about Charles King Newcomb. His kindly encouragement helped me over the bleaker expanses of thesis-writing, and his thoughtful criticism and suggestions have been invaluable.

J. K. J.

Montreal, August 20, 1945.

TABLE OF CONTENTS

THE JOURNALS OF CHARLES KING NEWCOMB

INTRODUCTION

CHAPTER ONE

BIOGRAPHY

Section I. Formative Years

WHEN Lieutenant Henry S. Newcomb died in a shipwreck, in December of 1825, he left a wife and six children. His eldest son, Charles, was five years old at the time. With the exception of Sarah, the other children were all younger.

Lieutenant Newcomb was the son of the Honorable Daniel Newcomb of Keene, New Hampshire. Before he joined the navy he had had two years at a college in northern New England and had, after two more years, graduated from Harvard. His steadiness and efficiency won him distinction in his profession and were several times noted in Cooper's *History of the Navy*.[1] His most important service was his share in the defence of Baltimore in 1812. There, commanding eighty seamen from the *Guerrière,* he held Fort Covington and kept up a lively fire which was instrumental in repulsing the attackers. The grateful citizens of Baltimore afterwards presented him with a golden sword.

Charles Newcomb's father was little more than a memory to him. Probably the only influence he had lay in the contrast which his son perceived between their two lives: the one healthy, full, and active; the other sickly, restricted, and studious. At the age of forty-six Newcomb had a rare moment of self-revelation; he wrote in his journal:

This son knows what his father's virtue must have been by the traits in himself which bear steady consciousness to his own shortcoming in conduct: the parent's blood runs flashing through the consciousness of the weaker child.[2] (J, IX, 139)

When Newcomb was a boy of nine, or thereabouts, he and his

---

[1] See J. F. Cooper, *History of the Navy*, 1840, II, 221-222.
[2] References to Newcomb's original manuscript works are given as follows: J, IX, 139, means Journals, volume IX, p. 139. CB, 1848, 162, means Commonplace Book for 1848, p. 162.

brother Henry were sent away to school in Plainfield, Connecticut. His mother's sister had been the first wife of the Honorable Joseph Eaton of Plainfield. It was with the Eaton family that the little Newcomb boys lived while they went to school.

Charles was his mother's favorite child; he was weakly, sensitive, and probably undersized. It is not especially surprising that he protested against being thrust out of the soft shelter of his home and into the less protected atmosphere of a school for young boys. Many years later he wrote that it was no wonder that men ranged far from home and became indifferent sons, brothers, and husbands

when they are ruthlessly torn, at early boyhood, from family influence & comfort, & thrown, during some of the tenderest & most formative years of their lives, into boarding-houses, boarding-schools, universities, & markets—until they are almost grown men. (J, IX, 249)

Neither Charles nor Henry enjoyed letter-writing, and, as might be expected, Mrs. Newcomb's earlier notes stress the importance of keeping up a regular correspondence. On December 30, 1829, she said:

I have not heard from you Charles, since you wrote me for the shirtee—I want you to keep the Journal you promised, & to let me know every thing about Henry & yourself—tell my dear little H. that he must write too—& that he must learn as fast as he can, & must not swear.[3]

She had to beg Charles not to get his older cousin, Giles, to write his letters for him, and once, after getting a rather impressive letter from Henry, she wrote:

If dear Henry wrote his, he has done himself much credit—for there is not a word misspelt—& for such a little boy it is a very good letter. I want you dear H. to write your own letters. . . . I want you dear Charles to write me what you think & feel, & whatever interests you will also me. (July 22, 1831)

Around Christmas time the brothers had tantalizing letters from their older sister, Sarah, who obligingly described the treats they were missing.

I had a delightful time Christmas at Mrs. Dorr's [she wrote] and I suspect if you had been here you would have been invited. We played . . . "Blind Man's Buff" and we had a Snap Dragon. Do you know what that

[3] The manuscripts of Mrs. Newcomb's letters are deposited in Brown University Library.

is? Well supposing you do not I will tell you. There was a basin put on
the table with some *Brandy* and *Raisins* in it; a piece of burning paper
was put in which caused the brandy to take fire and those who dared
thrust their hands in and take out the raisins had the most. (January 17,
1830)

Both Charles and Henry did well in school. They studied Latin
and composition and the other usual subjects, and their mother asked
that Henry, and also Charles if he had time, be taught Natural History. An intelligent and well-read woman, she took a great interest in
the education of all her children. Sarah, Charles, and Henry were all,
at one time or another, at the heads of their classes in school. The
three younger Newcombs, Elizabeth, Charlotte, and Bridgham, do
not seem to have been quite so studious. Less, however, is known
about them.

By the spring of 1832 Charles had grown most anxious to leave
Plainfield. In February he was ill, and in March, when he should
have been nearly well again, he wrote home despondingly that he
did not think that he would ever recover. Mrs. Newcomb, who was
most penetrating, may have suspected that her son's fears were encouraged by a dislike of his surroundings. In any case, she treated his
forebodings calmly and asked, with no sign of alarm,

& why do you think you shall not be restored in a short time? Cheer up
my Son, & remember you have a Mother who loves you dearly, & who
will do any thing for you to make you happy. (March 8, 1832)

In May he spoke of the unhappiness which life in Plainfield caused
him. By way of encouragement his mother told him that he and
Henry were spoken of as the best scholars in the school and she asked
if he could not make himself feel more contented there. His efforts
could not have been very successful, for in July she again urged him
to exert resolution and announced that she was going to change his
school when autumn came. Charles resigned himself to staying out
the rest of the term. And in the fall, according to his mother's
promise, he was sent to Andover to prepare for Brown.

Before observing any more of Newcomb's career it is important
to understand just what sort of woman his mother was, for Newcomb
was to be dependent upon her, financially, emotionally, and intellectually, for most, perhaps all, of his life.

She was the daughter of Christopher Mardenborough, who owned the plantation of Monkey Hill, at Basse Terre, on the island of St. Christopher's, British West Indies. Around the beginning of the nineteenth century her father sent her to the United States. Some years later she met Lieutenant Newcomb, whom she married in New York in 1814. Not long after his death at sea, she left her mansion at Newport and brought her young family to Providence to live.

The earliest anecdote about Rhoda Newcomb comes out of family gossip. Whatever its accuracy, it reveals her descendants' estimate of her character. The story is that when Rhoda and one of her brothers were sent to this country, they were each given a sum of money and asked to have their portraits done by Copley or some other good painter. The portraits of the two still hang in the Gallagher house in East Greenwich. One is a warm and sparkling picture of a young man with expressive eyes and curly hair. The other is a rather hard, flat portrait of a woman with unusually penetrating blue eyes and a rather masculine forehead. The theory about the pictures is that the young man went to a good painter while his economical sister went to some hack artist, paid him a small fee, and then pocketed the change.

Her dominant characteristics were a genuine love of intellectual pleasures, an unsatisfied literary ambition, and a selfish and often unscrupulous eagerness to keep her children dependent upon her.

As a girl she was an enthusiastic reader of Dr. Johnson, Addison, and the other eighteenth-century favorites. During the 1830's and '40's, however, she read the books popular in the Transcendental group in which she circulated. Her letters to her son contain excited accounts of her readings in Plato, Euripides, Dante, Shakspere, Ben Jonson, Massinger, Goethe, Schiller, and Kant; and she took great pleasure in the books of Emerson, Margaret Fuller, Sampson Reed, Bronson Alcott, Sylvester Judd, and other American writers. She was a member of the Providence Athenaeum and attended lectures at the Coliseum—and, at least once, read a paper to this group. She was also one of a literary côterie which included Sarah Helen Whitman, Anne Charlotte Lynch, Albert Gorton Greene, Thomas Davis, the antitranscendental Mr. Pabodie and other Providence celebrities. Before very long she was on comparatively intimate terms with Margaret Fuller, Emerson, and Alcott. When she was in town she divided her time between reading books and newspapers, writing in her journal, and calling on the Providence *literati*. The rest of the time she was "on the wing" to New York, where she felt really free, or to Concord to hear Mr. Emerson lecture, or to Boston, where she attended Miss Fuller's Conversations and usually saw a play or heard a concert before returning home.

Rhoda Newcomb's keen love of literature was accompanied by a recognition of the prestige of literary persons and by a decided literary ambition, at first for herself and later for her son. She wrote articles on Goethe's genius, the Letters of Goethe and Schiller, Carlyle, Coleridge, Ann Hutchinson, and the Pseudo-Critics of Providence. Most of them were published in the *Providence Journal* and in the *New York American*. Nothing of hers seems to have reached the pages of the *Dial* or the *Harbinger*, or the other more literary publications. Those of her articles which I have looked at contain the probable explanation. They have all the faults of Transcendental writing: floridity, chaotic enthusiasm, and emotional, rather than thoughtful, organization; and they lack the clear perceptions of truth and the purity of expression which mark the best writing of the period.

The ambition which her own work could not satisfy she appears to have transferred to her favorite son, Charles. Before he was in his teens she had him promise to keep a journal. In her letters to Plainfield she twice reminded him of the fact. At the same period she held up for his emulation a young Providence neighbor, of whom she wrote:

Henry Dorr is spoken of as a wonder—his compositions, which are numerous (for he hardly hears of a subject or thinks upon it without writing), are said to be equal to those of a man—his sermons are quoted for their excellence—& thought by no means inferior to Mr. Crockers! Now I think you might . . . by forming the habit of writing often, succeed as well as others . . . the habit of writing teaches us to express our ideas correctly—to arrange them in the mind properly—as well as to prepare you for whatever profession you may hereafter select—as for the Navy— dear Charles, which you fancy at present, I advise you to give up the subject for two or three years—then, when your mind is more mature, you will be more capable of judging. (February 23, 1832)

Throughout her letters one finds little hints that show what she expected of her son. Once, after a visit at home, Charles carried back to Brook Farm a quire of his mother's foolscap. When she discovered the loss, she wrote archly—and a little demandingly—that she expected "nothing less than a spiritual epic out of it." (July 11, 1844) In another letter she suggested that he might translate a Greek play for the *Dial*. In still another she told him that she had just read Hawthorne's "Select Party" in the *Democratic Review* and that Hawthorne's

favorite hero, who was to write the great epic or some other great production of this age, was described so much like a certain son of mine that I actually realised it for a time! (July 26, 1844)

Actually, Hawthorne's "hero" is but one in a series of allegorical characters and is described without too great detail as

a young man in poor attire, with no insignia of rank or acknowledged eminence, nor any thing to distinguish him among the crowd except a high, white forehead, beneath which a pair of deepest eyes were glowing with warm light.[4]

In the beginning, Newcomb's acceptance of a literary career seems to have been due partly to a vague inclination and partly to his desire to please his mother and to fulfill her hopes in him.

Mrs. Newcomb's least pleasant characteristic was her desire to dominate the lives of her children. Sarah, who became engaged to John Gallagher while she was at school in New York, was lucky enough to escape by means of an early marriage. Henry was firm enough to insist on joining the navy, and was seldom at home after the age of fifteen or sixteen. Charles and Charlotte were the chief victims of their mother's selfishness.

Rhoda Newcomb early instructed her children that their prime duty in life would be to look after their mother, to respect her, and to sacrifice their comfort and, if need be, their future happiness for her contentment. From some of her early letters it is clear that she knew instinctively how to make artful appeals to their sympathy. She impressed on them the fact that if they would "continue to be obedient & good boys" their mother would "always love you, & be glad to make sacrifices" for their benefit. (February 15, 1830) In 1830 she wrote:

have you heard of Mr. Cushing's death? it was very sudden—he rose in the morning & while washing himself fell & never breathed again! What

[4] Nathaniel Hawthorne, *Works*, Riverside Edition, Cambridge, 1882, II, 79.

a warning to us all! to do what is right, that we may be prepared for so great a change—his poor children are deprived of a good father—& the only way they can respect his memory will be to conduct in such a way as to make their Mother happy. (October 6, 1830)

Her next letter reinforced the point with,

Mrs. Bowen was here last Eve'g & told me she was surprised to see the kindness & attention of Mrs. Cushing's Sons to her—the elder boys instruct the younger & do all they can to assist their Mother—they are a fine family of Children—One of them you know has gone as Instructor to Mr. Hare's Children—another takes his father's place as agent in a Manufactory—you & Henry must do all you can to study & learn that you may relieve my cares & supply, in a degree, your dear father's place. (Post marked October 13, 1830)

Since the Newcomb nest appears to have been well feathered with bank shares, her anxiety for the future seems a trifle forced.

When Charles was a child his bad health must have made him grateful for the shelter which his mother's affectionate care offered him, and then as well as later his physical weakness probably lowered his resistance to her domination of him.

When he was older and had begun to cherish the wish of living independently, he dared not face the truth of his situation. He could hardly admit to his consciousness the thought that it was his mother who stood between him and the wife and home he hoped to have. Instead, he forced his resentment into other channels whence it emerged as hatred for literary life, scorn for strong-minded women and, in general, as distaste for some of the other things which his mother had represented. His directly personal relationship to her, on the other hand, was marked by an over-active devotion.

Only in one place in his writings is there any direct reference to the uneasiness of their relationship. It is found, scrawled in pencil, in the back pages of one of his Commonplace Books.

Mother &c. bad as before, but I not to despond but to do my part, to love & protect; to have a home & all in it. (CB, 1847, 162)

Newcomb was admitted to Brown University in September, 1833, and was graduated four years later, at the age of seventeen. The Brown curriculum at that period included ancient and modern languages, rhetoric, moral and intellectual philosophy, geometry, algebra, optics, surveying, navigation, and chemistry.[5]

[5] For a complete outline of the curriculum, see W. C. Bronson, *The History of Brown University* 1764-1914, Providence, 1914, pp. 216-217.

If his marks give us a fair means of judging, Newcomb was a comparatively poor student. He did his best work in Latin, Greek, and philosophy, but had a hard time with his mathematics. In the middle of his junior year, and in his senior year, his marks improved enough to raise him to the middle of his class. Until then he had had an average rank of fifth from the bottom in a class of about fifty. Judged by our present standards, his marks look very good, but all, except the last two sets, compare most unfavorably with those of his classmates. At that period, a boy at the top of the list was likely to have term marks which ran like this: Latin, 98; Mathematics, 100; Greek, 99. Newcomb's record is as follows:[6]

Freshman Year:

	Latin	Mathe-matics	Greek
Term I	88	87	90
Term II	87	81	82
Term III	87	79 (Algebra)	88

Sophomore Year:

	Latin	Mathe-matics	Greek	Rhetoric	Compo-sition
Term I	91	80	91		
Term II		80	92	89	
Term III	88	80		85	90

Junior Year:

	Latin	Greek	Rhetoric	Natural Philoso-phy	Chem-istry	Compo-sition
Term I		92	86	76		
Term II	94			90	90	92
Term III	No record for Newcomb					

Senior Year:

	Physics	Moral Philoso-phy	Paley's Evi-dences
Term I	96	96	
Term II			97
Term III	No record for any of the class.		

[6] Brown University Registrar. *Record of Standing, Absences, and Term Marks of Students,* 1827-1907.

During Newcomb's undergraduate days Dr. Francis Wayland was President of Brown. His long presidency was devoted to raising the scholastic standards of the college and improving the rather lax discipline. He raised the entrance requirements so as to include Caesar and Jacob's *Greek Reader,* and he added new courses in Classics, French, and astronomy. A fairly severe academic paternalism was imposed upon the undergraduates who lived in dormitories. During study hours, Wayland had the students inspected regularly by members of the Faculty. If Newcomb had lived at Hope College or at University Hall, perhaps he would have been a better student. As it was, he lived at home with his mother and sisters throughout his four years at Brown. Apart from the hours which he spent in the class-room, his membership in the United Brothers' Society seems to have been one of his few links with the other undergraduates. This club was similar in nature to the older Philermenian Society: it had a library which its members could use, and it met every week or two to debate some question which had been appointed at an earlier meeting. Newcomb debated on the affirmative side of: "Would the civil code be improved by substituting transportation for capital punishment?" And he helped win the negative of: "Is wealth a greater incentive to action than fame?" and "Are the Corporation under moral obligation to give the whole of the graduating class of 1835 degrees of A.B.?"[7]

By the time he was through college Newcomb had abandoned his plan of going to sea. He decided instead to become a minister. During the spring of 1836 he had spent several weeks in New York with his namesake, Charles King. There, probably with a view to becoming a preacher, he took a course to cure him of stammering. When he asked his mother for the money to pay the fee, she wrote approvingly,

should you succeed, a new world of pleasure & profit will be opened to you, dearest Charles: the pleasures of conversation & the advantages of yr favorite profession will then be at your command. (Undated, *ca.* April 9, 1836)

She enclosed the cheque which he had requested. This cheque caused

[7] See Brown University. United Brothers' Society. *Constitution and Records,* 1833-1837.

an amusing flurry of correspondence, for the letter in which it was sent was crossed by another from Mr. King which offered to settle with the stammering-master. Mrs. Newcomb immediately wrote to her son telling him to retain the cheque and to allow Mr. King to pay the bill. Charles, in the meantime, had already made his payment and was anxious to consider the transaction settled; but his mother insisted that he explain the situation to his host and accept a reimbursement were it offered.

Sarah, who had recently returned from her school in New York, congratulated her brother on having a chance to broaden his knowledge of human nature. She wrote:

It is good for a boy of your age to go into the world & be thrown upon his own responsibility; you have too dark & gloomy ideas of human nature & I trust that experience will teach you that though none is *good,* many have frank, open & generous hearts & sundry other good qualities by no means to be despised. (April 19, 1836)

That summer he spent August at Newport. His mother urged him to remain there for the sake of his health though he might "pant for home."

In 1837, after finishing his work at Brown, Newcomb determined to prepare himself for the ministry. Late in September he boarded the New York boat and commenced his journey to the Episcopal Seminary at Alexandria, then in the District of Columbia. His grieving mother, accompanied by Charlotte, followed him down to the boat, but, finding the crowd too dense, soon retired to a hill from which they watched the boat slip down the bay. His mother wrote that she went home to a "sad & solitary" meal with Mr. Gallagher, Sarah, and Elizabeth.

I miss you more than I can express, dearest C. [she went on], every motion I make reminds me of your absence—for you were always at hand, but should this change result in your benefit . . . I must not regret it. . . . Let health be your first object now—then study. . . . I look forward with much pleasure to the future, in connection with you, & I hope to spend many, many happy hours with my dear Son—Never allow yourself to be depressed—when the fit is coming on, go in the open air or seek the society of some pleasant companion. When I was at your age I was subject to fits of depression, & generally cured them by exercise & society.
. . . Charlotte hugs & kisses as much as ever, but I cannot be reconciled to the loss of yours. (September 28, 1837)

That Newcomb chose an Episcopal theological school was not especially strange. His current Commonplace Book contained extracts from the Roman Catholic breviary, the Latin Hymns of St. Francis Xavier, as well as from the writings of Saints Athanasius, Basil, and Gregory. It is very likely that, if Mrs. Newcomb and Margaret Fuller had not joined forces against him, Charles would have gone even further and embraced Roman rather than English Catholicism.

As Sarah once pointed out to her brother, it was strange that any of the young Newcombs should have taken a deep interest in religion.

Is it not singular, Charles [she wrote], that three of mamma's children should become interested in religion while she herself is rather indifferent to it? Do you not see & feel the hand of Providence in it? (April 19, 1836)

Sarah's willingness to marry John Gallagher, an Episcopal clergyman, surprised, even shocked, her mother. Whether or not the girl's conversion occurred before, or after, she met Mr. Gallagher, she felt her religion deeply and discussed it at length in her letters. It seems likely that she was influential in leading her brother toward the Anglican doctrine.

Newcomb spent but one year at Alexandria. He appears to have left the Seminary with the intention of returning after the summer vacation; for when he asked for permission to write only once a fortnight, his mother replied that he would soon be home and that she would in the meantime

expect to receive a letter from him weekly, as usual. Soon [she went on] we shall embrace each other, dearest—& be together at least two months! (May 19, 1838)

George Willis Cooke stated that Newcomb abandoned his intention of entering the ministry because he "found it impossible to be a sectarian."[8] That the young man's religious views were unsettled can be seen from sections of a letter written by Sarah on January 11, 1838.

And *is it so* my brother? Did I read rightly or have I dreamed it, that all you . . . are now "Certain of . . . [are] the duty of love to God & Man & the Resurrection of Christ Jesus from the dead"? Mother & Miss Fuller

[8] G. W. Cooke, *An Historical and Biographical Introduction to Accompany the Dial,* Cleveland, 1902, II, 146.

must then rejoice that a proselyte was so *easily* made & that at length you have cast into utter oblivion the "truth as it is in Jesus." . . . Do you remember, dear C—how bitterly I mourned on yr return from Alexandria at the change that had come so blightingly over your once evangelical views. . . . Little did I dream . . . that again I should find my head sick & my heart faint at the relapse of my brother into cold, heartless unitarianism denying the Lord who bought him. . . . Do you remember that when I came from Newport last summer I told you of the scheme formed by Miss F. to allure you from the Superstition of Romanism & how you ridiculed the idea? How little saw we that in [so] short a time her plans would have obtained a consummation even beyond *her* brightest hopes!

Six months after this letter was written, Newcomb was in New York. He was studying Catholicism under some professor in a seminary.[9] He remained there for only a very brief period, however, and soon returned to Providence.

Comparatively little is known about Newcomb's life and occupations during the years which elapsed between his return from Alexandria in 1938 and his installation, in 1841, as a boarder at Brook Farm. He read, saw a good deal of Margaret Fuller, wrote in his Commonplace Books, escorted his mother to literary functions, and nursed his health at Newport.

Hints in a letter which Margaret Fuller wrote to Newcomb in 1839 suggest that the young man, who was eighteen or nineteen years old, may have fancied himself in love with her around this time. Miss Fuller speaks of their pleasure in certain landscapes, and of their enjoyment of certain books, read aloud in the course of strolls in the country—of the usual pleasures, in short, of an intellectual friendship. On May 29, 1839, however, she wrote:

I think you were right at first and that we had best not correspond. But, as I hope not to be forgotten for some time, I shall hold myself in readiness to answer whenever you appeal to me for sympathy, or, if such I am able to give, for information.[10]

In November of this same year Newcomb's sister Charlotte visited her. Miss Fuller wrote to Newcomb,

I hope she will be your friend and companion, since I cannot be myself. I flatter myself she will be more to you for having been with me.[11]

[9] Rhoda Newcomb's letter of July 9, 1838.
[10] Among the Margaret Fuller manuscripts at Harvard University.
[11] *Ibid.*, November, 1839.

In his *Commonplace Book* for 1839 the entries are few but comparatively full. He concentrated on English and European writers of the late eighteenth and early nineteenth centuries: Shelley, Coleridge, Hazlitt, Goethe, Schiller, Lessing, Richter, and Rousseau.

Already a protégé of Margaret Fuller's, Newcomb became acquainted with her friend Emerson in the spring of 1840. Into his first copy-book he had entered several pages of Emersoniana obtained from Miss Fuller's note-book. There can be no doubt that he was eager to meet the great man. Emerson, for his part, had already heard interesting things about the young genius whom Miss Fuller had discovered in Providence. He recorded the beginning of their friendship in a letter of March 30. "Mrs. Newcomb," he said, "treats me like an old friend." Of her son he wrote:

With that San Giovanne I established friendly relations at sight but wind & rain & a multitude of persons have thus far hindered us of our projected walk which was to be the confessional.[12]

At the beginning of July, 1840, Charles spent several days with Margaret Fuller in Jamaica Plain. While there he had a severe attack of illness. The lack of fortitude with which he bore pain disgusted his strong-minded hostess. To Emerson she wrote of Newcomb:

He is wretchedly ill. I think he may die, and perhaps it would be well, for I doubt if he has strength to rise above his doubts and fears. Oh how I thank Heaven that I am made of firmer fibre and more resolute mind.[13]

The rest of the summer he spent at Newport. Here he read in manuscript some of the Reverend Charles Timothy Brooks' translations of Jean-Paul Richter. Brooks had already begun work on Richter's *Titan,* which he did not publish until the 1860's. Newcomb copied out passages from it and appended to them a note:

a fine specimen of his glorious descriptions—imagination & fancy—Natural orchard ones. (CB, October 25, 1839, 18)

It was not long after reading the beginning of *Titan* that Newcomb

[12] *The Letters of Ralph Waldo Emerson,* ed., R. L. Rusk, New York, 1939, II, 270.
[13] *Ibid.,* 310.

wrote, under its influence, his story, "Dolon," which was later published in the *Dial*.

Now that he had given up his plan of a theological career, Newcomb was anxious to find some other occupation. The one which occurred to him most readily was that of European travel. But his mother, while she had no intention of allowing him to go abroad without her, declared that duty to her daughters required her to stay at home. When she felt that her son was becoming restive, however, she made half promises of a trip, exclaiming as she did so, "What a happy time we shall have!" In the meantime she sought to keep him busy with other plans. She urged him to contribute some verses to the book of Providence poetry which her friend Miss Anne Charlotte Lynch was compiling. In a letter which followed, she set forth the suggestion that Charles might become a "Lecturer upon Ethics"— or upon any other subject which he might choose. Such a career would permit him to remain with his mother and would, therefore, "be best and happiest for both." (August 19, 1840)

The next time that he brought up the question of touring Europe his mother put him off with similar excuses, saying that they could perhaps go another season when dear Charlotte would "have taken to herself an help mete." (June 13-16, 1843) It is very much to be doubted, however, whether Mrs. Newcomb did anything but stand in the way of Charlotte's acquiring a helpmate. In the course of her letters to Charles Mrs. Newcomb mentions half a dozen occasions when Charlotte was "disappointed" by some young man. Sometimes the breach between them was caused by her mother's refusal to countenance an engagement; at other times the young man in question announced unexpectedly that he had never thought of Charlotte except as a friend.[14] At another time, when there was talk of going to Saratoga Springs Mrs. Newcomb explained that if Charlotte went she herself would also be obliged to go, because of the girl's "propensity for some particular beau." (July 10, 1845) It appears that

---

[14] It is hardly surprising to learn that, after a few such disappointments, Charlotte took advantage of a brief illness of her mother's to have clandestine meetings with Biundi, her Italian teacher. Evidently she felt that she had been at fault this time, for she was quiet but penitent. Ordinarily after some budding romance had been blighted she was intractable and mutinous toward her mother—as though she had sensed and resented interference.

she had no objection to her daughter's beaus, provided none of them was favored. There is no conclusive evidence to prove that Mrs. Newcomb was acting selfishly; indeed, it may be argued that Charlotte was impulsive and required protection from adventurers. It is, however, a suggestive fact that, although Charlotte was rather beautiful, and high-spirited, and was of a comfortably rich family, she did not marry until 1870—five years after her mother's death—and that Charles, the chief object of his mother's domination, never married at all.

SECTION II. BROOK FARM

It was around the first of April, 1841, that George Ripley, with his family and a few friends, moved into the farm-house of an estate in West Roxbury, Massachusetts. For some years Ripley had thought of forming a community of intelligent people who would like to enjoy the pleasures of intellectual association while supporting themselves by agricultural and domestic labor. For the first few months after moving on to the farm Ripley retained all the responsibility for the venture. By the end of September the project appeared so successful that there was no difficulty in transforming it into the "Brook Farm Institute of Agriculture and Education." The articles were drawn up; the stock issued to members, and backers; the officers of the organization chosen; and on October 11, 1841 a deed for the farm was obtained.[1]

Although Charles Newcomb never became a member of the Brook Farm Association, he was a boarder at the farm almost from the beginning. He arrived there about the twentieth of May, 1841, and remained there, with occasional absences, until the first week in December, 1845.

Whether it was Charles or his mother who first urged the benefits of going to West Roxbury, Mrs. Newcomb was heart-broken at his leaving. She had spent all of January in Boston whence she had several times written to "Dear Carolus rex" to tell him how homesick she was and to urge him to join her in Boston immediately, even if he felt obliged to get a new shirt and cravat first. Now, four

[1] See Lindsay Swift, *Brook Farm: Its Members, Scholars and Visitors,* New York, 1900, pp. 1-19.

months later, *he* was gone, and for an indefinite time. While waiting for his first letter Mrs. Newcomb wrote:

I need not tell you how often Sadness possesses me, when, in my lonely moments, I think of our separation . . . the sympathy of those I love is . . . essential to me—to be sure I have that from you where you are—but I miss the constant care & interest I had in yr health—only relieved by activity in its behalf. Still, I am . . . very *happy,* when I think how good are yr prospects of improved health—what refined & intelligent people are about you—& that to all human ken, you are in the very situation best adapted to yr present condition. (May 27, 1841)

In her letter of June 6 she made a further effort to point out to Charles the benefits of his situation. She encouraged him to become acquainted with Mr. George Bradford and wrote cheerfully of his recent pastimes:

I am glad you had so lovely a time with Miss S[turgis?]—when Miss Fuller comes, give my best love, & tell her I wrote her a note yesterday. . . . You & Miss S. must have had a romantic time in the woods—*is she engaged?* Although you find some discomforts, Charley Dear, if you find yourself improving in health, which is promoted by making some physical exertion—it is the very object gained for which you went—you could not prob^y be thrown in so pleasant a circle at Newport, besides other disadvantages there.

By the time that Charles had been two weeks at the Community he wrote that his health had so improved that he was able to work three hours a day and to take part in such strenuous exercise as tree-climbing. This letter contained another bit of information which puzzled, though it does not seem to have disturbed, his mother. We must suppose that a knowledge of her son's vagaries made it possible for her to reply, with no hint of alarm or expostulation,

So you mean to wear gloves & a veil to bed—do you remember Parson Hooper, one of Mr Hawthorne's heroes—who wore a black veil always & no one could see his face or divine the cause? (June 13, 1841)[2]

Some of Newcomb's idiosyncrasies annoyed Mrs. Ripley a little. His mother felt obliged to tell him that he ought not to wear his

---

[2] The purpose of wearing a veil might have been to keep out the pernicious, damp, night air. Twenty years later Newcomb advanced the theory that soldiers in camp would do well to sleep with handkerchiefs over their faces. It is hard to account for the wearing of gloves. Possibly the plan was unconnected with his physical health.

heavy calf-skin boots in the house. She added that he ought to consider other people's tastes to the extent of cleaning his finger-nails, and explained that such niceties were among the sacrifices we must make for the sake of our fellows. (July, 1841)

When it came to writing home, Newcomb was a reluctant correspondent. At first he tended to write upon abstract subjects, but his mother protested against his sending her compositions and demanded to know, instead,

who you have walked with, talked with, *loved*—enjoyed—& in fine, your thoughts & feelings. (July 13, 1841)

Later on, he chose other methods to free himself from these cloying demands: he took to leaving wide margins, or writing evasively on rather impersonal subjects. When he asked hopefully if he might write less often than once a week, Mrs. Newcomb would not hear of such an arrangement. She insisted on punctual answers to her letters, saying, in case of storm, "I can wait one day with patience, I hope." (January 17, 1845) In some letters he tried to be less reticent: in one he gave an enjoyable account of an "Aesthetic Party" which had taken place in the Community, and, in another, told how he had had a ducking in the course of a picnic on the river.

Margaret Fuller's young friend, Caroline Sturgis, often visited Brook Farm. Newcomb got to know her rather well; indeed, hints in the family letters and elsewhere suggest that he may have grown rather fond of her. Georgianna Kirby remembered finding Charles and Caroline reading Greek in the hay-mow.[3] Miss Sturgis seems to have been the "Miss S." with whom he walked so romantically in the woods. When his mother mentioned the occasion, she must have wondered how much her son liked this Miss S. for she significantly underlined the question, *"is she engaged?"* Charlotte, according to the habit of young sisters, teased him about "dear Caroline" when she wrote, and once said archly,

So your *beloved Caroline* is to come to see you all. Don't be *too* excited Charley. (June 12, 1842)

[3] Georgianna B. Kirby, "Reminiscences of Brook Farm," in *Old and New,* III, 436. Mrs. Kirby refers to the pair as "Erasmus" and "Sybilla." There is no doubt that Newcomb was "Erasmus"; and Lindsay Swift has identified "Sybilla" as Caroline Sturgis.

A year later, when Mrs. Newcomb was discussing the trip for that summer, Carry Sturgis's name came up again. Mrs. Newcomb was eager to go to Niagara, though they had already been there. Referring to Miss Sturgis's disappointment on seeing the falls for the first time, she concluded that

from what I know of Carry, I should think her love of the beautiful was greater than her sense of the sublime . . . simple Nature, children, & fairies, please such persons as Miss S. more than great water falls. So I think, though you may think it presuming in me to form an opinion of one about whom I know so little. (June 25, 1843)

An interesting, if unimportant supplement to these remarks is found in a letter Emerson wrote to Margaret Fuller. Apropos of nothing in particular he remarked that "Charles K. N. has gone to Niagara. Caroline, to Nahant."[4] It seems possible that Newcomb may have hoped that he, Caroline, and his mother could take their summer trip together. Such a supposition, however, is mere conjecture.

While at Brook Farm he was infected mildly by the general desire to experiment in costume and diet. In December, 1843, Mrs. Newcomb asked him if it were wise to wear linen pantaloons at this time of year. Several times his mother wrote advising him not to give up milk, butter, or cream, or various other foods; then, as later, his diet was largely a matter of whim.

Especially in the early part of his stay, he spent a good deal of time in writing. He probably kept a journal, though none for this period is extant, and none is referred to before 1843 or 1844. By 1841 he had also written several stories; one of these Miss Fuller saw and liked. This piece was, I think, a first draft of "Dolon," which appeared in the *Dial* the next year. It is certain, at least, that "Dolon" had been written some time before September, for in this month Mrs. Newcomb wanted to know if he had given up the sequel to it.

Emerson, who came to Providence in the following February, spent some time with his young friend and was made happy "by his conversation and his reading of his tales."[5] He invited him to come to

[4] *Letters*, ed., Rusk, III, 184.
[5] *The Journals of Ralph Waldo Emerson*, ed., E. W. Emerson and W. E. Forbes, Boston, 1909, VI, 162.

Concord for a visit and asked him to bring both parts of "Dolon," which Margaret Fuller had obtained permission to print in the *Dial*. The invitation was repeated several times without success.

"Dolon" was printed in July, 1842. It presented a serious problem to Elizabeth Hoar, who recopied and otherwise prepared the manuscript for publication. Late in June Emerson had to write an urgent letter asking the author for permission to make a few alterations in the punctuation of "Dolon," for in the entire first page of the story there was no period until the very last line.

Emerson thought that "Dolon," despite its "odious licences," had "more native gold than anything . . . since Sampson Reed's Oration on Genius."[6] The public was not so sure of its merits. George Willis Cooke gives us a fair notion of the contemporary opinions about "Dolon." It was, he says,

much admired and it was much discussed. It was also the subject of much merriment on the part of critics, being laughed at and caricatured almost as much as Alcott's "Orphic Sayings." Even so ardent a transcendentalist as W. H. Channing could write of it to Margaret Fuller: " 'Dolon' is full to crowding with truth and beauty, but alas! it has no key-note for earthly instruments. It is a song made for heaven's harps, sung to the spinet of the earth."[7]

Newcomb's sister, Sarah Gallagher, was among those who caricatured and laughed at the strange piece of writing. She had always enjoyed teasing her solemn young brother. Now, from Savannah, she wrote:

As "Dolon loved to go & sit on a large rock within a wood which bordered on an old potatoe moss-hilled field, separated from the house by a large hay field". . . [he] may again be seated on the same rock beneath the sky, the clouds, the branches & leaves, pondering not upon the nature of the root which was one day to materially contribute to the satisfying of some hungry body (for Dolon was too spiritual to eat) but upon the expansion of his soul into a transparent eye-ball, as the genial rays of the sun were vivifying & expanding & maturing the useful plant on which his physical eye now dwelt, while as he thought of : . . . reason & the ideal world, of the future passings of his . . . etherialized spirit from planet to planet, from star to star. . . . Dolon . . . was mortified to find himself guilty of a sensation resembling what in the days of his infancy he had heard spoken of as hunger. And yet how could it be? for his spirit was so pure, so truthful, so aspiring, so searching, so ardent, he enjoyed such precious communion with stars & waves & trees & blue skies & petri-

[6] *Letters,* ed., Rusk, III, 74.
[7] Cooke, II, 145.

fied forests. . . . With lizards, scorpions, cock-roaches & cabbage-leaves. . . . (*ca.* March 8, 1843)

This letter—which ends "Your affectionate transcendental sister"— hits off very well Newcomb's rambling sentences, his obscure phraseology, and the transcendental yearning expressed in the story.

Margaret Fuller made the most thoughtful and, I think, the most just, criticism of "Dolon." She wrote to Newcomb, in July, 1842:

Its succulent and involved style displeases, and hides, not drapes, the thought. On a third reading I am more than ever sensible that you must learn the art of choosing among your thoughts, and prune as well as water your vine.[8]

Dolon, the character in whom the sketch centers, was a beautiful boy who liked to "be much in the air" and who constantly sought communion with nature. Every late afternoon and early evening he could be found sitting on a large rock in a wood. On one such occasion he chanced to look into a pine-tree over his head, and there, sitting in the top branches, was a man in a crimson tunic. When Dolon's parents learned about this adventure they tried to make him promise not to return to the spot again, for they had heard it was frequented by a madman, who worshipped pagan gods. But Dolon, after having had a strange mystical experience, could not keep from returning to the rock one night. There in the moonlight he saw the strange man, who was now dressed as if for sacrificial rites. Taking a wreath from his arm, the madman placed it on Dolon's head; then he plunged his knife into the boy's breast, and after gazing down at the body "threw himself prostrate before the rock as before an altar." Just what Newcomb was trying to say in this rhapsodic story is hard to understand. He seems to have had in mind the closeness which he felt to exist between children, nature, and the Ideal.

The whole piece, which is written in the strained idiom of a prose translation, shows plainly the influence of Jean-Paul Richter's *Titan,*[9]

[8] Among the Margaret Fuller manuscripts at Harvard University.

[9] The following is one of the extracts from Brooks' Richter which is most like "Dolon":

"He had, often in May, climbed up into a thick-limbed apple tree which supported a whole green hanging cabinet, & had laid himself down in the arms of its branches. And when, in this situation, the wavering pleasure-grove swung him about amidst the shy sportings of the lily-butterflies, & the hum of bees & insects,

portions of which Newcomb had read not long before. The similarity between the two includes not only style but the romantic emphasis upon man's relation to nature.

The first part of "Dolon" was published under the following title: "The Two Dolons From the MS. Symphony of Dolon. The First Dolon." It is not known whether Newcomb completed the sequel to the tale. If he did, it was not printed.

Around this time Newcomb wrote an "Essay on Saints and Poets," which his mother read and admired. He also wrote a story called "Edith" and read Emerson "copious wonderful pages"[10] from it at Brook Farm. For a clue to its contents we have only Emerson's reference to it as "the riper study & prayer of Edith & her train."[11]

The bulk of Newcomb's early writing must have been in his first Journal, which we do not have. Emerson makes two or three references to having read sections of it. In June, 1842, he wrote:

His criticism in his "Book-Journal" was captivating and in its devotion to the author, whether Æschylus, Dante, Shakspeare, Austin [*sic*], or Scott, as feeling that he had a stake in that book . . . and in the total solitude of the critic, the Patmos of thought from which he writes, in total unconsciousness of any eyes that shall ever read this writing, he reminds me of Aunt Mary.[12]

Again, in 1849, Newcomb visited Emerson bringing journals which he had written in 1843. Emerson described the manuscripts with enthusiasm as

full of subtle genius. Intense solitude appears in every sentence. They are soliloquies, and the abridged stenographic wit and eloquence, like that or better than we are wonted to in M. M. E. [Aunt Mary].[13]

At this and at other writings Emerson noted his disappointment

---

& the clouds of blossoms, & when the flaunting top now buried him in rich green, now launched him into deep blue & now into the sunshine, then did his fancy stretch the tree to gigantic dimensions. It grew alone in the universe, as if it were the tree of endless life . . . the white & red clouds hung upon it as blossoms, the moon as a fruit, the little stars glistened like dew, & Albano reposed in its infinite summit, & a storm swayed the summit from day into Night, & from Night into day." (CB, 1840, 18.)

[10] *Letters,* ed., Rusk, III, 74.
[11] *Ibid.,* III, 55-56.
[12] *Journals,* VI, 213.
[13] *Journals,* VIII, 60.

in Newcomb's unwillingness to speak to an audience. In explanation of his attitude Newcomb preached the doctrine of use and referred his questioner to Swedenborg.

Although Lindsay Swift supposed that Newcomb must have been "something of a blight"[14] at the Brook Farm festivities, he seems, actually, to have been rather well liked by the other young people there. Marianne Dwight refers to the "fun" they had together with Dora Wilder; and Ora Gannett Sedgwick classed him among the boarders who "added greatly to the pleasures of the association."[15]

He was at this time a slight, dark young man, with a hesitant manner and a nervous laugh. He had a heavy mass of tangled dark hair which was always slipping over his eyes and being flipped back with an impatient gesture. Georgianna Kirby later confessed that she felt a strong desire to force Newcomb into a chair and give his unkempt hair a much needed brushing.[16]

Most of the anecdotes about Newcomb depend upon his eccentricities for their interest. The picture that they give, while amusing, is not particularly complete.

Perhaps the fairest impression of Charles as he appeared to people of his own age may be gleaned from the letters of Marianne Dwight. Her friendship with the shy young man was especially fostered by the fact that she was intimate with Anna Q. T. Parsons. Miss Parsons had a remarkable gift for reading persons' characters by pressing a letter or other manuscript of theirs against her forehead. She then received psychic impressions from the paper and described the character of the writer while someone else took down her words. Her sincerity, coupled with the striking accuracy of her "impressions," made her talent of great interest to Ripley, Emerson, W. H. Channing, and Margaret Fuller.[17] Charles Newcomb's character was one of those read by Miss Parsons. The record of what she saw is not available, but it was so favorable that Marianne Dwight begged Newcomb to let her keep a copy because

[14] Swift, 50.
[15] Ora Gannett Sedgwick, "A Girl of Sixteen at Brook Farm," *Atlantic Monthly*, LXXXV, 398-399.
[16] Kirby, III, 48.
[17] Marianne Dwight Orvis, *Letters from Brook Farm 1844-1847*, ed., Amy L. Reed, Poughkeepsie, 1928, p. xiv.

it is too good and too beautiful and too true to destroy! I hope it will not be done.[18]

Miss Dwight appears to have had a genuine liking for mysterious "C. K. N.," although her feeling was tinged with the faint awe which a girl is likely to feel for a solitary, romantic youth who is reputed to be both a mystic and a poet. Dora Wilder, who kept house at the Eyrie, was her friendly rival in caring for his wants.

Dora and I [she wrote] have more jokes with him than a few. You have no idea how we meet soul to soul in *fun*.[19]

She shared with many others the sense that Newcomb was "different" and that he therefore deserved especial consideration and privileges. He stood out from the others not as an eccentric but as a man of genius—one for whom allowances must be made. One evening at one of the Brook Farm dances he chivalrously brought a chair from across the room and placed it beside his that she might sit down. In describing the incident, she wrote:

From *him* I felt the kindness, and we all three sat there together the whole evening.—I wish you could have seen his heavenly smile when I left the room and he bade me good-night. Of course we sat together almost in silence.[20]

At the end of 1844 the Brook Farmers realized the necessity of stricter economy. They began a system of retrenchment in which the regular members of the association gave up certain foods. One long table, the "no-retrenchment table," was set in the old style, for boarders, scholars, and visitors, and "a few associates who feel that their health requires" it. At the others no tea, meat, butter, or sugar was to be served.

Charlie N. sat at the *no* retrenchment table at *one* meal, but has come home to us again [wrote Miss Dwight], and is excepted from the general rule and allowed to have tea and butter brought to him. Our breakfast these short days is ready precisely at seven and, in order to make people punctual, Mr. Capen carries the dishes off at exactly half-past. Here again, friend N. is excepted, as he ought to be.[21]

Newcomb, of course, was a boarder and was under no moral obliga-

---

[18] *Ibid.,* 20.
[19] *Ibid.,* 21.
[20] *Ibid.,* 47.
[21] *Ibid.,* 51.

tion to sit at the retrenchment table. Miss Dwight's point, however, is that he deserved special privileges because he was an exceptional person.

Charles' extreme sensibility caused even his invalid sister, Elizabeth, to make allowances for him. In the autumn of 1843 Mrs. Newcomb, hoping that a southern climate might help Elizabeth's ailment, decided to send her to Savannah for the winter. For some reason Charles was very much opposed to having her go—perhaps because he supposed that she would die down there without his being able to see her again—and he wrote her a letter which distressed her a great deal. She had hoped to see him before she set out, but the instability of his emotions made her think better of the idea. Instead she sent him her little crucifix and a note in which she said,

I would have been glad to see you, but knowing how deeply you feel think both had better be spared.[22]

It is easy to suppose that Newcomb was carelessly considered a genius simply because he had peculiar habits and made the most of them. Some such implication may be read into Hawthorne's faintly ironic description of a stage the youth went through in 1843:

We talked of Charles Newcomb, who, it appears, is now passing through a new moral phasis; he is silent, inexpressive, talks little or none, and listens without response except a sardonic laugh; and some of his friends think that he is passing into permanent eclipse.[23]

Other people, Emerson among them, were impressed by the extreme discernment of some of Newcomb's remarks. Emerson noted with particular satisfaction that Newcomb was one of the first persons to call attention to the French traits in Thoreau's character by comparing him to a French-Canadian *voyageur*.[24] Georgianna Kirby recalled his

genius for penetrating to the very core of a subject, so that a few words from him often impressed his hearers more than an hour's talk with one more healthily balanced.[25]

---

[22] Quoted in Mrs. Newcomb's letter of October 18-19, 1843.
[23] Nathaniel Hawthorne, *The American Notebooks*, ed., Randall Stewart, New Haven, 1932, p. 176.
[24] *Journals*, VII, 386.
[25] Cooke, II, 144.

One of the things which Charles especially enjoyed was his association with the children of the Brook Farm School. With them he
skated, played ball, and hunted for birds. One evening Rebecca Codman and Marianne Dwight discovered him in a shed back of the
wash-room, where some of the boys were gathered

around a barrel of potatoes they were cleaning. He sat with his back to the
door reading stories to these boys to their great amusement, so we stood
still and listened, to enjoy the fun of teasing him about it afterward. Pretty
soon he discovered us and shouted well, and fired potatoes at us,—and
after that didn't dare tell any more stories without now and then sending
a potato over his shoulders.[26]

The most striking anecdotes about Charles Newcomb have their
source in Georgianna Kirby's *Reminiscences of Brook Farm*. From
her we learn of his habit of reading Greek long after the other Brook
Farmers were in bed and of his "reciting the Church Litany at intervals through the rest of the night." Since the walls of the Eyrie
were extremely thin, there is no reason to doubt the accuracy of her
statement. She describes his room as being decorated with rushes,
ferns, moss, and garlands. On the walls were hung pictures of Jesus,
Ignatius Loyola, and Francis Xavier. In the space between Loyola
and Xavier another portrait was before long inserted: that of the
famous dancer, Fanny Ellsler, whom he had, somewhat reluctantly,
seen in Boston and had promptly admired.

Newcomb was once the unconscious cause of a great deal of amusement to his companions on a skating-party. Mrs. Kirby's story is
that as they skated down the river a church spire came into view, and
that at this instant they saw Newcomb

fall on his knees, clasp his hands together as if in prayer, and, after a few
moments, rise, take off his skates, and, fording his way through the un-
broken snow of the bank, approach in the direction of the not distant
church.[27]

One of the skaters, who knew him well, predicted that Charles
would proceed straight up the center aisle—quite unconscious of the
surprise his skating togs and sudden entrance were causing the respectable congregation—and kneel before the altar. Before long he

[26] Orvis, 24.
[27] Kirby, IV, 353.

returned to the river looking contented; and, after praising the simplicity of Catholic countries, where any poorly clad person was welcome to step into a church and ask a blessing, he replaced his skates and glided down the river.

He was very sensitive to the personalities of others. When Anna Parsons visited Brook Farm he preferred not to be introduced to her, but lingered in her vicinity most of the evening. Later he reported that the sound of her voice had pleased him greatly.[28]

It must not be supposed that during his five years at West Roxbury Newcomb saw nothing of his family—though there are indications that he tried to see less of them as time went on. He always spent Christmas at Providence. At the end of the first two summers he went home in September and did not return until almost the end of April. In the next two years, however, he cut his winter visits down to a week or two.

Mrs. Newcomb made many flying visits to Boston for Conversations and concerts. Sometimes she had Charles meet her there, usually at Miss Peabody's book store; at other times she would tell him that if it were convenient to the Ripleys she would come out to Brook Farm for the night. He was not in the habit of encouraging her to visit him at West Roxbury; in one letter she wrote:

Dearest Child,
. . . I have a nice plan in prospect.—I am going to Boston next Thursday, to hear a Conversation—In the afternoon . . . I shall go out to the Comm^y and spend a few days—i.e. if Mrs. R. says she will take me to board for a week. Now do not discourage me, or throw obstacles in the way—for I have long wanted to stay a few days and see for myself something about a Com^y. (February 15, 1844)

In August of this same year, 1844, she was offended by his evident reluctance to join her in a proposed trip to Concord, and she delivered a somewhat peevish ultimatum to the effect that,

Unless I receive a letter from you Tuesday morning saying you will meet me at Dedham with *much pleasure* I shall not go. (Postmarked July 27, 1844)

She did not hesitate to drag him away from the tranquillity of

[28] Orvis, 24.

Brook Farm that he might accompany her to New York or escort her about there. In February, 1844, she asked him to come immediately to Providence. Charlotte and Elizabeth were away, she told him, and she would be "very, *very*" glad to see him.

I perfectly long to have you with me—& do not think I ought to stay any longer without one of my children with me. (February 23, 1844)

By way of warning, however, she quickly added that he had better come prepared to accompany her to New York. He did so. It was the middle of March before he was free to return to Brook Farm. By April 25 she had another trip to New York planned. This time she recalled her son in order that he might stay with Charlotte while she travelled. He came. The next year she wrote again to ask him to join her in New York and escort her about town. Recognizing his unwillingness to leave Brook Farm, she added that he need not come if it did not "contribute most" to his happiness. Yet, almost in the next breath, she was careful to point out that without a beau she could not go out of an evening in New York. Still, she continued, if he really did not feel able to go he should remain where he was. In the end, he followed her wishes and divided the month of May between Providence and New York.

In the autumn of 1845 the Newcomb family moved to a new boarding house and began urging Charles to come home to live. The prolonged separation was becoming less and less agreeable to Mrs. Newcomb. She reminded him that their most recent journey (apparently to Keene, N.H.) had

drawn me nearer to you than ever, my dear child—the chords of sympathy are tighter & we are brother & sister, as well as parent and child. (Postmarked September 15, 1845)

The letters of the next two months offered him all sorts of inducements for coming home. Charlotte, probably at her mother's request, sent a letter which fervently hoped that they would be together soon. She warned him that he seemed to be growing morbid, and begged him to come home. *"Dear Mother,"* she exclaimed, "we may all yet be a comfort to her!" Five days later Charles had still sent no definite promise that he would return. Instead, he wrote to ask what sort of profession he was suited for. Mrs. Newcomb replied that the problem could be better solved when they were all together and could talk it over. He countered with the proposal that they might take a trip somewhere. His mother, however, rejoined that Charlotte did not like to travel. She concentrated on describing the pleasantness of their new lodgings, the ladylike manners of their landlady, and the small parlor with a fire-place, where Charley could be alone whenever he chose. November came without bringing Charles. The letters from home grew progressively urgent. One expressed fear of the small-pox epidemic at Brook Farm. Another told him of the sacrifices his mother had made for him: she had given up the mansion at Newport for the sole reason that he did not care to go there; and when the girls had begged her to move to New York, she had refused because she preferred to live near her son. She mentioned buying the long-desired, five-volume set of Plato; promised that she would finance for him a seat in the Catholic church; and reported that Charlotte was planning to attend the church and to read Shakspere with him. The siege of letters reached a climax with Newcomb's capitulation and his mother's joyous exclamation:

My heart is leaping. . . . Come, dear, your Mother waits, Plato waits, & Jesus waits—last, not least, of course. (December 4, 1845)

So ended Newcomb's life at Brook Farm. In the second week of December he set out for home. And Marianne Dwight wrote to Anna Parsons:

I regret C. K. N.'s departure more than I can tell. He has always been a conspicuous, or rather an important object in the picture to me. I can hardly think of Brook Farm without him. The sweet, sad youth! He will feel the change still more than we. Think of him in a city life, if you can. Oh! it will kill him, soul and body. Wherever he is, may God bless him and cheer him.[29]

SECTION III. IN PROVIDENCE: 1845-1865

Upon his return to Providence Newcomb settled down quietly as his mother's companion. There he remained until her death twenty years later. The few letters scattered through this period do not give

[29] Orvis, 142.

many clues to his way of life. With little doubt, however, his activities were those of his mother: reading, writing, attending literary salons, listening to lectures, and taking short trips to New York and longer ones to summer resorts. Some summers he stayed at Newport, where he spent the mornings walking and the afternoons in society. When October came around, he usually spent a weekend in Concord with the Emersons.

During the first five years of this period he took refuge in reading and study. He began his daily routine of memorizing the *Psalms* and passages from Shakspere's plays. He filled up the back pages of his earlier commonplace books with quotations from his current reading and with short notations of his thoughts on literature, marriage, and education. Three new commonplace books were also begun: in 1847, 1848, and 1854. Although each book was started in a different year, the notes were often made contemporaneously, so that in the volume dated 1848, for example, there are some entries made as late as 1857.

The reading he recorded in these books is quite varied. In the 1847 volume he concentrated on history, biography, and memoirs. He read histories by Michelet, Lamartine, Niebuhr, J. C. Campbell, Southey, Alexander Young, Prescott, and Samuel P. Hildreth; and looked into the lives of Louis XIV, Marie Antoinette, Fox, Burke, Scott, Byron, Charlotte Brontë, Beethoven, and Franklin. In the next volume we find a higher percentage of novels mentioned—especially those by Jane Austen, Susan Ferrier, Dickens, Thackeray, Charlotte Yonge, and Lord Normanby. The 1854 book was begun after his reading had started to dwindle; the result was that although it covers a long period of time, its entries are comparatively few. He dipped into Mary Mitford's *Our Village;* read novels by Charles Reade, Dickens, and Miss Yonge; and went through travel books about England, Paris, Germany, Turkey, Egypt, and Abyssinia. The last entries consist of several pages from Terence, whom Newcomb read in 1871.

Earlier, in June of 1845, Emerson had mentioned visiting Newcomb at Brook Farm. He described him as being

pained now, it seems, by the doubt whether he should retire to more absolute inward priesthood, or accept the frequent and to him dear solicitations of domestic and varied life. His idea of love, which he names so often, is, I think, only the wish to be cherished.[1]

By 1847, or earlier, all doubt had been resolved. There was no hesitation in Newcomb's mind as to which he would prefer: a celibate literary life, or an active married one. The attractions of literature, he thought, did not hold a candle to those of marriage.

It was not, then, without a prolonged emotional struggle that Newcomb settled down to a life of ministering to his mother's comfort. The outward signs of this conflict are few, but they are corroborated by his later development.

His chief problem was whether he could possibly get married and still fulfill the duties which his mother exacted from him. As he had been taught from earliest childhood, his first duty was to be a good son; and from things which had been said in letters and in conversation he realized that Mrs. Newcomb's conception of the functions of "a good son" would hinder, or destroy, his chances of contracting a happy marriage. Despite the intensity of his longing for a wife,[2] home, and children, he seems to have been incapable of analyzing the nature of the obstacles to his happiness. Even in those pathetic little notes which he scribbled, in the faintest of pencil, often upside down, in the back spaces of his commonplace books— even here, in the course of his frankest admissions, he skirted the edges of his difficulty. Unable to see or to face his problem at all clearly, he could not take independent action to remedy the situation. Instead, he wrote down fragmentary hints and cryptic longings like the following:

World—girls not for such as me: I to keep to routine of my youth: good like me. I would hate them in time.

Mother &c. bad as before, but I not to despond but to do my part, to love & protect; to have a home and all in it.

Fear not if soer [soever?] haunts me; so does rank, Lit, lust; life *supersedes* all. (CB, 1847, 161, 162)

Dear Charlotte coming in at Atheneum to day, reminded me with her natural loveliness & constitutional felicity (so that I could have found in

[1] *Journals,* VII, 60-61.
[2] So far as we know, Newcomb had no especial woman in mind for a wife. An attachment to some particular person *might* have led him to rebellion.

such a one a wife) of my own, in my family, privilege. I saw that such a one should keep his own ground quietly; waiting for a peer rather than mourning at not being a fellow to those around; above insult & neglect, in natural repose before willingness to ply nature & not to go beyond it for self or others.

I was reminded . . . to be all that was noble & generous as a son & a brother; to use my thoughts &c for use in letters.

I am reminded, also, to seek a home, & not to dally with meditations of time-killing. (CB, 1848, 137)

Actually Newcomb did make a vague attempt to remedy his predicament. He unconsciously realized that it was this literary career, which his mother desired him to pursue, that bound him to her so closely. Had he gone to sea, or entered the professions of law or medicine, as he had thought of doing, his rigorous training would have taken him from his mother's side and the time taken by the subsequent pursuit of his profession could have confirmed the freedom he had gained. Following his "genius" and accepting a literary life, however, could lead only to seclusion—a deadly seclusion in which his mother would continue to dominate him. Such feelings as these, lying unexpressed at the bottom of his mind, were, I think, the foundation of his enthusiasm for Swedenborg. From this philosopher Newcomb adapted two doctrines which seemed to him particularly true: those which concerned marriage and "use." One of Swedenborg's revelations had shown him the sanctity and perpetuity of marriage. Newcomb expanded this idea to mean that only in marriage could happiness, perfection, and unity with God be found. By the doctrine that man's highest degree of being is in "use" Newcomb was able to justify his dislike of the recluse life of "'abstraction" which he was leading.

In 1847 we find the first reference to this great admiration for Swedenborg which was to make Newcomb the enemy of literariness. The first mention of the new tendency was made by Emerson, who observed the change with misgiving:

Charles K. Newcomb, the fathomless sceptic, was here August 8th. Thought he defies, he thinks it noxious. It makes us old, harried, anxious. Yes, but it is no more to be declined than hands and feet are.[3]

[3] *Journals*, VII, 321.

Two years later he wrote, after another visit from Newcomb,

Ah, dear old Swedenborg, and is thy saw good, *"The perfection of man is the love of use"?* And this fine luminary, brightest of all, can ill conceal his dislike of a general remark, spends his mornings at Newport all summer, in walking; his afternoons, "in society"; and has read but one book, this year, namely, an old novel.[4] Dear Swedenborg, if you can catch this American sprig, will you not whip him soundly![5]

The passage of ten years did not decrease Newcomb's opposition to intellectualism. In 1855 he wrote Emerson what his mother referred to as a "'Swedenborgian, rhapsodical letter" and received a kindly but dampening answer:

My dear Charles,
You are surely a strange perverse son of the light fighting against light, and it requires all the resignation which days & the corrections of largest nature teach, to acquisce [*sic*] in the waste of your genius on I know not what theory of your dear mad master Swedenborg, that genius is perni- cious. . . . To be sure, it seems verbiage to praise light & defend thought. . . . But what extreme caprice made you their accuser! . . . Years ago, when I first knew it I lamented this overcasting of my brightest star, but, as it was frankly avowed—the creed, I mean, of suppression of all thought —there was of course no choice for me; I must submit to the silence of the wise lips I coveted to listen. . . .[6]

Shortly after this letter arrived, Mrs. Newcomb wrote to thank Emerson for reproving her son's "deluded thought." This year seems to mark the height of Newcomb's Swedenborgianism. After that, he gradually lost interest in Swedenborg but retained the two doctrines of use and marriage which he wove together and incorporated as the central points of his own philosophy.

Newcomb took one of the most drastic steps of his life in 1862, when he joined the Tenth Rhode Island Volunteers. This group was recuited mainly from the members of the Providence National Guard. On May 23 several military companies were asked to as- semble for three months' service in Washington. Four days later, the regiment, bent double by the unaccustomed weight of their packs and drenched by a sudden downpour of rain, assembled in Exchange Place and boarded trains for the South. During their sojourn at Washington the troops were posted at Tennallytown, D.C. and

[4] This statement was, to be sure, a little exaggerated.
[5] *Journals,* VIII, 61.
[6] *Letters,* ed., Rusk, IV, 516.

Alexandria, Va. Their task was to defend Washington if the Confederates should approach the city, but the rebels did not get close enough to make this necessary. The most active service in which the Rhode Islanders participated was the capture of a two-foot field howitzer which a rebel-sympathizer had secreted in his barn.

The men were not spared the prevalent hardships of ill-fitting shoes and uniforms, monotonous, and often sickening, diet, and epidemics of malarial fever. One of the company wits referred to his tent as the "Smithsonian Institute," because of the wide variety of bugs it contained.[7]

To the sheltered Newcomb the discomforts of army life were most beneficial. He hardened himself admirably to the duty of standing watch on rainy nights, sleeping in exposed places, and marching long distances. In the spring after his return to Providence, he began taking "daily morning walks of at least fo[u]rteen miles." (J, II, 269) After a week of this exercise he recorded that

On the 19th I walked, without stopping, in the course of my 15 mile walk, 10 miles, by mile posts, on the railway, in a little over 2 hours, 5 minutes: thus progressing from my first trials of 2.17; 2.13; 2.11. (J, II, 279)

On the twenty-sixth of May he walked thirty miles in nine hours. He now spent all his mornings walking briskly along the railroad or on the bank of some river. As he strode ahead he observed the clouds and trees, the color of the water, or—if it were winter—the ice-formations on the frozen ponds; and when he got home he described in his diary what he had seen.

More and more frequently he spent part of the day writing in the new *Journal* which he had started to keep in 1851. He was coming to write in it more and more often. Volume One had covered the years between 1851 and 1861, but Volume Two lasted only two years, and Volume Three was filled in eight and a half months. Before long Newcomb noticed that he tended to write upon a rather limited number of subjects, and he gave his journals the title of *Principles of Life illustrated in thoughts on Nature, Scholarship, Shakspear, Government, the war of the great American Rebellion, & Morals & Man in general.*

[7] William A. Spicer, *History of the Ninth and Tenth Regiments Rhode Island Volunteers,* Providence, 1892, p. 260.

On June 30, 1865, a great blow fell on Newcomb: his mother died. Her death occurred too late to release him for the pursuit of his own happiness. All he knew was that the foundation upon which he had constructed his life and habits had suddenly crumbled.

Faithful to his habitual mode of writing, Newcomb made no direct mention, in his *Journals,* of her death; instead he wrote impersonally:

The fact that the death of a loved, honored, & sacred person, with whom intercourse has been dear & near, in no wise affects the substantial character of the past, & seems, in comparison with it, as a transient &, in some sense, unreal event, indicates immortality. (J, VII, 84)

A good many months later, when the shock had worn off, Newcomb wrote several long passages praising the intellect, character, and appearance of his mother. He referred to her in these places merely as "a woman he had known."

She belonged to the tropics of humanity [he wrote], for she bloomed all the year round. Her mood was almost invariably bright, buoyant, & sweet. . . . Her good sense was famous. . . . She was innocent, as well as vivacious, as a child. . . . Her interest in reading, in chess, cards, & society kept her mind fresh & apt. . . . Her eye was more brilliant than a diamond, & softer than a diamond, veiled in an amethyst. . . . She sought society: she depended on her home; & she dreaded solitude . . . never failed of asking her children when they went out, to be at home at a designated hour: & looked out for them when she expected them. (J, IX, 140)

A few months after her death he decided not to stay in Providence. He did not go at once to Europe—possibly because he felt a little lost; instead, he moved to Philadelphia. In this city he had at least one close friend, Philip Randolph. Randolph had for some time owned a farm in southern Rhode Island. He had been introduced to Newcomb through a letter from Emerson and it may have been he who induced Newcomb to settle, for a time, in Philadelphia.

SECTION IV. PHILADELPHIA AND EUROPE

From 1866 to 1871 Newcomb lived alone in a Philadelphia rooming-house. About his life during this period we can be sure only of the details which he allowed to creep into his diary. When he moved to Philadelphia, he was half-way through the tenth volume of this diary; now, in the next five years, he was to fill seventeen more volumes. From the first it had been his habit to omit from his writing all autobiographical matter. His sole concern had been with literature, politics, morals, and nature. On those very rare occasions when he had mentioned members of his family, it was as though they were the most distant of acquaintances, and the only mention he made of himself was in connection with where he had walked that day or how fast he had covered a certain distance. The diary was what he called it: "A Diary of Thoughts." After he had been in Philadelphia for a time, however, personal details began to appear more often. They consisted mainly of notations on his diet, dress, exercise, and recreations. When he recounted an actual anecdote about himself, it was presented as being about some one of his acquaintance. And when he wrote about some one he knew, or had known—like Hawthorne—he often made use of a naïve device: he inserted the person's name above the line, and then crossed it out in such a way that it was still legible.

He lived quite by himself in a room in a lodging-house. Each morning he rose before sunrise, dressed, and went out to a near-by restaurant where he breakfasted on four eggs. Then, watching the sun as it crept above the roof-line and made the smoky sky glow like a pearl, he returned to his room. There he settled down to his task of memorizing the Psalms and speeches from Shakspere, and he wrote down any thoughts which occurred to him while he recited. In the summer he spent most of his afternoons at the base-ball park; if there was no ball-game, he strolled out of town into the country. In the winter he went skating on the Schuylkill or at Fairmont Park and diligently, if self-consciously, perfected his backward roll. During the first year or two of his sojourn in Philadelphia, he spent many of his evenings visiting the Randolphs and other friends whom he made in the city. He now and then mentioned dining out and once or twice inscribed in his diary some charades written at the request of a recent hostess.

Especially in the latter part of his stay in Philadelphia Newcomb was a constant theatre-goer. He saw Booth, Forrest, Fechter, and Davenport, as Hamlet, and attended other Shaksperian performances by Murdock, Barton Hill, Adelaide Ristori, and Mrs. Scott-Siddons. He went five times to see *The Black Crook,* an early spectacle play which was damned from many pulpits because of its prominent show of the legs of its female chorus. Operas, concerts, and lecture-series also attracted him. He took especial pleasure in Beethoven's *Fidelio* and Mozart's *Marriage of Figaro*. In January, 1871, he heard what must have been one of the earliest Philadelphia productions of *Tannhäuser* and disliked it for its romantic medievalism, until some months later he learned that Wagner was a liberal and decided that he must hear "the music of the future" again.

Although he avowed disbelief in the "mythologism" of the sect, and would have committed to flames the organization which sustained "popery and priestcraft," Newcomb surprisingly often found himself present at vespers and other services in the Catholic Cathedral. And although he occasionally scoffed at what he saw and heard there, he continued to return for more. The official explanation which he gives is that

A man's presence at a place in a part of his own is, in itself, a protest against the part taken by others. . . . Sorcery becomes jugglery when it is made a spectacle. (J, XVI, 206)

That he had by no means become entirely deaf to the voice of Catholicism may be seen from his admission that he had

stood prostrate in the Cathedral at vespers yesterday afternoon, suffused with tears even so early as the first Psalm, "Dixit Dominus Domino meo . . ." (J, XVIII, 295)

As months passed, Newcomb's social intercourse appears to have dwindled. It is not surprising to find that, in the course of his increasingly solitary life, the eccentricities of his youth multiplied. He saw few friends, read fewer books, and spent his many leisure hours inspecting himself and his habits with great curiosity.

He watched his diet with the intensest of interest. For several months he gave up coffee—a beverage which he had notoriously enjoyed at Brook Farm. After a period of illness, however, he was forced to take it with his dinner as a tonic, and he made a note of its effect on him, saying,

the reaction of that is bad, & I do not like its ruthless &, in the main, needless, seizure of the nerves. (J, XXII, 17)

The "seizure of his nerves" is only too clear from the manner in which his handwriting sloped off the lines of the page that night.

Some evenings he stopped at a groggery for a glass of lager beer before coming home to write of the evil effects of alcohol and of the inertia which it caused in him. At another time he ate no meat for twenty months. On resuming it he fancied that he found himself more vigorous, although he felt less resistance to cold. One morning he ate but two of his usual four eggs for breakfast and subsequently, when he began to write his diary, experienced unusual lassitude.

Newcomb still found it necessary to discuss the problem of whether or not to keep a dairy. There was a curious dualism in his attitude toward his writing: he began to look upon his journals as his life work and as his substitute for a more regular occupation; at the same time he did not abandon his earlier notion that there could be no adequate excuse for "diarisation."

In the fourteenth volume of his *Journal* he resigned himself to writing it, saying,

I now reconcile myself, so far, to my habit—in default & in abeyance of regular & desired occupation, otherwise—of diarising, by a sense of its subserviency to good, through . . . an intention of giving it means of its publication, if only after [my] death, to the public. . . . I now express my desire & design that it be given to the Massachusetts Historical Society. (J, XIV, 84)

Only a month earlier he had written that a man in his position

must not hesitate to say, "I will study no more. I will diarise no more in the hours which I should devote to a nurture & to a redress of my awful & momentous want." (J, XIV, 8)

And a year after reconciling himself to his "habit," he "resolved, henceforth, never to think of writing or to expect to write unless for some positive object." (J, XVIII, 120) Within a week, nevertheless, while thinking about the duty of all men to do some sort of work, he thought that "a diarist may be classed as a worker, possibly, on the same terms as is the reporter of a newspaper." (J, XVIII, 139) The difference between the two was that the diarist addressed posterity while the journalist addressed his contemporaries. There was no reason, he pointed out, why a diarist should publish his diary, for it could be published after his death: "otherwise the labor of a diarist would be enormous & onerous." (J, XVIII, 140)

Superficially, at least, Newcomb found it necessary to be conventional about clothing. He had developed strong ideas about the importance of dressing as other people do, even though he reserved the right to disapprove of the foolish costumes they wore. Among idealists like the Brook Farmers one could brave December weather in linen pantaloons, but in the midst of a great city like Philadelphia it was necessary to conform—or to appear to conform. Despite his prejudice against eccentricity, however, Newcomb did take minor liberties with his dress. The most amusing of these was in connection with his stockings. In August, 1868, he confessed:

I know not how to whisper it to my friends; but I took advantage of a difficulty with my stockings, a month since, to leave them off, & my feet seem to be grateful for riddance of the damp & clammy things; their room has been, indeed, better than their company. . . . Shoes are too small, already, without the packing of superfluous haberdashery. The feet ask, as their natural right, a little roughness of contact, & as much room & air as is possible. . . . It is as yet an experiment, & it is yet summer. (J, XVIII, 309)

Among the strangest of his minor oddities are the indoor exercises which he invented to take on rainy days—and later on pleasant ones as well. The purpose of the "gymnasty" seems to have been to justify his staying in his room with his journals instead of going out for an afternoon of walking or skating.

I am glad to find [he wrote] that, if I have no time for separate, mental & physical exercise, I can, in my room, by walking & posturing, while I write, or recite, or think, or read, take both in one, so far as in-door exercise can be called due exercise. (J. XV, 266)

Later, he discovered that

during my recitation of Shakspear, with inflated lungs & upheld arms, as I promenade my room, my chest upheaves as if it were a mountain of muscle. (J, XVIII, 239)

Sometimes, when he tired of his ordinary routine, he chinned himself on the cornices of his room. A couple of years later he varied his procedure by writing with his book

resting on the wall above the level of my chin, so as to avoid all scholar's fault of bending head & shoulders. The only fault seems to be the draining of blood from the hands & arms . . . and the loss of the promenade to which I have been accustomed while writing. . . . (J, XXIV, 295)

He concluded this passage by explaining that, although he was getting advanced in years, life still appeared before him as a "vast training ground of manly condition & conduct."

Since his arrival in Philadelphia Newcomb had ceased to read anything but newspapers and perhaps a few reviews. Apart from these periodicals the only new thing which he recorded reading between 1866 and 1871 was a poem which Dr. Furness introduced him to one afternoon. The poem was a "pretended translation of a Persian poem," written "in praise & recommendation of drink as the salve of scepticism and mortality," (J, XXVI, 249) evidently Fitzgerald's *Rubaiyat*.

In January, 1871, there was a recurrence of his interest in books. He mentions looking again into the *Inferno* and reading Terence, Plautus, Aristophanes, and Farquhar. He picked out Terence as "the first book I have read verbatim & seriatim for many years." (J, XXVII, 8)

It was in 1868 that Newcomb began writing his "Songs of Love," an unending sequence of feverish, erotic, doggerel verses. Between 1868 and 1871 he wrote 1015 of them, apparently as an outlet for his sexual frustration. Such an explanation can, I think, account better than any other for the immense number of the poems, their extremely physiological nature, and his willingness to include them in the *Journals*, which, he hoped, would one day be published. The reasons which he gave for writing them in his diary are convincing only to one painfully eager to be convinced; and yet Newcomb, despite the strong influence of his upbringing and the propriety of the period in which he lived, easily overpowered himself by his argument that his poems were not obscene but merely "natural." So thoroughly did he deceive himself that beneath one of the least printable of his poems he wrote: "These distiches would do for a bold, not bawdy, clown in a drama." (J, XVIII, 234) The theatre of the present day would not treat such verses as bold rather than bawdy, nor would it be likely to include them in any presentation. The Philadelphia stage of the 1870's can hardly be thought of as more liberal.

In the summer of 1869 his mind was almost entirely governed by feverish thoughts of sex. His obsession can be plainly seen in the first two hundred pages of Volume Twenty-two of the *Journals*.

Here, in addition to forty-four "Songs of Love," he wrote at some length on the mating of a pair of panthers, which he had watched in the Zoo at Central Park; the lechery of apes and monkeys; the laws against fornication in Philadelphia; the fact that in New York City the deaths exceeded the births; virility in old men; masculinity in writers; and the vicious extremes of pruriency and prudery. He developed all these subjects with the same emphasis. Because his thoughts were flowing in one channel he found sexual symbolism in the most casual of happenings—from the glance of some passer-by to the capture of a moth by a swallow.

The question has been raised by Miss Mary C. Harmon, in her unpublished paper on Newcomb, as to whether the erotic poems were not the expression of a licentious phase in his life. She wrote:

In later life, Newcomb evidently had an illicit affair, or possibly several, which moved him to write love poetry.[1]

As Miss Harmon read only a small fraction of the *Journal,* her assumption is understandable. I feel, however, that if Newcomb had been having an affair, he would not have had the impulse to write poems of this particular sort. The influences which formed his character suggest rather that he might have burst into morbid anxiety about his guilt.

Newcomb made a vigorous effort to avoid sublimating his desires. He constantly reminded himself that he must not allow his diarisation to take the place of a fuller and richer life; and yet, at the same time, he could not keep from writing at the rate of four and five pages a day. He often expounded the virtue and necessity of "mourning." When he did so he was not referring, as one might easily assume, to grief at his mother's death but to a persistent longing for marriage, or "full manly scope." Perhaps the most striking example of his tragic eagerness to keep his plight clearly in his consciousness was the prayer he wrote in 1867 after a short visit to Providence:

Let me, please Providence, so manage that I may not allow the loneliness & the homesickness, which I experience on my return from a visit to my family & relations in New England & New York, to this comparatively strange city, to become alloyed or allayed by any extraneous acclimation, nor by any diversion. Let me so endure, &, even, welcome the depriva-

[1] Mary·Catherine Harmon, "The Philosophy of Action," p. 23.

tions of homelike associations as to make them the incentive forces, not only of a home amongst relatives, but also of a home of my own; let me be careful against any demoralisation through a resort to diarisation, reading, or skating, of my capacity in heart & head for full manly scopes & life. (J. XV, 246)

The importance of his poems, with their innumerable revisions and word-substitutions, should not be underestimated; they contain the clue to Newcomb's state of mind and the key to many of the otherwise obscure sections in his system of moral philosophy.

On May 24, 1871, on the last page of the twenty-seventh volume, the journal comes abruptly to an end. Perhaps the reason for the abruptness is that the journal was actually continued somewhere else —on ship-board or in Europe. It was not long after this that Newcomb fulfilled his youthful wish of going abroad. When Emerson heard the news of his friend's departure he was amazed. He thanked Benjamin Wiley, his informant,

for the surprising news of St. Charles—[adding] I had thought he would content himself with dreaming, that is creating his Europe, without descending to the vulgar method of eyes. But he actually went to the war, & why not now to London? But being there, I doubt his early return. Nothing but bad news from his bankers would bring him home, him for whom old civilization has an endless charm, & America only a solitude.[2]

If Emerson's guess was correct, Newcomb never had bad news from his bankers—at any rate he remained in Europe until he died.

Little is known about the last twenty-four years of his life. He sent a letter to Emerson in 1872, in which he offered to lend or give him enough money to rebuild his house which had just burned down. The rest of the letter contained an account of his travels in Europe and the rather defensive assurance that even if he had not accomplished great things he had at least kept a diary.[3] In the fall of this same year he and Emerson had a visit in London.[4] Nothing is known of the nature of the meeting.

The only things which now remain of his European life are an anecdote, a packet of sketches, and four letters addressed to his sister Charlotte.

The anecdote is that when Dr. Bowen, a friend of the Newcomb

[2] *Letters,* ed., Rusk, VI, 191.
[3] *Ibid.,* 220.
[4] *Ibid.,* 226, f.n.

family, visited France, he looked up his old acquaintance, Charles Newcomb. When he happened to say that he was interested in Gothic architecture, Newcomb told him about a very lovely cathedral outside Paris and suggested that they visit it. One morning, accordingly, the two set out. Newcomb would not hear of going directly to the place, but insisted upon approaching it by way of a hill from which they had a very fine view of the cathedral. After some time they went down and into the building. Bowen wandered about examining all its nooks and alcoves, while Newcomb settled himself quietly in a corner and remained there. When Bowen was ready to leave, Newcomb said that, since he had not finished seeing the church, he would like to spend the night at an inn and come back the next day. His curiosity aroused, Dr. Bowen fell in with the plan. In the morning, to his surprise, he saw his friend return and sit quietly down in a different corner. Some days after the two men had returned to Paris, Newcomb presented Dr. Bowen with a fine sketch of the cathedral.[5]

Though affectionate, the four letters which Charles sent his sister from Europe[6] contain little personal news. The first two were sent from London in 1879, and they were chiefly concerned with the problem of legacies. The other two letters, which were sent from Paris, answer questions about family history and give a tourist's account of life and sights in France. In the letter of 1888 there is one question which is of no little interest. Charles asks Charlotte "to try & find out what became of my trunk of books & papers, which you left in the Casey garret." (December 11, 1888) He says that in the trunk were books presented to him by Emerson and Hawthorne, and that there were some drawings by Caroline Sturgis. One cannot help wondering if the volumes of his early *Journal* were also packed away in this trunk and if they were lost, along with the other contents.

Of the last two decades of his life nothing else is known, except that he died in Paris, in 1894.

[5] For this information I am indebted to Miss Sarah N. Gallagher.
[6] These letters are among the Newcomb manuscripts at Brown University.

CHAPTER TWO

THE JOURNALS

Section I. The Manuscripts

AFTER they were written, the Newcomb journals crossed the Atlantic twice. They junketed about the continent of Europe for twenty years before they were sent home to rest not many miles from where they were first begun.

The history of their rediscovery is interesting. In the course of his work on Emerson, Van Wyck Brooks grew curious about the "Book-Journal" of Charles King Newcomb, which Emerson had admired and praised. He at last discovered it in East Greenwich, Rhode Island, where it had been carefully preserved in the attic of Miss Sarah N. Gallagher, Newcomb's great-niece. The reference, in *The Flowering of New England,* to the Newcomb journal "that lay unpublished in a Rhode Island attic fifty years after his death"[1] caught the attention of Professor Randall Stewart. When he came to Brown University, he asked Miss Gallagher if she would deposit the Newcomb manuscripts at Brown. At his suggestion she sent them to Brown University Library.

The manuscripts consist of letters, seven commonplace books, four volumes of numbered moral thoughts, a keepsake book belonging to Charlotte Newcomb, and twenty-seven volumes of journals.

There are over three hundred letters, most of which were sent to Charles Newcomb by his mother. Those written in the years 1836-1837 and 1841-1848 are especially interesting because of the literary gossip which they contain.

Of the seven commonplace books six are by Newcomb. The seventh evidently belonged to a man of an earlier generation—perhaps his father or grandfather. Newcomb's copy-books are six and a half

---

[1] Van Wyck Brooks, *The Flowering of New England, 1815-1865,* N.Y. 1936, p. 244.

inches by eight. The paper, which is of fairly good quality, is bound between heavy cardboard covers. The first book was given to Charles while he was a junior in college by his brother Henry. In a flourishing and youthful hand the following inscription is written and rewritten on the first two pages:

Charles King Newcomb
Providence
R.I.
from H. S. N.—Dec. 14th 1836

Since none of the commonplace books is numbered, a list of them may be of some use. In the order in which they were begun they are:

1. December 14, 1836. 136 pp.
2. December 24, 1839. 119 pp.
3. There is no date on the fly-leaf of this volume. The first entry is dated October 25, 1839. Some entries were made as late as December, 1846. 171 pp.
4. January 2, 1847. 167 pp.
5. January, 1848. 171 pp.
6. May, 1854. Two-thirds of the 350 pages are blank.

Like the commonplace books the journals are six and a half by eight inches. They are written on very heavy paper and are stoutly bound in green or speckled covers, with leather backs and corners. Though they vary in length the average volume contains 360 pages.

The following is a descriptive list of the volumes, together with their length, dates of beginning and ending, and any pertinent notations to be found on the fly-leaves.

1. Charles King Newcomb, Providence, October, 1851. Principles of Life, illustrated in thoughts on Nature, Scholarship, Shakspear, Government, the War of the great American Rebellion, & Morals & Man in general, by C. K. N. . . . The contents of this Diary, so to call it, suggested, & only recently, the above title of Principles of Life, &c; the title, in no wise, suggested the contents. (Feb. 1865). (October 11, 1851-August 13, 1861. 350 pp.) [Every volume is inscribed with Newcomb's name, and the first twenty-one have the title, *Principles of Life*. . . .]
2. Providence, July, 1861.
   (August 22, 1861-June 27, 1863. 358 pp.)
3. Providence, June, 1863.
   (June 30, 1863-March 11, 1864. 360 pp.)
4. Providence, March, 1864.
   Morning Studies. [Evidently a suggested title.]

(March 2, 1864-September 9, 1864. 360 pp.)
5. Providence, September, 1864.
 (September 12, 1864-January 20, 1865. 360 pp.)
6. Providence, January, 1865.
 April 21, 1865. It is my purpose, after this date, as it has been, as a whole, my habit, not to alter, after the date has passed, what has been previously written in this diary: inasmuch as, even if it should be crude or, in any degree erroneous, it may be of value or interest as illustrative of previous experience, especially of that part of experience which relates to the affairs of the country, opinions are sometimes valuable as studies & illustrations, if for no other purpose. No changes will be made, unless grammatical, or supplemental, or statistical.[2]
 (January 20, 1865-May 16, 1865. 356 pp.)
7. Providence, R.I.
 Merely for manly culture & for memoranda of the laws of condition for self & others.
 (May 16, 1865-November 11, 1865. 356 pp.)
8. Providence, R.I.
 (November 13, 1865-March 19, 1866. 358 pp.)
9. Providence, R.I.
 Write with definite ends not only of conduct, but of address as of a man to his wife: so cherish manly marriage of mind & heart even in thinking, studying, & writing.
 (March 20, 1866-July 23, 1866. 370 pp.)
10. Philadelphia, Penn.
 (June 25, 1866-October 23, 1866. 362 pp.)
11. Philadephia, Pennsylvania.
 (October 23, 1866-January 8, 1867. 360 pp.)
12. Philadelphia, Pa.
 Newcomb on Morals, Politics, Shakspear, & Nature.—Whether to select a volume of notes on Shakspear, or to publish the diary as a whole.—Give all the volumes of this diary to the Massachusetts Historical Society for its archives: it may be curious, if not valuable, in coming times.
 (January 8, 1867-March 6, 1867. 360 pp.)
13. Philadelphia, Pa.
 Newcomb on Shakspear & Life. San Carlo's Diary on Shakspear & Life.
 (March 6, 1867-June 7, 1867. 358 pp.)
14. Philadelphia, Pa.
 This diary is disposed of on page 84. It is prefaced on p. 263, & qualified there,—provisionally.
 (June 7, 1867-September 26, 1867. 358 pp.)
15. Philadelphia, Pa.
 Title. Action, Life, Men, & Shakspear.

[2] This note was later cancelled by Newcomb.

Began to write, on feet, altogether, as before, somewhat, Nov. 9.
(September 26, 1867-December 21, 1867. 300 pp.)
16. Philadelphia, Pa.
(December 21, 1867-March 2, 1868. 356 pp.)
17. Philadelphia, Pa.
(March 2, 1868-May 16, 1868. 352 pp.)
18. Philadelphia, Pa.
A Diary of Generalisations on the Scope of Man
Mental Exercises by means of a Diary.
Moral Exercises of Mind in Memoranda of Life.
(May 16, 1868-August 31, 1868. 360 pp.)
19. Philadelphia, Pa.
(August 31, 1868-December 12, 1868. 360 pp.)
20. Philadelphia, Pa.
(December 12, 1868-March 22, 1869. 360 pp.)
21. Philadelphia, Pa.
(March 22, 1869-July 30, 1869. 366 pp.)
22. A Diary of thoughts on principles of life, by C. K. N.
[This title is repeated in each of the remaining volumes.]
(July 31, 1869-November 13, 1869. 361 pp.)
23. (November 13, 1869-February 17, 1870. 360 pp.)
24. (February 17, 1870-May 21, 1870. 356 pp.)
25. (May 21, 1870-September 22, 1870. 359 pp.)
26. (September 22, 1870-February 7, 1871. 362 pp.)
27. (February 8, 1871-May 24, 1871. 361 pp.)

It is not surprising that Newcomb's mother had difficulty in de-
ciphering his letters to her. His hand-writing is so pinched, and so
many characters are ill-formed or represented by a mere jerk of
the pen that only long practice makes it possible to read his script
with facility. On a page three-quarters the size of an average type-
writer sheet he managed to squeeze about 255 words. The average
volume of his journals contains about 99,250 words; the total number of words in the twenty-seven volumes must come to approximately three million. Of this great bulk less than one-fortieth is represented in the selections made for the present volume.

In the first volume Newcomb wrote at irregular intervals and seldom at any great length. The intervals at which he wrote may be
seen from a glance at the dates on the first twenty pages. They were
made on October 11, October 13, October 24, December 24, 1851;
March 4, March 21, May 24, June 14, July 27, July 28, and August
24, 1852. As early as Volume IV, however, he had settled down

A typical example of the way in which Newcomb revised his Journal.
See page 49 for an interpretation of this passage.

to writing every day but Sunday. Many volumes later he happened to spend a rainy Sunday in writing. Thereafter he always wrote on the Sabbath but made an attempt to write fewer pages on this day.

In one day's writing he usually made five or ten entries. Although the commonest length for an entry is about half a page, they vary from one or two lines to three or four pages. Each one forms a complete unit. None of them is divided into paragraphs, though dashes are occasionally used to indicate a break in the sequence of composition. This absence of paragraphing may have been due to a desire to save paper. On the other hand it may be a characteristic of Newcomb's style: "Dolon," as it appears in the *Dial,* has an average of one paragraph to a page.

The manuscript of the *Journals* is peppered with deletions and substitutions. It does not seem likely that these changes were all made at the time of writing, or in the course of any one systematic revision of the diary, but rather that they were added from time to time, as Newcomb mulled over sections of the journal which he had recently written. In some places one can find three distinct layers of readings. In a sentence on page 120 of Volume VIII we find a fair example of the way in which he changed his phraseology. Originally he wrote: "but they would also engage in occupation if it was offered to them by others or was prominently visible." He then changed it to read: "they would also engage in fuller manly occupation if it seemed opened to them, or if it was prominently visible." The final reading is: "they would also enter fuller, & really manly scope if it stood opened before them, or if it was accessible without toil." In general, the effect of his substitutions is to make his qualifying phrases longer or more numerous. Sometimes the style is improved; more often it is not.

Section II. Arts and Letters

Newcomb devoted more pages of his *Journals* to literature than to any other subject except moral philosophy. A large portion of his writing on arts and letters, however, is steered into moral rather than into aesthetic channels. His commonest method is to state a moral truth, which he has assumed or perceived, and to illustrate it

by citing an incident, or quoting a few lines, from one of Shakspere's plays. At other times he reverses the process by finding in
Shakspere a text which he develops into a brief moral discourse. A
very few passages show an unadulterated attempt to criticize or inter-
pret Shakspere's art. Later in his life, when he was living in Philadelphia, Newcomb regularly attended the theatre and saw many
Shaksperian productions, which he described, somewhat vaguely, in
his diary.

He outlined his own system of illustrating morals by means of
Shakspere when he wrote:

Exemplifying humanity by Shakspear, & collating Shakspear with humanity,
are different kinds of diversions. . . . A man may use Shakspear as Shakspear used the books which gave him his themes, plots, & models.[1]

In a similar vein he wrote, referring definitely to his own work:

If anybody ever reads this diary they may think that the criticisms &
moralisations on Shakspear are so many successive attempts to study &
illustrate the passages in his plays; whereas, in great part, they are the
record of references suggested by thoughts & sentiments that were initiated
in the world & only collated or connected with Shakspear, or referred to
him, or hung upon him.[2]

Even for a critic of the ethical school, his approach is a little unusual. A number of Shaksperian critics of the 1860's wrote about the
moral rather than the artistic aspects of Shakspere's work; but few
were so frank as to start with a moral subject and then to proceed
to illustrate it by lines from *Hamlet* or *Timon*. It is possible to
find in Newcomb's philosophy a basis for his curiously reversed procedure. His Swedenborgian hatred of intellect, of diarisation, and of
literary work in general, no doubt included a distrust of critical writing. He described the process by which he had reconciled himself
to spending so much time in criticism of Shakspere, when he explained how

The young man, who decries & ignores Shakspear's plays today, because
they give him less of real life than his own sentiments, aspirations, &
purposes suggest to him, may, after some years, be an interested collater
of Shakspear's text with life, through his very interest, determination, &
experience in life. (J, XII, 185)

[1] P. *115*. Italicized page numbers refer to the present work.
[2] *125*.

It is hard to avoid the suspicion that, when Newcomb started with a moral observation and illustrated it by an example from some great writer, he felt that he was not really guilty of indulging in literary criticism. He was, instead, coming closer to his ideal of "developing full manly scope"; he was attending to problems of conduct and of "action"; he was not losing himself in the dead end of abstraction.

We find him, in accordance with his system, generalizing—as Henry Giles[3] did four years later—about how vicious women exceed vicious men in depravity. He is subsequently reminded of the contrast between Macbeth and his wife: "Shakspear," writes Newcomb, "showed his usual verisimilitude to nature . . . in delineating Lady Macbeth, not only as the tempter of her husband, but as worse than him."[4] Pointing out that "unprincipled . . . women resort to the artifices of coquetry to develop or insure the positiveness in a man, which they know their mere characters will not suffice to foster,"[5] he drives home his point by referring to the difference between the caution of Cressida and the generous confidence of Juliet. "The facility with which men who are addicted to sententiousness & to saws are diverted from principles & ends" makes him think of the "ductility of Polonius in Hamlet's hands, through sheer wit."[6] Newcomb describes morbidness as

a moral malady in which the simple relations & responsibilities of life seem intricate, doubtful, & impossible, just as in physical malady the least movement in one's chamber seems long, & the ordinary amount of diet on one's plate seems monstrous.[7]

In this way he explains Hamlet's horror at his "exceptional plane & part."

In the opposite manner Newcomb refers to some phrase or nicety of characterization in Shakspere, and discourses on its moral truth and value. Hamlet is described as the only person in the play "who has any sort of moral object in view," although he is also the only one who has not "some definite sort of an object in view."[8] Speaking of Coriolanus as one who wishes "to confer, but not to receive, favors" he mentions the parallel case of his own mother who "was

[3] Henry Giles, *Human Life in Shakespeare*, Boston, 1868. See Augustus Ralli, *A History of Shakespearian Criticism*. London, 1932, I.
[4] 104.   [5] 115.   [6] 132.   [7] 137.   [8] 110.

lavish in lending, but not in borrowing, books."[9] In order to convince us of Shylock's "strength of wit & even of character,"[10] Newcomb goes on to discuss the imagination and the resolute endurance of privation which must accompany miserliness.

Both of Newcomb's methods result in approximately the same quality of criticism; for, though the two techniques are superficially opposite, they have but one aim: to estimate Shakspere's genius as a moralist. Both succeed about equally well in their purpose; both manage, about equally often, to enrich our understanding of some character in the plays.

By proceeding from the abstract to the particular he sometimes shows great ingenuity in explaining Shakspere's choice of incident or of words. After pointing out that "eccentricity in dress . . . shows a dangerous disregard of relations to society," he says that a woman realizes that she can have more confidence in "a pliant conformer to fashion" than in one who dresses according to some peculiar theory. The connection between an odd costume and an odd mind persuades Newcomb that it is Malvolio's general eccentricity which leads the humorists of *Twelfth Night* to make him an eccentric in costume.[11] Newcomb also noticed that uneducated people

are often close observers, by virtue of their position, & shrewd observers, by virtue of their curiosity. . . . The parlor is as a stage-scene to the kitchen. . . .[12]

From this observation he was enabled to understand why it was that servants played such a prominent part in the drama. In Shakspere's plays, especially, they were "something of a chorus."

Illustrating Shakspere by morals, it is clear, was not very different from illustrating morals by Shakspere. One suspects, indeed, that Newcomb occasionally went out of his way to think up a moral generalization with which to introduce some remark which he wished to make about Coriolanus or Macbeth. It is difficult to suppose that he actually thought of "ambitious men" as being "prone to superstition through the forwardness & image-making tendencies of their perverted imaginations . . . idolatrous in sentiment as in acquisitiveness,"[13] before it occurred to him that his description fitted the char-

[9] 136.   [10] 135.   [11] 121.   [12] 113.   [13] 104-105.

acter of Macbeth and explained Macbeth's relationship to the Witches. In this example, as in a few others, it seems likely that Newcomb deliberately shoved the cart before the horse in an effort to remain constant to his anti-intellectual principles.

There are a few discussions of Shakspere which are concerned more exclusively with artistic value and interpretation. Such a passage is the one in which he discusses the structure of *Timon*. Shakspere, he says, is here obliged,

in verisimilitude to Timon, to conform his dramatic action, from the more general conventionalism of the usual drama, to the almost epic narrative of a monologue.[14]

A more impressionistic bit of interpretation is his sketch of the atmosphere with which *Lear* opens. He finds it

thick with the conspiring elements of a horrible storm. Lear's fitful heat; Cordelia's sullen temperateness; Goneril & Regan's vigorous heartlessness; Kent's impetuous indignation; Gloster's stagnant sentiment; the suitors' hushed expectations . . . prepare & prelude a violent outbreak. Preparation . . . procures the presence of active forces.[15]

Newcomb had a good sense of artistic pattern and repetition, even though he did not appear to pay much attention to the form of an entire play or work of fiction. He noticed that Shakspere's plays had

commonly . . . a sort of series of personages, in which the lesser virtues of some foil the greater virtues of others, & the greater [*sic*] vices of some foil the greater vices of others.[16]

He discerned that Biron, Amado, and Costard, in *Love's Labor's Lost* were "but parts of a long line of homogeneous & various impersonisation in the same play." In *Romeo and Juliet* he found that Lady Capulet, the Nurse, and Juliet illustrated each other; with less justification, I think, he saw in *Hamlet* another such series: Osric, Polonius, Laertes, Horatio, and Hamlet. Newcomb laid to Hamlet's responsive impressibility his "quick & abandoned" call, "Hillo, ho, ho, boy! come, bird, come." He explained that in a moment of tension Hamlet was simply answering, in kind, Marcellus's cry of "Illo, ho, ho, my lord!"[17]

In Newcomb's Shaksperian criticism there is a tendency to find

[14] *109.*   [15] *135.*   [16] *145.*   [17] *149.*

common traits in different characters. In one place he asserted that
Hamlet and Macbeth were in the same moral predicament; (J. XV,
215) in another he says that Timon "is Hamlet run to seed"[18] in
respect to morbidity. Iago and Falstaff he compares as examples of
different degrees of viciousness: "Fallstaff is parboiled in vice; Iago
is frozen in it."[19] Most successful of his parallels is the prolonged
contrast which he finds between *Romeo and Juliet* and *Troilus and
Cressida.* According to his custom he expresses in moral terminology
the difference which he finds between Troilus and Romeo. Where
Romeo was groping for the truth of love, Troilus sought the good
of love before its truth, and thus "fastened upon Cressida for the
sake of experience before principle."[20] Observing the difference in
the partings of the two pairs of lovers, he saw that Romeo and Juliet
"would as soon think of doubting each other's love, as of making
professions of constancy to each other."[21] Cressida, however, feels
obliged "almost [to] exhaust the eloquent rhetoric" of lovers "in
her attempt at makeweights for her superficial sentiment."[22]

Newcomb never developed a strong sense of Shakspere as a
dramatist. Few, if any, plays were given in Providence. Boston had
some Shaksperian productions. There, in his early twenties, Newcomb went twice to see Macready in *Hamlet.* It was not until he
moved to Philadelphia, however, that he had a chance to become a
regular theatre-goer. He was then in his mid-forties, and his attitude toward Shakspere was already set. When he saw the plays on
the stage he saw little more than what he had read in his study; and
his description of a performance generally referred to the timbre of
the actor's voice, to some of the words prudishly or carelessly substituted for Shakspere's text, and to the instructive qualities of the
drama. His criticism of the acting is anything but specific. When he
says that Edwin Booth's Iago was "too pensive & isolated . . . too
much like Hamlet, in reflectiveness,"[23] and that his Hamlet had "too
mobile & demonstrative an impatience & restlessness,"[24] it is hard
to be sure what his criticism means or how valid it is. His descriptive
phrases are vague and abstract in meaning: "splendid & suggestive,"

[18] *101.*   [19] *123.*   [20] *139.*
[21] *145.*   [22] *145.*   [23] *120.*
[24] *123.*

"impressive & picturesque," "intense & interesting," "remarkable & effective in the personisation of Lear . . . without maintaining a free range & conduct of general relation to it."

Newcomb's criticism is rather like that of a few English writers who flourished in the 1860's. Like most of them, he treats Shakspere as a moralist. With Thomas Kenny[25] he believes that Shakspere's skill in understanding and reproducing the feelings of his characters was largely due to the passivity and femininity of his nature. Because he had no character, Shakspere could easily creep into characters stronger than his own.

Although Newcomb resembled interpreters of Shakspere like Cowden Clarke and Thomas Kenny, he does not seem to have written under their, or anyone's, influence. He thought and wrote out of his own isolation; and the faults as well as the originality of his criticism may be partly accounted for by the fact that his thought lacked that abrasion which is provided by contact with the thought of others.

By the time that he started his *Journal,* Newcomb was beginning to lose interest in general reading. The great part of his criticism, therefore, is confined to Shakspere, whom he continued to memorize and recite.

As he had done in the case of Shakspere, he generally judged other writers by moral criteria. He condemned the sonnets of Petrarch as "tainted with moral adultery,"[26] and thought their fame illustrative of the moral indifference of the intellectual world. Jane Austen he censured, not for her playful malice but because in *Emma* she allowed women to fall in love first with the men "without its being condemned";[27] and although he admired and enjoyed her novels he doubted the propriety of her having published them. He read Dante and was greatly pleased by the *Inferno* and the *Purgatorio.* In the *Paradiso,* however, he found "a tendency . . . to end in the . . . passivity of postural & sensational ritualism";[28] and he deplored the fact that here Dante

who had been something of an observer in the interest of morals, becomes more or less of a vague intellectualist, a spiritual abstractionist, like one lost in reverie before . . . painted windows.[29]

[25] See Ralli, II, 309-311.   [26] *99.*   [27] *96.*
[28] *103.*   [29] *103.*

After seeing a production of Bulwer's *Lady of Lyons,* he remarked that, although it was not preëminent in genius, it "showed some aspect of genius . . . in the moral—which was the republican—motive of the piece"[30] and that it was "an effective play, on this ground, for the cultivation of self-respect in the audiences." It was like Newcomb to discover genius by such a touchstone.

With various other writers he was more discerning. He imputed the floridity of Ruskin's style to a habit of writing during the heat of thought. "If Ruskin," he said,

had waited a year or two before writing his Modern Painters, he might not have felt like writing at all, but if he had then felt like it, he would have been much less diffuse, excited, & elaborate, & wordy than, intelligent & suggestive as his book is, he was at first flash & time when he wrote it.[31]

Later he added that it looked "as if Ruskin had got into the habit of incontinently proclaiming & printing whatever he thought."[32] Longfellow's translation of Dante gained praise for its "simplicity, preciseness, & reproduction." "Longfellow," he said, "seems to be just poet enough to make a nice translator."[33] Newcomb made some interesting remarks on what he considered to be the sham delicacy with which Dickens catered to the taste of the Victorian period:

The fact that fully discreet virtue has much less to do with the, so called, delicacy of his romances, as compared with those of some others, is suggested by his congenial, as well as professional, treatment of drinking, intoxication, & social, apart from sexual, scrapes.[34]

He noticed the likeness of Pickwick and Sam Weller to Don Quixote and Sancho Panza, and found that Pickwick was "a commonplace simpleton, however sweet in sort, compared with Don Quixote: in that he has less of any kind & degree of manly ambition & activity."[35]

From Newcomb's impressions of Hawthorne an apparently correct impression of the man can be extracted. He had read little of Hawthorne's work[36] and was judging him on the basis of their brief intimacy at Brook Farm. He called Hawthorne "a loafer in the ways of genius."[37] He found in him "the indiscriminateness & other imperfections of a child."[38] Newcomb could not help wondering if

[30] *156.*
[31] *142.*
[32] *157.*
[33] *129.*
[34] *143.*
[35] *154.*
[36] *149.*
[37] *139.*
[38] *149.*

back of Hawthorne's reserve lay some "suppressed & partly overcome, or otherwise more or less superseded, malice or ill-nature." It was with surprising insight that he wrote:

His diary will be his best production, I think, because it is more of himself under natural & social influences, than are his elaborate romances.[39]

He also discovered what seems to me to be the key to some of Hawthorne's faults as an artist: "He was so chronically & chiefly self-conscious that every thing he thinks & writes is a reflex of the personal man himself."[40]

About the other arts he wrote at less length. His interest in architecture was strong; but in writing of it he limited himself to developing the contrast which he saw in the spiritual backgrounds of Greek and Gothic architectural form. In a Greek structure he saw "something of the rude cave" undermining a rock; while in the Gothic he found the inspiration of the "wild forest" and the upheaving mountains. (J, II, 226) He suggested that the "inventors of Greek architecture had evidently been accustomed to groves, gardens, & plains," while the early Gothic architects had been familiar with "vast forests of odorous pines & somber hemlocks."[41] There was philosophical significance in the two kinds of construction: the straight, rigid, Greek column showed an isolated, uncoöperative individualism; the Gothic pillar, with its curved and spreading top and its way of interlacing with other pillars, represented a "social & reciprocal" spirit.[42]

While Newcomb enjoyed music he seems to have taken less pleasure in it than in the visual arts of architecture and painting. On several occasions he mentions Mozart with approval, but appears to have enjoyed him chiefly because he recalled having heard his mother play Mozart on the piano. In general, his appreciation of music was determined by his conception of the composer. He speaks of acquiring a new interest in the work of Beethoven after hearing that he "was susceptible in affection, never being without passion for some woman." (J, XXVI, 223) At his first hearing of Wagner he was reminded of Tractarianism and of "revived medievalism." He condemned the new music for its "ritualism" and moral romanticism; for, as he later confessed, he had had the idea that Wagner was "a

[39] *149.*   [40] *150.*   [41] *133.*   [42] *133.*

sort of popish dilettanti."[43] When he found out that the composer was a liberal, he determined to hear him again and prepared to like him.

As we have seen, Newcomb seldom attempted to judge any work of art on aesthetic grounds. This was, very possibly, because his aesthetic appreciation was keenest in the visual field. Forms in nature, architecture, and painting meant a great deal to him, and he was able to write more fluently and directly about them than about forms and mediums, which he wrote about at length but valued only after an effort. In his discussions of Shakspere, and of most other writers, he treats them not as artists but as moralists. His criticism, therefore, does little to add to our understanding of their technique and purpose. On the other hand, his ingenuity in discovering new or unorthodox shades of characterization often enriches our conception of some of Shakspere's dramatic personages; and now and again, as he might have put it, he is "splendidly suggestive."

SECTION III. NATURE

Newcomb's descriptions of landscapes, trees, sunsets, or winter scenes constitute some of his most successful writing. His observation of nature was subjective, aesthetic, and intense. Perhaps because they originated in strong aesthetic emotion, his delineations of natural scenes abound with his freest and most original figures of speech.

Since nature is one of the vastest quarries from which metaphors and similes are ordinarily hewn, figurative descriptions of it are of peculiar interest. If an author would avoid monotony, his illustration of natural objects by comparing them to other natural objects must be sparing and well chosen. He needs, then, to seek other sources for the greater part of any figurative language he may use. Newcomb solved the problem by likening nature to man and to things of human manufacture.

He was quick to notice in the landscape resemblances to parts of the human body—especially to the eye. The barren, desert-like ocean impressed him as being like a "great lidless eye."[1] He saw in the early sunrise "the dim sort of beauty of a half-closed eye"[2] and con-

---

[43] *156.*   [1] *163.*   [2] *181.*

trasted with it noon-day, "the eye of the giant in his strength."[3] Sailing home from New York once, he noticed how the landscape appeared to pivot about the moving ship, and he noted keenly that "the aspect of nature follows the observer like the eye of a portrait."[4] Mountains appeared to him to "rise like warm pulses."[5] When he looked at the flashing of the sun on the rippling surface of a lake, it seemed to him as if he saw "the lakes . . . tossing up their thousand hands in play with the sweet vernal winds."[6]

At other times he endowed earthly phenomena with human attributes. The mountains, he thought, stood "like the aged good, partly divested of their earthly body, as if entering the next world to which they are near."[7] Their tops were "worn by the tread of the stars."[8] Spring, with its sequences of rain and shine, reminded him of "a young parent, who cannot be all smiles to its offspring";[9] and the chilliness of this early season recalled the "apparent indifference of a newly married couple to everybody but themselves."[10] The sun, the stars, and the seasonal changes seemed to march across the earth like Titanic beings. As he watched the sun rise he felt that it trod "over the earth on a golden floor of its own light, like a hero marching amid his own glory."[11] The large dried leaves of autumn crossed "the air of October, with resounding tread, as athletes, swollen with muscle, & spent with achievement, walk heavily after a campaign in the arena."[12] What a contrast they presented to the little, juicy leaves of April which tossed buoyantly in the air "as children . . . agilely toss & spring about in the arms of their smiling parents."[13]

In a Thoreauvian mood he found in nature a purposeful consciousness, and wrote:

As the farmer spots the trees on his estate in token that he is to cut them down, so the earth sprinkles the trees with mould, even before their prime, to convert them in due time into loam.[14]

That his attitude towards nature was deliberately unsentimental may be seen from a notation he made in June, 1863. In the course of a walk to Quidnic he observed that

The fields & woods were as truly . . . busy as the operatives in the factories

[3] 181.	[4] 177.	[5] 178.	[6] 162.
[7] 166.	[8] 165.	[9] 180.	[10] 185.
[11] 173.	[12] 182.	[13] 182.	[14] 168.

which lined the Pawtuxet valley . . . or as the farmers who were tilling the ground by the wayside. . . . Nature cannot, if it would, stop to entertain the aimless stroller, any more than can the working husbandman or mechanic stop to entertain him.[15]

The contrast between the natural and the artificial is enforced by some of Newcomb's metaphors and similes. The dwellings, tools, manufactures, and arts of human society comprise a vast source for comparisons. The bare trees of September were "dismantled, like untenanted houses after a conflagration."[16] In the clearing of the air which followed a storm of several days "the dome of the sky . . . appeared as if . . . [it] had been retouched & cleansed."[17] Much of his nature-writing is enlivened by vivid references to household articles and habits. He speaks of the cracks in the ice as "seaming it like a carpet."[18] The heavy April rains "beat out, as with a mallet, the twigs into leavelets, & the buds into blossoms."[19] The dust of skate tracks is "piled in heaps like corded wood."[20] The first bird-songs of the spring sounded to Newcomb "as if the bird was drawing up with its tongue, as with a bucket, the vernal music out of its winter depositary."[21] Noticing the way in which the tree-leaves seemed to sprout out in the direction of the sun's beams, he wrote,

The sun sucks up vegetation through the trees as through syphons. It lets it fall again, as in suspended movement, toward the mother earth.[22]

After seeing a blazing sunset he declared that it had "the common & practical beauty of a baker's oven."[23] Thinking, in October, of the infancy of fruit he wrote: "Blossoms are the swaddling clothes of young fruits."[24]

A very few of his similes involve food and drink. In one place, however, he speaks of the way in which "the summer air gradually tones down in temperature, like a long standing drink of spiced wine,"[25] so that its warmth and its chill could be simultaneously felt. Elsewhere, he writes, "For the last two nights but one,—the white stars have been deliciously mingled with red auroras, like pieces of ice in rosy wine."[26]

[15] *166.*   [16] *178.*   [17] *173.*
[18] *164.*   [19] *166.*   [20] *169.*
[21] *175.*   [22] *180.*   [23] *167.*
[24] *185.*   [25] *181.*   [26] *189.*

When he revisited the ocean after a long absence from it, he expressed the familiarity of his sensations by saying that it "fell upon my senses . . . as calmly as an old shoe."[27] In 1867 it came into his head for the first time that

the soughing sound of autumnal winds was owing to the stiff age of the foliage. It reminds one of the creaking of a old vessel, laboring in a storm, on the tossing ocean, which is about to engulph it.[28]

Observing the effects of the summer's drought he writes:

The summer, before it evacuates for the winter . . . lays the train of a fire in its rear which shall, of itself, consume the vegetation before it falls into the cold & uncongenial hands of the invader.[29]

Newcomb most effectively likens natural sounds and appearances to those created by musicians and painters. He speaks of how the "treble of the frogs" composed with the "tenor of the sky"[30] to remind him of the great harmony of landscape and nature. The sound of the cracking of the ice at Mashapaug Pond made "a natural symphony" in which could be heard "the tuning of violencellos. . . . Drums, cannon, stringed instruments"; and the seams in the ice formed "the strings of the music which they sounded in breaking."[31] He often thought of a natural landscape in terms of a painted one. The haze in the atmosphere looked to him like the "gloss of a new picture,"[32] and the evening star shone out "like a cumulating dash of fresh pigment."[33] One night the crude soft yellow of the sunset could be compared only to "such a pigment as children use."[34] At another time, as in "The Rime of the Ancient Mariner," the "clouds look[ed] dry & hard like clouds in a picture."[35] Occasionally he perceived a sculpturesque quality in the scene, as when he saw the moon filmed over with clouds, and thought that "it was cased like the face of a statue draped in a marble veil."[36] Elsewhere he spoke of frozen water-lily leaves as playing at architecture because they appeared to hold up "the floor of the ice . . . like brackets or columnar entablatures."[37]

He was especially fond of comparing clouds, ice, and the surface of the sea to jewels—to the Oriental splendors of porphyry, amber,

[27] *172.*   [28] *182.*   [29] *185.*   [30] *170.*
[31] *164.*   [32] *168.*   [33] *167.*   [34] *170.*
[35] *178.*   [36] *170.*   [37] *169.*

agate, and pearl. Narragansett Bay in the afternoon sunlight resembled a "mass of porphyry frosted with silver light."[38] On another day the ocean looked "like a desert of broken crystals";[39] and at still a different time it blazed like a "molten fire of porphyry, silver, emerald, & ruby." Sometimes the clouds lay in strata in the evening sky, "compact, like things in amber,"[40] or the branches "streak[ed] the clear amber of the air like veins in agate."[41] Newcomb spoke of ice as "an orebed of pearls & diamonds."[42] The moon in the early evening "hung resplendent in a sky of bridal purity of tint, like a pearl in a delicate & open shell."[43] Even in these, the most conventional of his comparisons, he contrives to introduce some freshness and novelty.

Although Newcomb illustrated most of his impressions by figures drawn from sources outside nature, he was quick to perceive many inter-relationships between elements and animals, hours and seasons. The brilliance and the murmuring of water recalled the shimmering feathers and the twittering voices of birds; the waves of the ocean seemed to "chatter aloud like uneasy & gossiping sparrows."[44] In the course of a stroll on an oven-hot day he noticed how the bay seemed to rest "on its cool bed like a beast in a pasture."[45] Lily-pads made him think of the broad feet of diving ducks. The summer he referred to as "spring's noon"; autumn was its sunset; and "winter, perhaps, its night."[46] Clouds he compared to dolphins; when he saw them scatter and form new clouds, he thought them "like spiders weaving webs out of themselves."[47] During a walk in the White Mountains he noticed the rich black soil there; and when he returned to his hotel-room he wrote:

A tree does not fall but vegetation seizes hold of it like a worm, & covers it with loam & moss, as with spittle before it absorbs it.[48]

Ever since the days when, in the midst of reading *Titan,* he had exclaimed over Richter's "Natural orchard" descriptions (CB, October 1839, 18), he had been deeply impressed by the beauty of trees. When he wrote about the beauties of nature it was most often

---

[38] *163.* [39] *172.* [40] *161.*
[41] *169.* [42] *164.* [43] *173.*
[44] *176.* [45] *177.* [46] *162.*
[47] *168.* [48] *171.*

about the shapes and attitudes of trees. He said that they rose from the ground like fountains, that the earth sent them up like rockets, that they were wooden flowers; in winter they resembled "mountain streams glaciered by the frost,"[49] in summer they "shone like singing birds,"[50] and in March they crouched and curved "like tigers arching their backs & purring under the riding Bacchus."[51] He spoke of them, too, as "the shelter[s] of darkness," because "the shadows which sit under them in the day seem to have mounted into them in the night,"[52] and he wrote that "shadow seems in its nest among spruces, & has in them some of its darkest affinities."[53]

Good as they are, Newcomb's pictures of nature do not show to the best advantage in their present form. Because of the rambling sequences of the figures of speech in them, they are better suited to some longer narrative. As they are, they are like a haphazard mosaic, which composes neither picture nor design but a mere miscellany of brilliant dots. Almost every section is sprawling in form and lacks real unity. An absence of form, to be sure, can be expected in a diary. Still, where a division into sections exists the reader is usually right in hoping to find that conscious selection, rather than free association, has guided the construction.

Newcomb's manner of descriptive writing seems to have had its source in his own feelings rather than in the style of some writer whom he admired. A fairly close likeness to Newcomb's method, however, may be found in Sylvester Judd's *Margaret*. Mrs. Newcomb read the novel in 1845, the year in which it was published, and recommended to her son the "exquisitely beautiful pictures of scenery in it." (October 2, 1845) The following quotations from both writers show a similarity in language and in method, though they are by no means parallel passages.

JUDD: The Chesnuts [*sic*] shone in the sun. . . . [54]
NEWCOMB: . . . the golden chestnuts shone like singing birds.[55]
JUDD: . . . the snow that for a moment is ammassed upon it [a tree], falls to the ground like a harvest of alabaster fruit.[56]
NEWCOMB: The trees are dismantled, like untenanted houses after a

---

[49] *169.* [50] *172.* [51] *175.*
[52] *165.* [53] *172.*
[54] Sylvester Judd, *Margaret,* Boston, 1845, p. 166.
[55] *172.* [56] Judd, *160.*

conflagration. Fruits are thrown down from them like treasures that should be saved & moved.[57]

JUDD: . . . the scattered trees were all foaming with ice, and the rain having candied them over, trunk, branch, and twig, they shone like so many great candelabras.[58]

NEWCOMB: . . . in the narrow wooded road, a silver leaved ash stood, illuminating the darkness like a candle-labra.[59]

    Little buds come out on the candelabra-like trees like the first dim flames of newly-lighted tapers.[60]

JUDD: ". . . I can count you crimson gooseberry, flaming maples, claret sumach, yellow birch and what not."

    "Those are garnets, topazes and sapphires set in a dark rock of polished steel . . . would it not seem as if the trees extracted all the colors of the earth, cobalt, umber, lapis-lazuli . . . chrome, copper and gold . . . and dyed every leaf . . .?"[61]

NEWCOMB: . . . the golden tufts of grasses illuminated the side of the rail way with dark carroty gold. . . .[62]

    The husbandman would be starved if the soil of his farm turned to crystals & garnets, & none of it to apples & turnips. . . .[63]

Newcomb's knowledge of nature is more restricted than is that of Judd. Like Thoreau, Judd can name all the trees, birds, and animals in his forest. Newcomb, on the other hand, mentions but three or four common varieties of trees—the elm, the ash, the pine, and the oak. Of wild animals he referred to few besides the lynx and the tiger; and although he declared that he liked birds, almost the only ones which he named in his writing were crows, sparrows, robins, and ducks. Newcomb's landscapes are those of the painter: a silvery tree silhouetted against a black storm cloud; a haze of moonlight resting on young leaves; or a cluster of hills rising from the ground like "prolonged cadences."[64]

Newcomb's attitude toward nature is not curious, like Thoreau's, nor tinged with romanticism, like Emerson's. It is closest to that of Bronson Alcott.

Thoreau viewed nature from many directions. As a naturalist he was interested in the species and habits of wild life. Indefatigable in watching, describing, and discovering, he was, nevertheless, anxious to keep before him the idea that "mere accumulators of facts" studied nature incorrectly unless they strove continually to perceive "her true

[57] *178.*
[58] *Judd, 171-172.*
[59] *163.*
[60] *170.*
[61] *Judd, 285.*
[62] *165.*
[63] *174.*
[64] *178.*

meaning."[65] There is a strange contradiction in Thoreau's philosophical relationship to nature. Sometimes he confesses that by

intimacy with nature I find myself withdrawn from man. My interest in the sun and the moon, in the morning and the evening, compels me to solitude.[66]

or that "I love Nature partly *because* she is not man, but a retreat from him. . . . He is constraint, she is freedom to me."[67] At other times he approaches a more humanistic attitude. In such a mood he writes: "A lover of Nature is preëminently a lover of man."[68]

Emerson's interest in nature was philosophical, perhaps religious. In his journal he wrote about it most often as a projection of God, an exposition of the Divine Mind; and he listened for its message and its song. When he considered the material aspects of nature, he had the true romantic preference for wild scenes unmarred by man.

Among Newcomb's New England contemporaries Alcott came closest to sharing his views. Although in his earlier journals Alcott showed the conventional romantic attitude to nature, his more mature view was that

I love nature much but man more, and enjoy the landscape and society only as these are meliorated by genius and remind me of the art which humanizes and liberates nature.[69]

Contrary to the suspicion of Lindsay Swift,[70] Newcomb was not in the habit of spelling "nature" with a capital. There was nothing undisciplined about his admiration for natural beauty. He believed that there was "no beauty in nature so splendid as beauty in man."[71] The chief reason for the existence of nature was that man might use it for good purposes. Cultivated land was more beautiful than the ocean or the wilderness or the untamed mountains, because it was man's. "The rural country, not the sea shore, is the place for homes,"[72] he wrote. Even indifference must be preferred to an over-valuation of nature:

The simple rustics, who make no ado about the beauty of nature, are, so

---

[65] *The Writings of Henry David Thoreau, Journal,* ed. Bradford Torrey, Boston, 1906, I, 18.
[66] *Ibid.,* IV, 258. [67] *Ibid.,* 445. [68] *Ibid.,* 163.
[69] *The Journals of Bronson Alcott,* ed. Odell Shepard, Boston, 1938, 229.
[70] Swift, 200. [71] *179.* [72] *163.*

far, wiser in their relation to it than are the sentimental abstractionists, who make too much ado about it.[73]

The farmers used land instead of sighing over its beauty; theirs was a sound relationship to nature.

It is strange that Newcomb, who diverted almost all of his discourses on literature and society into moral channels, should have read comparatively little moral meaning into nature. Although he declared that "Nature is redundant with moral suggestion & analogy,"[74] he ordinarily limited himself to an aesthetic consideration of the subject. Occasionally he revealed a philosophical position which was tinged with Swedenborgianism and he emphasised the theory that nature was intended for "use." Of the "spectacles of wondrous art . . . in all nature," he wrote: "In use they live & move, & for use they were formed."[75] The purpose of nature was evinced by its "working aspect": the lily of the field, Newcomb could well see, was not slothful, but busy as a mill-hand in a factory. All nature was a manifestation of God's love and an instance of the way in which He worked. "Man must look upon what is called Nature, as the constant work of Providence that is ever going on. His own affections of uses will thus be ever encouraged, cherished, increased, & elevated." (J, I, 63) Besides that of "use" nature had another important function: it reflected Divine Love. Newcomb found evidence of this reflection in the seemingly intelligent actions of animals. He felt that they had no "intrinsic intelligence" and that they acted no more independently than did a puppet when its tongue was pulled and it was "made to squeak, by the showman of it."[76] Looking at the mountains, Newcomb felt that they were emblematic of the "divine origin of the earth," for they connected "the two worlds of heaven & earth."[77]

By far the most of Newcomb's writing about nature, however, ignores the moral implications of the subject. His nature is dependent upon man, for it is man who uses the fields, the ocean, and the forests; best of all, perhaps, it is man who enjoys the beauty of the landscape, the changing of the seasons, and the sense that the vast workings of nature were instituted for his use and enjoyment.

[73] *180.*   [74] *172.*   [75] *162.*
[76] *181-182.*   [77] *165.*

SECTION IV. SOCIETY AND GOVERNMENT

Under the heading of "Society and Government" may be placed Newcomb's discussions of national and foreign politics, his theories about social reform, his ideas about the morality of war, and his pictures of contemporary scenes and habits.

As one might expect, Newcomb's political sympathies were with the Republican party. He was, indeed, more than a sympathizer: his ardent support of the Republican North made him an unusually bitter enemy of the Democratic South.

The *Journal* refers especially to the administrations of Lincoln, Johnson, and Grant. It is interesting to observe his changing attitude toward these men. He was slow in acquiring confidence in Lincoln's government. To him the President seemed too lenient and too tolerant. Newcomb wrote, with severity, that "The President should long ago have arrested such men as Fernando Wood . . . . & now this disreputable man is elected in New York to Congress."[1] He railed at the "want of vigor," "the impotence," "the inefficiency & incompetency" of the administration and regretted that the Constitution did not provide against "disloyalty or imbecility" in the executive, so that posterity might be spared "the evils of Lincoln as well as of Buchanan."[2] So sceptical was he about the country's leadership that he spoke of the dearth of great men in the present age, saying that "America has no Washington, no Adams, no Jefferson, no Hamilton, no Marshall."[3] In attempting to discover the source of Lincoln's shortcomings as president, Newcomb concluded that they resulted from the habits of a lawyer. Lincoln, it seems, based his decisions upon the impartial study of facts instead of upon more emotional values; and he showed a legalistic

tendency to decide from an obvious or gross array of facts, rather than from a fine sympathy with a cause that induces impressions which assist the mind to a subtle & rapid judgment, & predispose it . . . in a right direction & to right bias.[4]

The character of a true statesman, Newcomb thought, "is a balance between that of the judge & the general."

Newcomb began to see signs of greatness in Lincoln in 1863,

[1] *191.*   [2] *192.*   [3] *192.*   [4] *195.*

after the Gettysburg Address had been reported in the newspapers. Among the first to recognize and admire the President's speech, he described him as, "doubtless, the greatest orator of the age."[5] Not long after this time, Newcomb spoke admiringly of Lincoln's "political tact," but regretted that it did not suffice to keep him from attending "the lecture of a female orator in the Hall of the Representatives."[6] In the election of 1864 Newcomb voted for Lincoln's re-election and described him as "upright, prudent, sagacious, & trustworthy, in his kind & degree," and added that his character as a statesman was unknown "only in the respect that his character was progressive, & that his policy kept pace with his character."[7] Newcomb deeply regretted Lincoln's death but blamed it on the President's fatal "facility." Grant, he pointed out, did not feel obliged to go to the theatre on that night, although his presence, like Lincoln's, had been announced. With hints of regret, he wrote that, had Grant been present, "the murderer might have preferred him for a victim."[8]

Andrew Johnson was not a favorite with Newcomb. Almost the only good word said for him in the entire *Journal* was written shortly after the Vice-President's inauguration, when Newcomb dismissed as defamation and slander the charges made by the "factious democrats"[9] that Johnson appeared drunk at the inaugural ceremonies. Subsequently, however, when Newcomb was bitterly opposed to Johnson's policy of Reconstruction, he found no little satisfaction in the President's "reported intemperance." (J, X, 241) By 1867 he was referring to Johnson's "treachery, double dealing, & impracticability." (J, XIV, 323) The diary gives us a sketch of Johnson's awkward delivery of his public speeches. As he stood on the balcony of the Continental Hotel in Philadelphia, he appeared to be "clouded with anger & ugly predetermination"; he "lifted his hat in his hand up & down in salutation of the crowd, stiffly & angularly."[10] After hearing him speak, Newcomb wrote that "President Johnson is so egotistical &, withal, so ill-at-ease, his speeches read, in parts, like soliloquies."[11] He compared his relation to Congress to the situation of a "vicious & cowardly rider, carried by the trained & eager horse,

[5] *196.* [6] *196.* [7] *200.* [8] *202.*
[9] *201.* [10] *207.* [11] *207.*

which he rides but cannot manage, into the very front of the field, from which he, in vain, endeavored to turn him";[12] and he ended by calling him "a patriot in disguise" who had served the national cause which he had tried to betray.

Grant, a man of action, was fairly well liked by Newcomb. In Philadelphia, in the company of President Johnson, the "tempered thoughtfulness & sweetness"[13] of Grant's face attracted Newcomb's attention. Later on in the *Journal,* however, there are several passages censuring the extravagance and luxury which had been introduced into the Washington circles. "I grieve to see," he wrote, "that Grant does not carry his personal simplicity & prudent economy into the White house. . . . This is, neither first rate manhood or first rate republicanism."[14] And when he saw Grant at the Chestnut Street Theatre, he "was sorry to see him in kid gloves."[15] These objections, however, were minor. He liked him for his energy and determination and observed that these qualities were tempered by thoughtfulness and deliberation. Though Grant was not, in Newcomb's opinion, a model president, he was "admirable in kind."[16]

It is hardly surprising that, as a New Englander, as an Abolitionist, and as a volunteer in the Federal Army, Newcomb felt an antagonism toward the people, the politicians, and the manners of the South. On the other hand, the extent and the duration of his bitterness occasionally seem a little shocking in a man who does not seem to have suffered a great deal from the conflict. He wrote against the Southern rebels as though they had been the most ruthless of foreign invaders. He thought that "spurious magnanimity to the enemies of the country is a sort of sentimental treachery to country," and that persons

who proffer forgiveness, without condition of repentance, to murderous traitors & who hasten to take by the hand those whose unwashed hands are reaking with the blood of patricide & of martyred patriots, compound with damnable sin.[17]

He also felt that

The Providence in the delay of reconstruction was . . . illustrated by the punishment-like humiliation in which the suspense kept the subjugated rebels. (J, XI, 23)

[12] *213.*   [13] *207.*   [14] *227.*   [15] *231.*   [16] *231.*   [17] *200.*

Election frauds were to be expected, almost as a matter of course, from a party which was allied "with malignant sectionalists & secessionists."[18] Fraud in the Republican party, he pointed out, was committed only by "irresponsible persons," or "in self-defence, or locally."[19] Three years after the end of the Civil War, he wrote that never in any war "was such unexpected & admirable punishment inflicted upon a worsted & wrong side as was inflicted by the north upon the south . . . & without revengefulness of motive."[20] Even later than this, when writing about the shooting of birds, he said:

These birds could have been better spared than those rebels; for they were innocuous, useful, & not unnatural; they lived, & let men live, while the rebels were slayers of men as well as stealers of men, & were intolerant, venomous, fanatical & insane.[21]

Toward foreign countries his attitude was more serene. He regarded England with friendly feelings, when he was not angered by her Southern sympathies. He admired the country chiefly for the domestic virtue to be found within it, for its national Protestantism, and for its strength as a nation—which he compared to a rocket: "small in the stick but large in the expansion of discharge."[22] He found little to admire either in Napoleon or in Louis Napoleon. The first, he could see, lacked the republican virtue of a leader like Washington; for Napoleon considered, first, himself and, second, the state under himself; while Washington thought primarily of the state and considered himself to be governed by its good. Louis Napoleon Newcomb dismissed as an imperialist who delighted in crude pomp.

Newcomb theorized less about the nature and duties of government than about the structure of society. In general, he favored a republican form of government and felt that it should exert a strong, benevolent control over living conditions. The English Parliament he thought negligent of the public good. He pointed out how everything that "it has granted in civil franchise has been wrung from it by the pressure of the people."[23] It had been rumored in 1864 that some English Corporations had reduced the wages of their laborers upon the excuse that the men were depositing savings in the bank. "Respect for man as

[18] *220.*   [19] *220.*   [20] *221.*
[21] *225.*   [22] *196.*   [23] *197.*

man," Newcomb commented, "is impaired & almost ignored, in an oligarchy."[24]

He recognized the fact that American working hours and wages were in serious need of reform. The bar-keeper at his hotel, he informs us, was on duty eighteen hours a day and received but eight dollars a week for his labor. A little boy who waited on table at a restaurant also worked under pitiful conditions: he rose at three, and sometimes at one, in the morning, and worked until he went to bed at nine or ten at night. "Such practices," said Newcomb, "make a bondage & a fatuity of industry."[25] He realized that money could not entirely

compensate for forced & unnatural labor: but large wages evince something of consideration on the part of the taskmasters who take advantage of the urgent wants of men to impose bondage upon them.[26]

He approved of the eight-hour movement, but supposed that "most business men will oppose it, because they pervert the industrial system unto a mere scheme of money making."[27] He was struck by the similarity between the "rapacious kings & barons" of the middle ages and the "rapacious speculators & middle-men"[28] of the Gilded Age.

The thin, haggard faces of many of the young men whom he passed in the streets of Philadelphia revealed a lack of food and of sleep. In restaurants, Newcomb noticed that these young men bought twenty-five cent meals that, even to him, looked slight. Food sold at grocery stores was often of a poor quality. A loaf of bread which Newcomb bought had a nasty, clammy smell when it was broken open. He was so disgusted by it that he would have thrown it out of his window, had it not been for fear of poisoning the hens that were gathering their food in the street. Some government supervision was sadly lacking: "such is the diet provided for people by this improvident system of society."[29]

At the period when fortunes were being made from lumber by speculators who stripped the land, without government restriction, Newcomb recorded a protest against the avarice which was "one of the sluices through which desolation & deprivation shall stream like a flood."[30]

[24] *197.*   [25] *209.*   [26] *209.*   [27] *208.*
[28] *211.*   [29] *219.*   [30] *219-220.*

In his youth, in Providence, Newcomb had been something of a radical. He had joined the least conservative club at Brown, and had sympathized with the cause of Thomas Dorr, who led a rebellion in an effort to extend the franchise in Rhode Island. Though he favored certain political and social reforms, he was opposed to any change in the position of women. He condemned Lincoln for his mere presence at the talk of a female lecturer. In Philadelphia, a furor in the medical school was caused by the presence of some women students at a clinic. Newcomb blamed the clinical demonstrator for allowing them to disrupt his class. It was weak, he said, for "men to succumb on the mere question of delicacy—saving . . . what natural & proper aversion there may be on the part of men to having women scientifically posted in such matters."[31] He was, of course, greatly opposed to the extension of the franchise so as to include women, and argued, without much originality, that women were amply represented by the votes of their husbands. Widows and spinsters, he explained, must expect to count lack of representation as one of the many hardships of their situation.

He blamed the licentiousness of both the very poor and the very rich: "The one class feel a sort of independence because they have an abundance of money; the other class because they have none." To remedy this situation he suggested that

The state should bind both classes to the common weal, by a heavy proportional tax of the rich, & by circumspection about the industrial interests of every class.[32]

"The moral significance of rank" was a subject in which Newcomb took a great interest. He compared life to an army and said that all men must keep their places in it. (J,V, 124) Superficially, rank might seem to be a petty social system; actually, it had a moral base. There was, according to Newcomb's argument, no reason why a "manly & industrious poor man" should

feel himself belittled by his seclusion from the parlors of the rich any more than a manly & patriotic soldier in the ranks feels himself belittled by being precluded from the tent of his superior officers.[33]

Newcomb's philosophy of rank would give a man a chance to act like a snob without feeling that he actually was one.

[31] *226.*   [32] *195.*   [33] *199.*

Newcomb regarded war as a counterpart of peace, rather than as its opposite. He proved the closeness of their relationship by calling attention to the fact that an "unjust peace partakes in its character of the evils, & of the most perverted quality, of the war which was . . . weakly refused . . . in the name of Peace."[34] There could be no security in peace itself without the possible backing of war. Furthermore, human beings were naturally bellicose. After watching one of the daily ice-fights which were carried on all winter between two groups of young men who lived on opposite sides of the Schuylkill, Newcomb concluded that a war for some real and moral cause was a benefit to men. It was better that they should fight for their country's safety than simply for the sake of petty quarreling. Upon seeing a group of negro soldiers at drill, he was pleasantly surprised. While he disliked seeing negroes in a white man's uniform, preparing to defend a white man's country, he felt that the drill "was not humiliated but ennobled by its effective good," because a "race once accomplished in martial matters will never allow themselves to be enslaved."[35] Military training, he thought, should be part of the training of every citizen of a republic. Armies should be chosen by conscription; and exemption from service should be given only for major physical defects, since too "rigid exemptions set a premium on diseases & infirmities."[36]

The follies of the time were scrutinized in the *Journal*. Newcomb was especially opposed to the use of tobacco, to the constraints of fashionable dress, and to the luxury of pretentious society. He wrote long and often against the evils of smoking. Once, when he passed a boy who was leaning against the wall of a house, faint from his first attempt to smoke, he offered him a "kindly rebuff" by saying, "O, you little fool!"[37] Tight lacing of the waist was another evil of the time. Newcomb tells of how one young woman had slept in her corset; as a result of her folly she died, and "her ribs were found overlapping each other." The diarist's comment was, "How senseless a thing is sin; & how sinful a thing is senselessness."[38] The large and gloomy brown-stone fronts of Fifth Avenue both amused and disgusted him. As he walked down the street he could not avoid thinking that

[34] *199.* [35] *194.* [36] *193.*
[37] *224.* [38] *224.*

a man would, probably, be considered as eccentric who should keep his blinds open & have no window curtains, in these palaces of tradesmen, as he would be if he wore no coat in the streets & went barefoot. Yet light is healthier, needfuller, & cheaper than Saratoga-water & sea-side baths: but it is not the fashion, & never will be, amongst people who delight in cosmetics, carpets, upholstery, & false lights.[39]

Newcomb occasionally gives sketches of contemporary Philadelphia: the filth of the streets, the prudery of the citizens, and the poisonous flavor of the food. The first thing which struck him after he moved to the city was the "net work of streamlets . . . discolored & odorous with the refuse of sinks."[40] In summer the city stank from the stagnant water in these open drains, from the rotting garbage which was carelessly emptied into streets, and from the dirty stables. It was impossible, at any time of year, to step out of doors without wetting the feet, for the citizens of Philadelphia were endlessly busy washing their white marble steps. When the "stinking sinks of malaria" drove him out of the city, he escaped for the summer to New York where he wrote, "New York is noisiest, but Philadelphia is foulest."[41]

Newcomb found a great deal of fault with the prudery of the period. He exclaimed against the narrow-minded Y.M.C.A. of Philadelphia, which excluded from its shelves the plays of Shakspere. Despite his New England boyhood he defended, in many parts of his *Journal,* the morality of the theatre. When the scant costumes of *The Black Crook* incurred the abuse of "silly prudes, & of mongering conventionalists," he declared that the Creator "of man is maligned . . . when the mere form of men & women is stigmatised as indecent."[42] In answer to those who objected that the presence of courtesans made the theatre an immoral place, he replied that such women had "little or, rather, no moral opportunity, in way of thought & culture" other than what they got there. [43]

American cookery, in his time, was spoiled by an excessive use of baking soda:

One is surer of having poisoned bread, cake, & pastry proffered to him by his housekeepers, landladies, & hosts, than a traveller is of having rats served up to him in China, or an old John Bull of frogs served up to him in France. . . . The stomach is eaten up by what it should eat.[44]

[39] *224-225.* [40] *205.* [41] *225.*
[42] *219.* [43] *230.* [44] *208.*

In the loaves which one bought at bakeries, fungus could sometimes be found, and, according to Newcomb's testimony, they were often marked by a strong alkaline flavor. He hoped for a day when flour or meal should be cooked, Indian fashion, in water alone.

Newcomb's scattered comments on society and politics seem, on the whole, to be just and sensible. They are interesting, as one man's impressions, but they lack the interrelation which they might have had if they had come out of a more completely developed social philosophy.

SECTION V. MAN AND MORALS

Newcomb's philosophy was not systematic because it was expounded according to emotional perceptions rather than developed according to careful, logical thought. It was focused upon the doctrine that "There is no morality but marriage:"[1]

It seems to me that home is everything, the end of life itself, the flower of the universal beauty in proper form. Before it, arts & literature are but arts & masquerades led by children. The Swedish seer has made a terrible science of that which I always felt.[2]

In the early parts of the *Journal*, too, he praised Swedenborg for being one of the few who had called attention to the divine nature of marriage and of the home. In Swedenborgian terms, he discussed the importance of "use"—that is, of a practical relation to nature and to life—and he described a type of man who, instead of developing himself for use, lived a life of "abstraction" and of solitary study. A little later, he introduced his ideal type: the "man of action," who made vigorous and full use of his life. For a long time Newcomb described the man of action in only the most baffling of terms: over and over again he described him as one who understood the importance of use, and who sought "full manly scope" and a "practive sphere." Only toward the latter part of the *Journal* did he explain that the man of action was one who combined vigor with virtue; and that by "full manly scope" he meant the sexual relations which were to be had in marriage.

[1] *282.*
[2] May 15, 1848. This letter is in the Margaret Fuller collection at Harvard University.

He wrote that marriage was the "normal condition & necessity of man." It was the reverse of that unhealthy isolation which "makes man a monster, & unmans him," and, since "isolation is death, marriage is life."[3] The evil of celibacy was that it had "its pivot in self." Even if he strove to amend his condition, the celibate could do no more than imitate the life of a married person, "like a would-be volunteer running after soldiers," without ever being brought into the casual "play of unselfish relations."[4] Newcomb had an answer for those who might argue that, because many married people were unhappy, it was dangerous to estimate marriage so highly as he did. From the very dissatisfaction of ill-mated couples he argued "the truth & good of marriage," since their discontent showed that they expected and ought to be happy together. "Domestic infelicity," he said, "is no more argument against wedlock, than dyspepsia is against food."[5]

In addition to being a solitary celibate, the man of abstraction was a recorder of thought, perhaps a genius. The evil of thought was not innate: it lay in the deadening effect which it had upon the will. The careful thinker weighed his actions and his motives and often quite forgot to act. "Literary abstraction," Newcomb wrote, "is dangerous, because the mind wanders from the body, loses it centre, & is detatched from will."[6] He compared excessive thought to a telescope, which at once "strains the eyes & shuts out collateral objects."[7] Undue thinkers he likened to "overused & untimely-used horses" which "lose their mettle & shape . . . become hacknied, sparse, dry, bony, spiritless, abject."[8]

The intellectual fault upon which he was most severe was that of "diarisation," which was a pure abstraction from life. Such a habit

is injurious because it prevents the truths from assimilating with the will. It tends to externalise the thoughts expressed, tearing them from fostering relations, altering their associations, giving them a place without the affections or the causes which disclosed them. . . . A thought should ripen in the man. . . . But when the mind quickly seizes it & plucks it, it plucks it from the tree which should ripen & keep it ripe & fresh.[9]

Thoughts, wrenched from their environment, could not retain their true meaning. A diary of the autobiographical type caused an "unduly concentrated & abnormally isolated consciousness," but a journal of

[3] 233.   [4] 235.   [5] 284.   [6] 231.
[7] 249.   [8] 249.   [9] 232.

thought, such as Newcomb wrote, was not much better. Both kinds tended to "disintegrate life by forcing an analysis of it."[10]

"Diarisation" bore the brunt of Newcomb's attack because it was the failing which he could not resist. He did not, however, overlook the dangers of scientific thought or of creative genius. He compared the man who subsituted learning for life to one who "studies corn & water & does not partake of them."[11] Speaking of how Kepler worked for sixteen years over unsuccessful hypotheses before he found a true system, he suggests that Kepler's faith in the existence of laws was much more important than his discovery of any of them. Newcomb remarked that

the stars studded the skies in vain to astronomers so far as they gave up their lives to the mere study of them; for they fulfilled their ends, whether or no the secret of their plane & procedure was known by man.[12]

The sickliness of creative genius, such as that of Shakspere, lay in its desire to "find basis for its incorporeality in a living form of another than itself."[13]

A striking counterpart to the weakly abstractionist was the active man. By man of action Newcomb meant more than one who was an axe-swinger, a ditch-digger, a gymnast or a hunter. His conception of action included "all the qualities of a man, in its broad, profound & full scope."[14] An active man was one who asserted himself, who was fully masculine, who joined physical development with moral motive, and who, "last, first, & throughout," remembered that he would "have only what he gets & takes."[15] The man of action must have undergone moral culture; his strength must have been tempered by virtue. Looking at the butchers in the stock-yards of New York, Newcomb saw

a sort of athletic monsters: bullies whom indiscriminate violence & vehemence had partly tamed, & whose demonstrative ardor the nothingness of vice had partly sobered. . . .[16]

From the appearance of these debased, though sinewy, men he concluded that "Gymnasty without morality turns muscle into stone."[17] The trained prize-fighter had meaningless splendor of physique. Newcomb compared him to a "gnarled tree, stripped for the encounters

[10] *254.*	[11] *238.*	[12] *292.*
[13] *232.*	[14] *249.*	[15] *245.*
[16] *248.*	[17] *248.*	

of winter" and lacking the "graceful symmetry" and "genial verdure" proper to the finest type of tree. So, in the highest order of men, "the muscles, which gymnastic & other collateral exercises of body develop, must be appropriated by manly motives & courses of life."[18] He later explained what these motives were, when he pointed out that the

end of manly force & beauty is favored, not attained, in gymnastics. The power of a man as a lover is the full significance & scope of his power as an athlete, & of his beauty as a show.[19]

Perhaps the man of action was best exemplified, in real life, by a trained soldier, fighting for a good cause.

He observed that "Reproduction is a primary law of all life"; and, calling our attention to the generative processes in nature, he drew from them the moral that "the primary & full joy of life is in love." Men of genius showed their subtle understanding of human needs and interests "by making love the pivot of the plots of their dramas . . .& philosophies."[20] In his theory of "mourning" Newcomb suggested that the abstractionist could not convert himself into a man of action by seeking sexual relations anywhere but in marriage. A man who was still single or who was for some reason forced to remain so, should mourn for a home and a wife. He should keep in his mind the thought of marriage and should cherish it. Those men who put aside ideas of marriage preferred to "conform themselves to privation, rather than suffer a healthy craving for nutritive meat."[21] Newcomb was certain that mourning should not be a melancholy state: it was to be marked rather by "vivacious & vigorous hope," than by "vacant & dreary despair."[22] Its virtue was in keeping "the heart free & open as a load-stone" so that it could "feel for what is near it, or comes within its range, but might, if the heart was not in a vigilant & attractional condition, stay, or pass by."[23]

Only by inference did Newcomb tell us that he was a victim of the abstraction which he so dreaded. Though he wrote constantly in his diary and lived in isolation, he evidently felt that in realizing the dangers of his situation he in part avoided them. Even at the age of fifty he still thought of himself as preparing for "full manly scope." Addressing the "Fortunate young man, whom a fair young woman gladly greets & joins," he warned him that close behind him was one

[18] *275.*   [19] *285.*   [20] *242.*   [21] *259.*   [22] *272.*   [23] *274.*

who observed his "felicity with eyes of sad fire,"[24] who was "perfecting himself" in discipline and aspiration, and who stood ready to overtake and pass the luckier man, if he lagged. Actually, however, he was no more than the "man of thought" who could "hear something of the music to which the march of life is set"[25] but who merely "beat time with his feet" instead of marching in the parade of heroes.

Newcomb's philosophy is especially important because it colors much of his other writing. An understanding of it lightens the obscurity of some of his critical opinions. When he criticized Shakspere's "passivity," he meant that Shakspere was at fault for wasting his life at writing plays instead of devoting it to some more active sort of career. To Newcomb a life spent in writing was a life lost. When he attacked Roman Catholicism and Tractarianism, it was their medieval elements which he distrusted: their exaltations and ecstasies, and the former's support of celibate orders.

In addition to developing his moral philosophy Newcomb made many scattered moral observations, some of which show unusual discernment or plain good sense. There is a great deal of insight in his defence of persons who try to be what they are not:

Sometimes, sham is to be taken for the reality which it counterfeits. Affectation often expresses the secret & earnest bias of a man. Many men should be taken for what they would be taken, because they will soon be that which they heartily assume to be.[26]

Like a true New Englander, he gave a good reason for his strong interest in genealogy, saying that

It does a man service to know who & what his ancestors were. If they were of the right mould, he gains secret self-respect, confidence . . . & self-identification. If they were deficient, he is specially reminded wherein to be vigilant, cautious, & active.[27]

Towards drinking and smoking he had the view conventional in his time. He was less severe upon them as moral transgressions, however, and regarded them more as unhealthful practices in which the man of action could not afford to indulge.

In general, Newcomb's moral philosophy was clearly the result of his thinking about his own unsatisfactory life and of his effort to direct it into a more happy sphere.

[24] *263.*   [25] *260.*   [26] *239.*   [27] *281-282.*

CHAPTER THREE

NEWCOMB AND HIS AGE

ALTHOUGH Newcomb aroused great interest and speculation among those who knew him, he has had little attention in our century. VanWyck Brooks' *Flowering of New England* seems to be the only literary history in which he is mentioned. Slightly more extensive accounts of him have been given in G. W. Cooke's *An Historical and Biographical Introduction to Accompany the Dial* and in *American Authors, 1600-1900,* edited by Kunitz and Haycraft. His name has also occurred in several biographies of Margaret Fuller, as well as in descriptions of Brook Farm and its inhabitants.

Since Newcomb remained something of a mystery, even to acquaintances and to friends, there is a traditional variance of opinion as to what sort of person he was. Dr. Codman called him "solitary, self-involved," "mysterious and profound."[1] Georgianna Kirby handed down amusing accounts of his habits, but paid tribute to his "genius for penetrating to the very core of a subject, so that a few words from him often impressed his hearers more than an hour's talk with one more healthily balanced."[2] Ora Gannett Sedgwick spoke of Newcomb as one who had contributed to her pleasant memory of Brook Farm. And it is clear that Marianne Dwight was fascinated by the poetic sensibility and kindly reticence which she observed in him. Orestes Brownson was often seen with Newcomb about the Farm. He did not mention the young man in his article on the Association, but he did introduce him into his novel, *The Spirit-Rapper,*[3] as Mr. Murton. In the novel the superficial side of Newcomb is shown, as can be seen from the nature of his conservation:

[1] See George W. Curtis, *Early Letters of George Wm. Curtis to John S. Dwight,* ed. G. W. Cooke, New York, 1898, p. 24.
[2] See Cooke, II, 144.
[3] This novel, published in 1854, was a *roman à clef.* Emerson, Alcott, and Theodore Parker were among those represented in its pages.

"As long as I remember my mother or my sister," said Mr. Murton, "I would never meet a woman, however high or however humble, without taking note of the fact that she is a woman."

. . .

". .Life is made up of little things, and he is a sad moralist who has no leniency for trifles. I love, myself, to look upon a pretty face, and find no great objection to those pleasant nothings which are the current coin of well-bred conversation between the sexes."[4]

The "Murtonesque" side of Newcomb's personality is generally ignored by modern historians of Brook Farm, who usually represent him as conversing about the beauties of Saint Augustine. Although both Hawthorne and Thoreau knew Newcomb, neither had much to say about him. In 1843, Hawthorne jotted down a report of the "new moral phasis" through which Newcomb was passing;[5] and Thoreau noted in 1854 that he "Went to R. Williams's Rock on the Blackstone with Newcomb & thence to hill with an old fort atop in Seekonk, Mass. . . ."[6]

It is in the writings of Emerson that we find the most extensive references to young Newcomb. They generally take the form of whole-hearted praise. "Charles," he wrote, after knowing him for a short time,

is a Religious Intellect. Let it be his praise that when I carried his manuscript story to the woods, and read it in the armchair of the upturned root of a pine tree, I felt for the first time since Waldo's death some efficient faith again in the repairs of the Universe, some independency of natural relations whilst spiritual affinities can be so perfect and compensating.[7]

Although many of the inhabitants of the Farm regarded Charles as one of the more eccentric of their number, Emerson felt that the young man had a "sanitary and retentive" influence on the "intellectual Sansculottism" of the place. He heard that "Charles Newcomb . . . was greatly respected, and his conduct, even in trifles, observed and imitated,—the quiet, retreating, demoniacal youth."[8] After visiting Brook Farm in the company of "C. S." (Caroline Sturgis, probably), Emerson described Newcomb as

too full of his prophecy, once to think of friendship. . . . A purer service to

[4] Orestes A. Brownson, *The Spirit-Rapper, an Autobiography,* Boston, 1854, p. 104.
[5] *The American Notebooks,* ed., Stewart, p. 176.
[6] *Journals,* ed., Bradford Torrey, Boston, 1906, VII, 79.
[7] *Journals,* VI, 214. Emerson wrote this in 1842.　　　[8] *Ibid.,* VI, 374.

the intellect was never offered than his,—warm, fragrant, religious,—and I feel when with him the pertinency of that Platonistic word, "all-various."[9]

In his later discussion of Brook Farm in "Life and Letters in New England," Emerson described Newcomb rather fully, without, however, mentioning his name. He said that he could remember

one youth of the subtlest mind . . . the subtlest observer and diviner of character I ever met, living, reading, writing, talking there, perhaps as long as the colony held together; his mind fed and overfed by whatever is exalted in genius . . . a man of no employment or practical aims, a student and philosopher, who found his daily enjoyment not with the elders or his exact contemporaries so much as with the fine boys who were skating and playing ball or bird-hunting; forming the closest friendships with such . . . yet was he the chosen counsellor to whom the guardians would repair on any hitch or difficulty that occurred, and draw from him wise counsel . . . puny in body and habit as a girl, yet with an *aplomb* like a general, never disconcerted. He lived and thought, in 1842, such worlds of life; all hinging on the thought of Being or Reality as opposed to consciousness; hating intellect with the ferocity of a Swedenborg. He was the Abbé or spiritual father, from his religious bias.[10]

In 1849 Newcomb visited Emerson, and brought with him some six-year old manuscripts. Emerson found them remarkable for their "abridged stenographic wit and eloquence," but he was beginning to wonder about the nature and extent of a genius which was deliberately hidden by its possessor. He wrote at some length about his puzzling young friend:

He is Brahmin existing to little use, if prayer and beauty are not that. Yet he humiliates the proud and staggers the dogmatist, and subverts all the mounds and fortification lines of accustomed thought; eminently aristocratic beyond any person I remember to have met, because self-centred on a deep centre of genius,—easy, cheerful, condescending,—condescending to the greatest, and mortifying Plato and Jesus, if it were possible, by his genuine preference of children, and ladies . . . to all their fame and

[9] *Ibid.*, VII, 61, June 7, 1845.
[10] *Works*, Centenary edition, X, 362-3. After this lecture had been reported in the newspapers Newcomb wrote in his *Journal:* "Few men have learnt the art of squarely breasting the special currents of praise. Perhaps most men can bear dispraisement better than they can bear eulogy; but scarcely a man can nicely balance ordinary self-respect with extraordinary respect from others. . . . A man's deadliest foe had best try the daggers of commendation before he tries those of slander in evil against him; for the chance is the former will do more mischief than the latter, possibly, in unsteadying & decomposing him. . . ." (J, XIX, 265-6). Newcomb continued in this manner for some pages, and in later volumes of the *Journal* made several further references to Emerson's praise of him in this lecture.

sanctity. . . . But though Charles's mind is unsounded, and the walls actually taken out, so that he seems open to Nature, yet he does not accumulate his wisdom into any amounts of thought: rarely arrives at a result—perhaps does not care to—so that I say, It seems, instead of my bare walls, your surrounding is really landscapes and perspectives of temples: yet they avail no more to you than if they were landscape paper-hangings or fresco pictures of temples. Newcomb is my best key to Shakspeare, and he is just beyond authorship.[11]

Just below this entry Emerson made a list of "Big-endians" and "Little-endians." The second group consisted of "Alcott, Very, Newcomb, Channing, R. W. E., Thoreau."[12]

By 1853, when Newcomb was at the peak of his Swedenborgian phase, Emerson began to despair of the young man's maturing into a fully developed genius. He wrote:

Only of Charles I would give much to know how it all lies in his mind; I would know his inmost sincerity; know what reserves he makes when he talks divinely. I would rather know his real mind than any other person's I have met.[13]

It was four years later that Emerson paid his highest tribute to the promise which Newcomb had once shown:

I keenly enjoyed C—'s pointed remark, after we had both known Charles Newcomb, that "no one could compare with him in original genius," though I knew that she saw, as I saw, that his mind was far richer than mine, which fact nobody but she and I knew or suspected. Nay, I rejoiced in this very proof of her perception. And now, sixteen years later, we two alone possess this secret still.[14]

In the *Memoirs of Margaret Fuller Ossoli,* Emerson described some of Margaret's friends. Newcomb he spoke of as a

youth . . . of invalid habit, which had infected in some degree the tone of his mind, but of a delicate and pervasive insight, and the highest appreciation for genius in letters, arts, and life. . . . His turn of mind, and his habits of life, had almost a monastic turn,—a jealousy of the common tendencies of literary men either to display or to philosophy.[15]

It is Margaret Fuller, herself, who gave us what seems to be the least biased judgment of Newcomb. While she admired the delicacy of his genius, she was also fully aware of his shortcomings. Since she was a shrewd observer of people, it is probable that her impression of Newcomb's personality is correct, as far as it goes. She did not

[11] *Journals,* VIII, 60-62.   [12] *Ibid.,* 62.
[13] *Ibid.,* 395.   [14] *Ibid.,* IX, 199-200.
[15] *Memoirs of Margaret Fuller Ossoli,* Boston, 1852, I, 209.

share Emerson's indulgent attitude toward her young friend. Early
in their friendship she became aware of the instability of his thought
and emotion. During his illness in 1840 she wrote that she doubted
whether he would prove strong enough to "rise above his doubts and
fears. . . . No sharp pain can debilitate like this vacillation of mind."[16]
Emerson gave us the other side of Miss Fuller's feeling about Newcomb
when he quoted her as saying that

'His mind should be approached close by one who needs its fragrance. All
with him leads rather to glimpses and insights, than to broad, comprehensive views. Till he needs the public, the public does not need him. The
lonely lamp, the niche, the dark cathedral grove, befit him best. Let him
shroud himself in the symbols of his native ritual, till he can issue forth on
the wings of song.'[17]

Twentieth-century writers who have said anything about Newcomb
have recapitulated the amusing tales handed down by Georgianna
Kirby or have re-echoed the high praise found in Emerson's *Journals*.
George Willis Cooke, who knew Newcomb through hearsay, regretted that "only a few anecdotes remain" of this "brilliant and
erractic" young man. He concluded that Newcomb was "an American
pre-Raphaelite"[18]—a title which Newcomb would have repudiated
with disgust. Lindsay Swift admitted that the odd young man must
have been "gifted to an unusual degree," but emphasized the fact that
he was a "sentimental devotee of unattached Catholicism,"[19] and, in
general, he suspected him of being a *poseur*. Swift's somewhat un-
favorable opinion was further developed by Katherine Burton, in
Paradise Planters.[20] She depicted Newcomb as an affected youth who
commonly brooded in corners and sighed dramatically before speaking. Where Swift's interpretation invites us to see Newcomb as a
kind of Transcendental Archibald Grosvenor, Katherine Burton's
flippant treatment reduces him to a Reginald Bunthorne. Van Wyck
Brooks classed as extreme individualism Newcomb's midnight chanting and the shrine-like appearance of his room in the Eyrie. Taking his
cue from Emerson, he called him a "young Providence mystic."[21]

From the assertions of people who were acquainted with him and
from the assumptions of people who were not, Newcomb has been
thought of as a disciple of Emerson. Whether they called him a

---

[16] *Letters*, ed., Rusk, II, 310.   [17] *Memoirs of Margaret Fuller Ossoli*, I, 209.
[18] Cooke, II, 143.   [19] Swift, p. 200.   [20] Published in 1939.
[21] Brooks, p. 243.

mystic, a pre-Raphaelite, or a mere eccentric, they appeared to take it for granted that he was a Romantic Transcendentalist, and that he was completely under Emersonian influence.

Judged by the *Journals*, however, none of these suppositions is altogether correct.

From his writing it is clear that Newcomb was no mystic. He made no references to trances, to immediate perceptions of God, or to any mystical experiences. Even the possibility of having such experiences did not appear to interest him very highly. On the contrary, he distrusted all ecstasies or raptures, and he dismissed the visions of his favorite Swedenborg as hallucinations resulting from an overloaded stomach.[22] In his disparagement of "ecstasy" he made it clear that he meant any

state of pietistical abstraction & emotionalism. . . . A life, a chronic condition, a flighty mood, &, in general, a plane of unbalanced, onesided, headlong, encyphelical, infatuous, & visionary emotionalism, rapture, quietism, fanaticism, & sensationalism, & all that sort of thing. . . .[23]

Just as it shows no mystical elements, so his *Journal* suggests no leaning toward pre-Raphaelism or toward any of the kindred movements which turned to medieval life for their inspiration. Medievalism, with Newcomb, was often responsible for "abstraction." Wagner's music displeased him because it reminded him of "tractarianism . . . of revived medievalism." After hearing *Tannhaüser*, he wrote: "It was no more wonder that the young king of Bavaria was infatuated by such music than that some of the young nobles of England were by Puseyism."[24] He cared just as little for the medieval romanticism of Sir Walter Scott as for the medieval abstraction of Dante's *Paradiso*.

Whatever Newcomb may have been in his early twenties, he was no Emersonian after the age of thirty. The followers of Emerson believed that man was intrinsically good and that he was infinitely perfectible, provided he acted according to his intuition of what was right. They supported civil and religious reforms: abolition, women's rights, temperance, Unitarianism. Since man was essentially good, unrenovated social institutions were a drawback to his proper development.

The religion most closely allied with the Transcendental movement

---

[22] *129.*   [23] *287.*   [24] *155-156.*

was Unitarianism. The religion which attracted Newcomb—although he affected to abhor the "ritualism & mytholigism" of the sect—was Roman Catholicism. In Brook Farm days, when Newcomb was passing through his most religious phase, Emerson referred to him playfully as "our young Catholic Fra Carlo." It was around this time that Mrs. Newcomb had trouble in dissuading her son from the priesthood. Although Newcomb grew away from the Church as he became older, he never altogether freed himself of its attraction. In Philadelphia he often attended mass, and yet he damned priests and papistry, and compared the "bedizzened" bishop to "an ugly magician." It must not be thought, however, that he went to church simply for the pleasure of hating Catholicism; for he once mentions having stood at vespers, with tears in his eyes, "as early as the first psalm." (J, XI, 297) His attitude toward the Church must have been completely ambivalent: although he did not quite approve of going, he could not keep away.

Newcomb's conception of human nature differed greatly from that of Emerson and the other Transcendentalists. Emerson taught men to rely upon themselves and to be confident of their inner power for good. In the "Divinity School Address" he urged his listeners

to go alone: to refuse the good models even those which are sacred in the imagination of men, and dare to love God without mediator or veil. Friends enough you shall find who will hold up to your emulation Wesleys and Oberlins, Saints and Prophets. Thank God for these good men, but say, 'I also am a man.'[25]

In "The Young American" he called upon his audience to obey its heart and to become "the nobility of this land."[26] He held that "the great man is he who in the midst of the crowd keeps with perfect sweetness the independence of solitude,"[27] and that "in the solitude to which every man is always returning, he has a sanity and revelations which in his passage into new worlds, he will carry with him."[28] Newcomb, on the other hand, had a more realistic concept of man and his relationship to other men. He wrote that "Heaven is ever true, whatever man is. Truth is bright & fair, however men receive it."[29] Because of the very nature of man there was a danger in self-reliance: "Sin conspires with solitude, in that it makes a man sole arbiter, in him-

---

[25] *Works*, Centenary Edition, I, 145.   [26] *Ibid.*, 387.
[27] *Ibid.*, II, 54.   [28] *Ibid.*, III, 86.   [29] 251.

self, apart from principle, of character & conduct."[30] He warned his reader against flight "from the world which is evil, despite good in it," because it was tantamount to flight "from the world which is good, despite evil in it." Men who attempted to live in solitude and to narrow their relationships with other men, because of the wrong practices of society, were "irrational and insane."[31] There was no doubt that

The world is the common, normal field of men. The privilege & duty of life in the world, involves the sequence that, on the one hand, all who live in it, as they are bounden to, must expect to be exposed to the evils prevalent in it, & to all evils incidental to human nature: &, on the other hand that all who are conscious of the particular or general evils in themselves have not only the right, but also are bounden, to live in it, notwithstanding the injury which their evils may inflict on others.[32]

Implicit in this fear of solitude is, of course, the assumption that man is not, by nature, good. If he were, solitude could preserve him from corruption. In this respect, Newcomb is nearer to the position of Hawthorne, or even of Jonathan Edwards, than to that of Emerson.

With their optimism and their confidence in the aspiration of man, the Transcendentalists discounted the problem of evil. Newcomb's discussions of sin and of hell showed an extremely un-Transcendental field of interest. He was less morbid than Hawthorne, but he would have agreed that as long as the human heart remained unaltered there would always be evil abroad in the world. "Hell," he wrote,

is a generalisation of the ultimation, & of the tendencies of moral evil. Evil is, in itself, hell: evil men are, by virtue of their condition, in hell. Practive philosophy cannot, as visionary optimists pretend to go, go beyond the fact that evil & hell are, & always will be, correlative words. The Eternity of hell is but another name for the chronicness of evil. . . . Truth to science required Swedenborgh to assume the eternity of hell, just as it required him to assume the eternity of humanity as it is.[33]

Newcomb's interest in reform was very slight. The nearest he came to joining any movement or group of reformers was when he went to live at Brook Farm. Here, however, he remained a boarder, without ever joining the Association. He found in the Community a refuge from his mother, and a pleasant, rural place where he could quietly lead the studious life he enjoyed. Even here, in a very hot-bed of reformers, he escaped the contagion.

[30] *284.*   [31] *283.*   [32] *240.*   [33] *262-263.*

Abolition had always seemed to him to be desirable; but he never grew very excited over the cause. He was intensely interested in the prosecution of the Civil War, not because it was a war to end slavery but because it was a war against traitors who had attempted to secede from their country; and a dislike of slavery seems hardly to have entered into his strong dislike of the South. When he joined the Tenth Rhode Island Volunteers, it was to help crush rebellion rather than to promote freedom.

In many other reforms of the time Newcomb's interest was lukewarm. He often wrote in his *Journal* against smoking and drinking. In his youth Newcomb had been accustomed to smoke, however; when he was at Newport for his health and while he lived at West Roxbury, his mother sent him a bottle of wine in almost every bundle. Later in Philadelphia, he as often as not prefaced his remarks about the poisonous nature of alcohol by saying that he had stopped for a glass of beer on his way home. The true upholders of temperance at that time favored total abstinence. The main difference between Newcomb's attitude and theirs was that he thought that enjoyment of alcohol and tobacco was unhealthful, rather than immoral.

As we have seen, Newcomb was opposed to the entrance of women into public life. He shared this attitude with the majority of citizens— who did not happen to be under the strong influence of Transcendentalism.

There was one reform with which Newcomb did have sympathy: he was deeply concerned at the long, ill-paid working-hours which the law then allowed. Under such conditions, he declared, freedom was undistinguishable from slavery; and he praised Grant for insisting that wages should not be lowered after the eight-hour working-day had been introduced. In his writing on the subject of hours and wages he occasionally showed reasonable indignation but he refrained from sentimentalism.

Unlike most of the Transcendental writers, Newcomb did not care for romantic wildernesses, but preferred the quiet, domesticated landscape prized by the pre-Romantic writers. His descriptions of nature were, within limits, objective and realistic. To see the reserve of his writing, one should compare it with Margaret Fuller's *Summer on the Lakes,* where she described her approach to Niagara Falls. She emphasized the solemn awe which imperceptibly stole over her, the "choking sensation" which rose to her throat, and the "thrill" which flooded her veins.[34] Newcomb found in nature a deep satisfaction rather than inexpressible thrills; he quietly enjoyed natural beauty without being overcome by it.

While the *Journals* give us the fullest available record of Newcomb's attitudes and beliefs, there are, naturally, in that vast amount of material many contradictory opinions. In spite of the confusions, however, it is not hard to conclude that the mature Newcomb was a realist and that he saw man as part of a large environment. When he was younger and more impressionable, on the other hand, he may easily have undergone a strong influence from Emerson and from Margaret Fuller. The most important evidence for this period—the *Book-Journal* which captivated Emerson—has been destroyed or lost. "Dolon" and a few passages in the *Commonplace Books* are the only internal evidence of Newcomb's early Romanticism which remains. "Dolon"—with its long sentences, its vague aspiration, and its suggestion of the bond between youth and the divine elements in nature —is surely the product of German Romanticism. A few parts of the *Commonplace Books* are similar in tone. Around the age of twenty-seven he entered a Transcendental cry:

Up. Up as a man. Be & do. Ennoble life by consciousness of birth & of brotherhood, & love of human race, spite of wrong doing & of disorder. Waste & consume not Energy & Health & Mind in idleness & morbid thought. (CB, January, 1848)

But here, although the tone is Emersonian, the meaning may not be. It is perfectly possible, for instance, that he was giving a deliberately vague expression to his personal problems. So, in the *Journal*, the inverted style, the Carlylean word-coinages, and the ambiguous phrases might easily be taken for Transcendental writing simply because their meaning is not obvious.

The truth probably is that Newcomb was strongly under the influence of Emerson around 1836-1846, when he visited and talked with him fairly often. After his Swedenborgian phase began, however, Newcomb seems to have moved out of the Emersonian sphere. In 1850 he admitted to Margaret Fuller that he was "not familiar with" Emerson's essays.[35] Emerson's influence on Newcomb must have

[34] *The Writings of Margaret Fuller,* ed., Mason Wade, New York, 1941, p. 11.
[35] Letter of February 19, 1850, in the Margaret Fuller manuscripts at Harvard University.

depended upon personal contact, so it is not surprising that its strength waned, with geographical separation and the passage of time. Although Newcomb used the very Transcendental medium of a Journal to express his thoughts, the thoughts which he expressed were usually anything but Transcendental.

It has been seen that the Newcomb we have come to know through his *Journals* is in many ways unlike the mysterious young genius who puzzled his friends and contemporaries. The *Journals* contain little of his "abridged stenographic wit" or of the "genius for penetration" praised by his associates. His moral philosophy is highly personalized and unsystematic; his description of society is interesting, but his discussion of it is uneven; his literary criticism is ingenious in its subtle appreciation, yet it hardly seems to warrant Emerson's declaration that Newcomb was his best key to Shakspere. Perhaps in his pictures of nature we find traces of the man who "talked divinely."

It may be that Newcomb was consistently overestimated by those who knew him. The diary which survives is full of symbolism, contradiction, and obscurity. Persons who characterized Newcomb as subtle and profound may have been expressing an admiration somewhat baffled by conversations whose significance escaped them. A man like Emerson, however, may have made the more complex mistake of reading into Newcomb's cryptic phraseology meanings which originated in Emerson's own mind.

Although Emerson was eager to befriend young men of exceptional talent, his eagerness was hardly so great that he would have imagined genius in a man who was completely mediocre. The "Book-Journal" which Emerson read may well have been the expression of a precocious originality and intuition. If so, the later *Journals,* instead of amassing and developing the earlier thought, amended and diluted it. It is not uncommon for youthful talent to lose its freshness and to fall green from the tree. It seems probable that Newcomb's was such a talent.

SELECTIONS FROM
THE JOURNALS OF CHARLES KING NEWCOMB

Section I. Arts and Letters

[1847]

Plato, the subtle logician, rich in rhetoric, in his inward mental activity saw the ill & danger of poetic culture & of nature-loving reverie; but—as the one was an intellectual imaginative excess, he fell into intellectual spiritual excess, & rose to a height which, while it summoned him from lower inactions, centred life too inwardly in thought. His relation to the oversoul[1] is too mental, & his method is too abstract because his end is abstract . . . his end is too exclusively & abstractly divinity rather than man, spiritualism than socialism, thought than life. Socrates makes man a medium of mental imagery of which he & other philosophers are a midwife. . . . The mind which in Homer is content with form, goes within, in Plato, to the Ineffable. Truth is not to be abstractly & unduly gazed at: we are men & are to make our forms the ends of all truth through which we commune with the spirit whence is its life. . . . (CB, 1847, 100-101)

October 30, 1847

I do like literature very much: I always find pleasure & interest in it; always is there food for suggestion & observation. *Poetry* is well to refine the faculties, but it is dangerous in bringing mental images with which the mind feeds on itself, & in preoccupying the mind; & history is well to give us our past; in the great & good we find nature tho only as in fellows: I take pleasure in religious musing over the Paradiso, in momentary uses of Laura & Beatrice, in Homeric vision of beauty; but life is all in all, & on a bright day, as is this, I should say to a scholar—"I like it very well—but it is for a by-hour only."

To read with use, one must read with the aim of perceiving relations to, & method of, life: as with eye on the end & only reality of all government, all being, we see truth & error. This motive is prac-

---

[1] This is one of the few places where Newcomb uses the word, "Oversoul," which occurs so frequently in Emerson's writing.

tical, giving us the summit of insight & of self possession, of moral exercise, & encouragement, of mental power, at once. Thus, reading is excellent & indifferent at the same time; it is like perception of people about us, & reflection on human nature & on divine law. History will thus be a record of men & states valuable to profit. (CB, 1847, 83-84)

[1847]

I do not like critics to make so much of Shakspear because his virtues are those of a nature whose imperative need is high tide of life, & of which action in him is but a pledge.[2] The Dramas of S. are but moods & states of man who passes on to full action. His persons are sweet-voiced, sweet active, but they must together seek life; & to end in reading him is as if they all found life in each other, & men in drama. (CB, 1847, 124)

[1847]

Chaucher[3] is a specimen of the English character in natural times before the world was yet so worldly, when there were green lanes & healthy socialness, preserving his youth to the last. His Cant. Tales, written at 74, are of the bloom of youth. And he is exquisite for his simple relations to nature as in the Cock, & c. His compositions has the union of imagination with the fancy of youth, as in the Knights Tale. (CB, 1847, 138)

October 11, 1851

Have decided to look into the greater Classics for a while, till something better fills time. Impatience may prevent a full appreciation, but a will bent upon activity may give a broader eye. I am impatient to be part of that life which is the image of heaven. Man possesses & knows the good in that of which the Poets discourse, or he takes possession & knows. A man, worthy of the name, who can appreciate the best in Poems, has sensibilities that impel him to a Home which is the centre of all Nature. That which pleases & catches

[2] Newcomb many times voices the opinion that Shakspere should be valued for what there is of nature in his work, rather than for what there may be of art. See February 5, 1866, *115*.
[3] Newcomb's customary spelling of Chaucer.

his eye in reading is the recognition of central truths, of moral sensibilities, of spiritual & intellectual & practical uses of nature, the undertone of primal order & beauty acting, like inspiration on the instincts of the author's human nature. Real Genius is the harmony of feeling & intellect; it is sensibility which elevates the mind & gives nearness to the high morals of Nature & of Life, & access to human nature; it is, in a way, near God &, therefore, in a way, near man: sensitive to good, it is sensitive to evil, so that it is master, more or less, of the ideal & of the actual, of Men as they should be & of men as they are. (J, I, 1)

October 24, 1851

Lately finished *Dante*. Cary's blank verse after Carlyle's[4] literal translation was offensive: it is a prose poem built out of Dante's sweet Italian. A prominent characteristic of Dante, with which I do not now sympathise, is the graphic scenicness. What interests me now in Literature is chiefly human nature, as in society, character, &c.: one point of interest in which is the reality that there is flesh & blood, & that you are given to sweet human nature. I do not think I could read *Scott* now, because he does not give men & women from a moral or social eye, but from a fancy, as if he took the people whom you were observing & carried them out into some romantic adventure. We have enough fancy of our own. We can easily imagine in merely picturesque positions, kings & queens, nobles & peasants, roundheads & cavaliers, but the recognition or perception of men & women in practical life pleases and instructs. Sight is better than vision. (J, I, 9)

September 27, 1852

Have lately been reading *Swedenborgh's* [*sic*] *Conjugial* [*sic*] *Love*. No wisdom in Books I have seen is so practical, so vital as his: no one before has seen & expressed life; only youth may have felt its depths in some respects but no youth has known the discipline of good & evil which are the completeness of it. No one im-

[4] Henry Francis Cary's translation of Dante's *Divine Comedy* appeared between 1805 and 1812; John Carlyle's prose translation came out toward the middle of the nineteenth century.

presses me with wisdom, manhood, life, as he does—or anything near it. Never before was Moral Philosophy written; never before was order expressed. Man will be man when such wisdom is made part of his education. . . . (J, I, 23)

December 1, 1852

In lately looking over *Shakspear,* I saw, not without some feeling, as from a previous part or similar experience, the terrible tragedies but as past: they were seen below me, like thunder clouds & storms from the mountain tops. (J, I, 27)

April 18, 1854

I do not enjoy this old reading & am glad that I do not:[5] for it would be unwise & a loss to become too interested in it. It is not pleasant to me to be carried beyond my own time, or to such themes. True art should be associated with practical & enlightened life. Taste should be commensurate with wisdom. Moral [?] completeness is the height of beauty & manhood, & so of all art. These Greek & Latin arts may have been a preserving influence for mental culture & refinement in the externalism of the middle ages, but, as models, should be superseded. As one would not go back to states of their own life, agreeing somewhat with old art, so they should not retrograde in literature. (J, I, 42)

July 24, 1854

Lately read *Emma.* Some of it gave me great pleasure, & it has many remarkable charms. But the book is alloyed by the women falling in love with the men without its being condemned. This is too bad, &, in one of Miss Austen's power, vexatious. Its naturalness makes it a good model for illustration of character. The book shows how useful novels might be. *Pride & Prejudice* is less complete, but interesting, like it, for natural charms. . . . The moral in neither is prominent.[6] The naturalness is too merely natural, an almost entire absence of exalted aim. . . . (J, I, 44-45)

[5] Compare with October 11, 1851, 94.
[6] Newcomb cites the text of *Pride and Prejudice* for an example of its lack of morality: "Elisabeth was forced to give in to a little falsehood here; for to acknowledge the substance of their conversation was impossible." (J, I, 45)

September 29, 1858

Shakspear knew human nature no better than other men; not so well as some others; less than professional men, who have opportunity to see men more as they are. He acted human nature; this was his knowledge of it. . . . His plays all show the unpractical, generalising character of Hamlet. . . . Hamlet is the key note to all the plays. What a testimony it is to the natural evil of human nature that any man can act evil in his own imagination, spontaneously, freely, copiously.[7] It shows that the same human nature is in all men; that its natural estate is evil; for nothing but religion can rule this seething capacity of evil & overcome it. It shows the need of regeneration & illustrates it: for good affection & principle are voluntary & deliberate acts of adoption. . . . (J, I, 111)

November 17, 1858

Plato affirms certain abstract principles: this is what strength there is in his philosophy. But what limit & deficiency of observation of these, & of application of them & of deduction from them. What a waste of rhetoric & composition, what words without souls, or rather with bad souls. He is entirely ignorant of the principles of human nature: of the relations of man to God & man, to Goodness & Wisdom. He knows nothing of what life is, nothing [of] what man is: he knows nothing of wisdom but a little wise logic, nothing of goodness. He has the monkish abstraction, the most anchoritish ignorance of the plan of life: of use, marriage, & all of man & life. His doctrines & principles awfully pervert man & society. His Republic would make a hell instead of a good state. What a contrast is Plato's poor philosophy to the angelical wisdom of Swedenborgh.[8] . . . (J, I, 123)

December 14, 1858

Opened Romeo & Juliet the other day, to see how much of man &

---

[7] An example of very un-Emersonian philosophy.

[8] In 1855 Newcomb was so deeply impressed by his Swedenborgian readings that his mother was worried about his "deluded thought." In a letter of July 9, 1855, Emerson warned him against the "waste of your genius on I know not what theory of your dear mad master Swedenborg, that genius is pernicious." *Letters,* ed., Rusk, IV, 516.

woman there was in it. . . . I thought how poor the world was to have such tragic dramas among its most vaunted literature. . . . (J, I, 125)

January 6, 1859

Rochefoucault's Maxims, however false as moral law, are true as transcripts of the laws of the unregenerate: they are valuable confessions of the motives of irreligious society. Thus, out of its own mouth, the unregeneration is condemned. It is so long since I read in them, I must look at them again to see if I am right in this characterisation of them. (J, I, 135)

December 15, 1859

What exquisite fineness & gentility in *George Herbert.* No gentleman could surpass the high tone of his breeding; no courtier the delicacy of his address & tact; and no poet his subtle finenesses. . . . Skating today on the ice before the fellows came, his Discipline, Longing, Invitation, made a May day in the mind as I called them up in memory. (J, I, 199)

March 15, 1860

Noticed the contrast between English & continental literature, in reading lately *Manzoni's I Promessi Sposi.* In the English novel, love, home, their incidents & relations, form the main design & part. Love is the warfare & the battle-cry in them. In this Italian novel, love is made the small centre of a large & complex web: home is the object of the conspiracy & action, but domesticity, such as it is, is not the theme; courtship & bethrothal, the relation of two souls, are only as an external groundwork of the story. . . . (J, I, 212)

May 26, 1860

Noticed at a concert last night the fine effect of the trumpet amongst stringed instruments. It infused a gentle, persuasive, heartlike influence into the music. It was like the warm breath of a full-hearted being. Its fullness & softness are womanly. The violins have a masculine mentality & muscle in their sounds. This is the case with all stringed instruments, whilst the wind instruments have the mellowness & softness & genial roundness of feminine flesh. How the trumpets rouse & cheer the affections. The flute has the delicacy of a woman's voice; violins are like the tongues of scholars. Notwithstanding, the air, like affection, has a part, such as it is, in both classes. . . . (J, I, 223)

August 8, 1860

What a commentary on the moral quality of the intellectual world, that there is so little consciousness that Petrarch's sonnets were written on another man's wife, & that they thus are tainted with a moral adultery, & are a standing illustration of violation of the tenth[9] commandment. . . . (J, I, 239)

November 17, 1860

Imagination is subtler in relation to fact than is fancy. To the imagination impressions are more imparted; to fancy they are rather suggested. Imagination is more unitary; fancy is more composite. In the one there is more insight; in the other more invention. Imagination has more of synthesis; fancy of analysis. Imagination records more by impression; fancy by composition. The one is symbolical; the other is metaphorical. . . . (J, I, 268)

October 12, 1861

Hamlet represents a large class of men because of their common moral inertia.[10] There is a general tendency to abstraction, to vague moral sensitiveness, to passive relations, to philosophical observation without personal interest in the relation of truth & principles to life. . . . (J, II, 20)

January 24, 1862

Shakspear's mental activity & sensitiveness are so great that he rants at times from mental irritation & excitement. He swells with mental stimulus roused by emotion & is carried along with it, as the big mouthed actor is carried away by his part. . . . (J, II, 50)

[9] It is the seventh commandment which forbids adultery.

[10] It seems probable that Newcomb found Hamlet representative of a "large class of men" because he felt that Hamlet's failings were his own. See below the entry for November 18, 1863, *101*.

November 8, 1862

Hamlet's morbid love of ease is a mainspring of his evil & woes. Call to action disturbs him. He is too conscientious to flatly decline or to wantonly forget, & he is not conscientious enough to manfully comply. . . . Hamlet is one of the best illustrations in literature of a man unbalanced between two worlds. Shakspear did not see the moral, & the result is the result of want of positive thought & choice. . . . (J, II, 97)

March 6, 1863

It is a good of poetry, that it enlists the sympathies, without the delays & risks of didacticism. It interests men before it convinces them. It gives them pleasure before it extorts their consent. It illustrates by experiment. It is an evil of poetry that it develops the feelings disproportionally to the understanding, & the sentiments disproportionally to the principles. . . . It develops prematurely & partially. . . . It is a relation of impulsive affinities, rather than of steady counterpartship.—It may be said in favor of poetry, that it is a genial & finished idiom of the feelings. . . . It may be said in favor of prose that it is a language of character. . . . Life is its deed, rather than its song. . . . (J, II, 218-219)

March 16, 1863

Shakspear is one of the few authors in whom force is composite: in whom the finess of details is in large ratio to the aggregate. His paragraphs are constituted of various expressions, like a mosaic outline of which each stone is a gem. His plays are made up of little plays. His beauties are beaded. . . . (J, II, 231)

March 17, 1863

The mien of the mind, unblended with the feelings, is cold & angular, ungraceful & unmelodious. This is seen in the contrast between even Shakspear & Ben Jonson. . . . (J, II, 234)

April 2, 1863

. . . One reason that readers of Shakspear prefer such plays as Hamlet, Othello, Lear, to Timon, is because impulsive defects &

vices are more common than more systematic & didactic defects & vices. There is eloquence in Timon, but the reader recoils at philosophising misanthropy. Morbidness inactive [?] is evil & piteous in Hamlet; but morbidness discoursive, in Timon, is more harsh & grating. It is more agreable also to learn order & principle from the conduct of men in action, rather than in harangue. A perverted understanding shocks as well as bores. Timon, in some respects, is Hamlet run to seed. . . . Timon shows in his moral dyspepsia the results of having, as he himself aptly & pithily expresses it, "had the world as my confectionary."[11] . . . Life is not a toy or a play, but is meat & action. (J, II, 256)

November 4, 1863

Medieval misconceptions of religion leave traces of their abstraction occasionally in Shakspear, as well as in Geo. Herbert. Thus Ophelia speaks of "the steep & thorny way to heaven."[12] . . . Human experience counteracted, to a great degree, the perverted & pestiferous influence in society at large of these abstractions—as in the case of marriage & life in the world, both during the dark ages & since—& of similar abstractions in previous ages. Human life not only preserved the law of life in these respects better than did a false church, but conserved it until the world more fully felt & saw that what is of humanity is also of religion & that the earth is a type of heaven. . . . (J, III, 142)

November 18, 1863

Hamlet also represents a large class of men in a tendency, on the one hand, to a merely natural or passive routine of life, &, on the other hand, to eccentric & radically abstract relations to duty. Like him, they either follow, as a matter of course, the beaten track of life, in the way of nature; or else they pervert the call of higher principles, which should base them firmly in natural life, into an abandonment of normal ways for extravagant & abnormal relation to truth & sentiment. . . . (J, III, 165)

[11] *Timon*, IV, iii, 260.
[12] *Hamlet*, IV, iii, 48.

December 8, 1863

There is some art in Shakspear, but it is softened & overshadowed by his redundant humanity, such as it is. It is art in nature, like affectation in children. Its traces are so delicate that it requires almost the subtlety to detect them that it does to recognise some of his beauties. His art is unstrained & offhand. (J, III, 198)

December 19, 1863

Shakspear shows originality in its subtle aspect of inventive appreciation, or discursive observation. His images are from nature, & are such as would occur only to a fine apprehension. They are grouped only as they could be grouped by a composite mind.[13] It requires experience, almost, to take them in their full sense. . . . (J, III, 223)

December 28, 1863

The comparatively graphic scenery in the Inferno & Purgatorio, as compared with the vaguer outlines of the Paradiso, in the Divina Comedia, attests the difference of the relation to the external & to fact, in passion, judgment, & moral discipline, from that in the more abstract intellectual. The mind is less at large & discursive in the subject that is more directly connected with experience, & knows, in kind, its ground. Dante's persistent grasp of figures is also notable. He feels his way by them as he goes along. He interprets his thoughts by imagery. He reproduces, to some degree, principles in their embodiment, & invests moral spheres with natural scenery, especially in the Inferno & Purgatorio. He was, to a degree, practically, somewhat, an analogist. Without thought, he took the counterpartship . . . of the worlds as a matter of course. Dante's comparatively liberal relation to the medieval theology is also notable. He was, while a citizen of the world, too much of a man . . . to be satisfied with, or absorbed in, the more romantic sentimentalism of the church of that day. . . . As he passed on through Inferno & Purgatorio & went farther & farther from the world, he approached a sphere about which most men, & especially the medieval creed, are addicted to

[13] Compare this with the preceding selection.

abstraction itself; &, perhaps, the Paradiso shows a tendency in him to end in the very passivity of postural & sensational ritualism whose influence, during his early course . . . his more active relations checked & even, to a great degree, counteracted & precluded. He ends as in a large cathedral, & he, who had been something of an observer in the interest of morals, becomes more or less of a vague intellectualist, a spiritual abstractionist, like one lost in reverie before pictures & painted windows. The theme which rightly treated, would have drawn him back to the world, & nearer to it than before, drew him, as he treated it, away from it. . . . (J, III, 242-243)

February 5, 1864

Shakspear's frequent habit of using in one sentence words in different senses, proceeds from persistent & large grasp, & from rhythm of thought, not from mere rhetorical alliteration or verbal witticisms. Thus, Constance, in her fine & solemn lines on the relation of principle to wants, plays on the word "need," "that need must needs infer this principle."[14] . . . So in Valentine's play on the words "life & death" in 2G. of V.[15] . . . He sometimes rolls a word, like a sweet morsel, over & over, in his mind, with keen relish, as if to digest it fully, or in vivacious appreciation of the many sides of the relation of the thing denoted by it; "If love makes me forsworn, how shall I swear to love?"[16] . . . & in the fine sonnet in the same play . . . on study, "light, seeking light, doth light of light beguile."[17] . . . (J, III, 310)

March 12, 1864

Vicious women are apt to be more depraved than vicious men because their more affectional & emotional natures are more singly & thoroughly pervaded by evil than are the more discursive & composite natures of men. They are more rapt & absorbed, more impulsive, less reflective. The very antagonism of harsh evil to the

[14] *King John*, III, ii, 213.
[15] *Two Gentlemen of Verona*, III, i, 170, ff.
[16] *Love's Labor's Lost*, IV, ii, 109.
[17] *Ibid.*, I, i, 77.

normal natures of gentle womanliness favors, when perverted, a more defiant, obstinate, & hearty adoption of it. Their excess of evil is a counterpart to their superiority in good, as compared with men. . . . Shakspear showed his usual verisimilitude to nature, & accordance with sacred & secular tradition, in delineating Lady Macbeth, not only as the tempter of her husband, but as worse than him. . . . (J, IV, 17)

March 19, 1864

. . . The Newcomes, written by Thackeray . . . is an instance of a work, the reading of which is almost precluded by the initial, prominent, & persistent sentimentalism & humanity-worship of the writer. Instead of simply drawing his characters, he associates with them, fondles them, feels with them. . . . Although Thackeray is not wordly in respect of money, tuft-hunting, or bullyism, he is worldly in not regarding the end of life in the world. . . . He is not a mere intellectualist or a mere sentimentalist; but the blending of these two traits, without direct principle, becomes what may be called mawkishness. . . . (J, IV, 38-39)

March 23, 1864

In one deep sense of the word, tragedy itself is a comedy, inasmuch as it, indirectly, shows the success of order by showing the intrinsically demoralised character & inevitable failures of disorder. It shows the conflict of evil against the Providence which is the good of man, & that evil is worsted in the conflict. . . .(J, IV, 46)

March 24, 1864

One essential difference of pagan & Christian tragedy is that, in the one, man struggles against an arbitrary & inexorable Providence, &, in the other, man struggles against a wise & beneficent Providence. In the one system man misconceives Providence; in the other system he rebels against it. In the one, he is ignorant of Providence; in the other, he ignores it. . . . (J, IV, 47)

April 20, 1864

Ambitious men are prone to superstition through the forwardness

& image-making tendencies of their perverted imaginations. They tend to delusion in thought as in desire. They are idolatrous in sentiment as in acquisitiveness. The apparition of the Witches makes more impression upon Macbeth than upon Banquo, who saw them with him, because they were more congenial in their general economy, as well as in their decoying suggestions, to his character. They owe their prominent part in the drama to the prominent evils of one person in the tragedy, Macbeth himself. . . . (J, IV, 110)

April 25, 1864

The entertainment of evil thoughts habituate a man to their appearance so that they seem less & less strange, repugnant, & unnatural to him. He is less shocked by the fact that they address him, & less sensitive to their character. So the restless & turbulent sea slimes its shores & deposits its weeds like eggs, in its own excrement, & thus rolls in with smooth facility over its beds of weeds. Macbeth is aptly represented by Shakspear as but once appalled at the mere thought of crime; "My thought, whose murder yet is but fantastical, Shakes so my single state of man."[18] . . . (J, IV, 120-121)

June 8, 1864

Comedy is more generic & comprehensive than tragedy, as the history of a victorious war, as a whole, is more so than is that of a disastrous campaign in either a successful or unsuccessful war. The difference is not merely relative, but, if such be the case at point, intrinsic, as heaven differs from hell, or day from night. In comedy the cold storms are succeeded by warm sunshine. In tragedy the cold & the storms are perennial like ice at the poles or like darkness in tombs. It is the difference of a man, sometimes sick & sometimes well, from a man chronically & organically diseased.—The prevalence in the world of the head-strength, waywardness, & morbidness, with which many men pervert the sweet & blessed comedy of life into a tragedy for themselves & others, is connected with the fact that most dramatists tend to throw themselves with more force into their tragedies than into their comedies. . . . (J, IV, 219)

[18] *Macbeth,* I, iii, 139-40.

September 30, 1864

Faults apparently opposite are apposite, because the mind & feelings are so much distrained & forced in one direction as to bring together qualities which, under usual conditions, are relatively remote. Thus Hamlet is so over-cautious & obstinate in the matter of killing the king, that he is impetuous & rash in killing Polonius.[19] He is so irritated at his chronic passiveness, that he rushes to eventuate a sudden impulse before he can began to palter & reflect. . . . (J, V, 54)

November 3, 1864

Men like Hamlet get into doubt because, in some respects, & amongst other evils, they seek doubts. They tamper with truth & lose its front: they turn it over in wanton & morbid activity & are bewildered by its obverse: they play with it & lose their respect for it: they detach it from its end & lose its significance: they run counter to it, & are staggered by the force with [which] it meets & overwhelms them. . . . In some points they are like children who tear a toy to pieces, to see how it was made . . . they are like men who lose, or impair, their own identity by curiously & passively personating others in their consciousness. . . . (J, V, 122)

November 5, 1864

Shakspear has illustrated the sensual & the heroic, in the characters of Falstaff & Henry 5[h]. In doing this, he has illustrated the sensual in both of these men, & the heroic only in one. He has shown in one, at large, that there is a sensuality especially cognate to the depraved & unmanly will, & in the other that there is a sensuality which, though unmanly & unheroic, has more to do with wanton & reckless energy than with confirmed & aimless inclination: that what is a wild & heedless play in one is a systematic & artful labor in the other. Henry & Falstaff diverge from an apparent community of sensualism at the pathway of civil duty. . . . The experience of Henry attests that sensuality is alien to heroism, & that of Falstaff attests that heroism is alien to sensuality. Henry puts off sensuality by put-

[19] *Hamlet*, III, iv.

ting on the heroic; Falstaff assumes only the mock heroic because he adheres to sensuality. . . . (J, V, 130)

December 20, 1864

Humanity is the scope of all faculty, the focus of all range. Shakspear's mind, after an exercise of imaginative power, in the interview between Prospero & Ariel, that is indicative of a mental strength unparalleled in literature of its kind, returns, in the pathetic words of Prospero, to his womanly daughter, "Awake, dear heart, awake"[20] . . . as to its nest. This refrain of recognition & address, in the midst of that wild & wonderful scene, is like the culmination of a terrible storm in the falling of a dew drop on a rosebud: it is like a patch of a warm & flowery mead beside an ice-berg: it is like the glance of an eagle from the bleak & tempestuous air to its sheltered eaglet. (J, V, 279-280)

December 26, 1864

. . . A man who is uneasy about himself is prone to be uneasy about persons who are like him. . . . Hamlet is impatient at Polonius because he is impatient at himself. Polonius is as a talker what Hamlet is as a thinker. . . . (J, V, 296)

January 16, 1865

. . . Shakspear, Dante, Milton, & Swedenborgh, are incomparably superior to Homer, Eschylus, Aristotle, & Plato, because the Bible had developed the spiritual faculties of mankind in those who received it or also lived under its influence. (J, V, 351)

January 30, 1865

The ends & rules of reading are, in brief: 1st, to get at truth as principles & as facts. 2d, to cultivate, exercise, & form the understanding. 3d, to develop & train the mental powers, & with them the moral powers. . . . 4th, to get the mental & moral diversion, sport, relief, assimilation. 5th, to generalise the mind & feelings. 6th, to get the benefit of the powers, experience, suggestions, & range of other

---

[20] *The Tempest,* I, ii, 305.

men. 7ᵗʰ, to study & know men, the world, & human nature. 8ᵗʰ, to enlarge the scope of both relations & observations. 9ᵗʰ, to study & illustrate life. 10ᵗʰ, to study & illustrate morals in general, by the thought, conduct, & experience of men both as they have been, are, &, above all, should be. . . . (J, VI, 29)

January 31, 1865

It is a bad style which says more than need be said. It is a symptom of immature relation to thought. It is diffuse because the thought is not yet absorbed. The thought is made much of in expression, because it is a stranger to the consciousness. It is elaborated, through desire to substantiate it. Life-time is so summary & mind is so prolific [that] men want to read much in little. Amplification has its office in eluci-dating, spreading, & assimilating, but maturer men ask for the cen-ter, & immaturer men should be taught to look to the center. . . . The best writer writes briefly because he writes maturely & for cause. He does not artificially condemn his thought, nor sentimentally ex-pand it. . . . The expression of thoughts should be, in a great degree, expression of principles. Like corrolaries in geometry, it should rather sum up the problem & accompany & suggest it, than, in itself, work it out. . . . Many writers bore their readers & injure their influence by thinking through writing. . . . Ruskin . . . thinks too much as he writes, & is hence diffuse. Wordsworth studied poetry, & presented all his essays to the public. . . . (J, VI, 30-31)

. . .

Shakspear is, in some respects, more of an American than he is of an Englishman. He belonged to the age in which the tide of prin-ciples began to turn & swell, that, at its full, in the next age, surged to New England & was there received on the congenial shores of nascent democracy, whilst it subsided in the relatively uncongenial & hardened spheres of old England. . . . In his English Historical Plays he showed English loyalty, English tenderness for royal tradition, & English conservatism, but, also, unbiassed regard for the energy & general fitness for office which is one of the early prognostics of republicanism. . . . (J, VI, 32-33)

February 6, 1865

The music of the soft sweet voice of a woman ran through the music of the rough pointed voices of a choir of boys, in church yesterday, like a stream of ripe oil through a stream of crude wine. Rosewater & brine were not more different than these notes. . . . [A] choir of boys is not appropriate to a church, because they can sing with neither understanding or mellowness. . . . (J, VI, 50)

February 7, 1865

It is one of many differences between Shakspear & many other playwrights, that he uses art in the ends of nature, & that they use nature in the ends of art. Shakspear is not without cunning & artifice, as seems to those who see his naturalness more than they see his tact: but he suborns them to nature, as a brave soldier suborns strategem to service, or as a fisherman suborns his fancy tackle to fish-catching . . . he sets out his vases because he has wine to pour into them. . . . (J, VI, 53)

March 10, 1865

. . . Even Shakspear, who dramatises his [Timon's] career, is obliged, in verisimilitude to Timon, to conform his dramatic action, from the more general conventionalism of the usual drama, to the almost epic narrative of a monologue. It was a poor exchange that Timon made of hollow society for barren solitude: of crude sympathies for crude antipathies: of thoughtless fellowship for thoughtless alienation: of shallow joys for shallow sorrows: of unintelligent gluttony for unintelligent starvation: of fond trust in men for fond distrust of men . . . & of aimless philanthropy for aimless misanthropy. . . . (J, VI, 145)

March 30, 1865

Men of some thought & feeling see more than men of less thought & feeling, because their scope is more comprehensive. They see more because they feel more. . . . They mean more because they have more sense. . . . They use language in larger & subtler significance. They assume some things for granted, & are fully apprehended only by their fellows. They purposely hold in reserve things which they do not intend to fully express & this reserve puzzles men who do not keep pace with them in experience. The blunt & ready reply of Troilus, to Pandarus' protestation "I speak no more than truth," "Thou dost not speak so much"[21] . . . is a fine & suggestive, though not full, illustration of this distance of meaning between men of more & less feeling. . . . (J, VI, 213-214)

July 17, 1865

. . . what was a monotone in Polonius was a mood in Hamlet. He was disgusted with him as he was disgusted with officious scruple, with abstract metyphysics, & with overactive mentality in himself. Polonius was a type of onesided men, who creep in the deep ruts which they have worn in their limited relations, & who seldom or never move in accord with the mobile mass of men. Hamlet more decidedly saw & more energetically repelled abstraction in another than in himself. (J, VII, 96)

August 28, 1865

The only person in the tragedy of Hamlet who has any sort of moral object in view is the man after whom the play is named: & yet the only person in it who has not some definite sort of an object in view is Hamlet. One direct cause of the crudity of a man like Hamlet is the fact that so few men are even turned toward the direction in which he reluctantly & slowly goes. . . . (J, VII, 173)

September 19, 1865

An inverted & antithetical style, unduly used, is disagreable in that it evinces a sort of formality in thought, & of consciousness in sentiment. It is not wholly affected for it is the result of mood & position more than of ambition & vanity. Men who write much adopt it partly for the sake of facility & point, & partly from pleasure in resonant expression. . . . There is in it a pleasing & expressive feature of balance, as there is of rhythm in metre; but carried to excess, & used as a habit, it becomes posturing & formal, like danc-

---

[21] *Troilus and Cressida*, I, i, 64-65.

ing in a person who thinks too much of his steps. . . . (J, VII, 228)

September 21, 1865

Juliet's reluctance to have Romeo leave, & her remonstrance against his leaving, is an exquisite instance of the tendency of women to tempt men at the price of permanent welfare for the sake of imminent pleasure: "Therefore stay yet; thou need'st not to be gone."[22] . . . (J, VII, 233)

October 6, 1865

The mere natures & experiences of men do much to assist their judgments & conduct. Men, especially as they are, may often receive valuable hints from their feelings. The feelings are sometimes truer than the thought, because they are less tampered & perverted. It is thus that a wife is frequently a trustworthy counsellor to a husband: she is more the creature of feeling than he is. A man's condition more or less indicates & suggests his needs.—This principle is illustrated in Rosalind's apt reply to Celia's advice to wrestle with her affections for Orlando: "O, they take the part of a better wrestler than myself."[23] . . . (J, VII, 261)

October 11, 1865

False theories do not stand the brunt of even false desires. Men who prate about chance are the men who trust to it the least when their pleasures are concerned. "If chance will have me king, why chance may crown me, Without my stir,"[24] said Macbeth . . . yet Macbeth would not wait on chance, though his alternative was a monstrous crime. (J, VII, 274)

November 13, 1865

Most men are neither natural or normal; they do not either adhere to mere nature or follow due grace. Children are more pleasing, because they are at least natural, & in such sort that normalism is suggested & illustrated by their condition & conduct. They have the

[22] *Romeo and Juliet*, III, v, 16.
[23] *As You Like It*, I, iii, 22.
[24] *Macbeth*, I, iii, 143.

bounding vigor of animals & the refined presentments of men.[25] The fairies in Midsummer's Night's Dream are interesting as a sort of organised children. (J, VIII, 2-3)

November 30, 1865

Truth is like a jewel that all men can put on, but that is becoming & seemly only in manly men. The morbid Timon, the surly Appemantus, the ugly Thersites, all the fools in Shakspear, & the blunted Sancho Panza in Cervantes, say smart, & often profound, things, but they do not say them with prestige or commensurate effect, because they do not say them in due scope. (J, VIII, 40)

December 16, 1865

Alliteration sometimes tempts the thought with a sudden diversion of contradistinction. It is a sort of logical, imaginative fancy. It is weak & silly as a habit, for it is a onesided & low range, when regarded merely in itself:[26] but it is a relief & a play when it is intermixed & timely. "Their fraction is more our wish, than their faction,"[27] said Nestor, in the latter scope, in Troilus & Cressida. . . . (J, VIII, 56)

December 29, 1865

. . . Montaigne nurses his thought like a woman nursing a baby, or like a girl playing with dolls. He keeps house as in a study. His habits are those of invalidcy, & he glories in them. He pets himself as young females pet men. He regards himself as in a mirror. He studies himself as doctor-ridden women study their symptoms & prescriptions. He is the reservoir of all his reflections & studies. He aims all literature & sentiment at himself. He lives in the luxury of his own self-consciousness. The garrulity of his race is modified by

[25] Compare with Newcomb's sketch, "Dolon," *The Dial*, July 1842, pp. 112-123.

[26] In some of Newcomb's later journals there is an excessive amount of alliteration. He must have been conscious of his fault, for he several times tried to justify it by calling attention to alliterative passages in Shakspere. Among his entries for July 19, 1867, appears a discussion of alliteration, followed by this sentence: "I am resolved, henceforth, to avoid it, though I never played with it against meaning." (J, XIV, 135) Later, this note was crossed out—perhaps because Newcomb realised that neither half of it was true.

[27] *Troilus and Cressida*, II, iii, 107-108.

his character into writing. . . . His essays are notable for the natural wit which they evince, & for the natural candor of their communicativeness; but they are unsurpassed as a depiction by himself of the unmasculine tendency & nature of his mode of thought. In another mood, Montaigne might have published his Essays as Confessions. . . . (J, VIII, 83-84)

December 29, 1865

It was an ingenious hit in Fallstaff to call purse-taking his vocation & then to say that it was "no sin for a man to labor in his vocation"[28] . . . many, so called, businessmen of modern times could say little more, in extenuation for their morally disreputable transactions in speculation, than this. (J, VIII, 85)

January 9, 1866

Miscegenation is so abnormal & so repulsive [that] Shakspear shows verisimilitude in making Desdemona's father especially averse to her match with a Moor. A parent would naturally see the evil sooner than a mere theorist or indifferent person would see it. Shakspear took the misalliance from the story; doubtless he forgot it while he gave Othello's & Desdemona's part, as probably most readers of the play have always done: like Desdemona, he saw the visage of the Moor in his mind. The reader must be content with the play as one of character apart from individualisation, in this respect of race & complection. All Europeans have never regarded the matter as all Americans regard it, because of less familiarity with it. Charles 5th gave his daughter to the Duke of Tuscany, said to have been a Mulatto. (J, VIII, 108)

January 23, 1866

Illiterate or debarred people are often close observers, by virtue of their position, & shrewd observers, by virtue of their curiosity. They do not participate but look. The parlor is as a stage-scene to the kitchen; the line is as a pageant to the rank & file. Servants have prominent parts, such as these are, in the drama of all nations. In Shakspear's plays they are something of a chorus. Sancho Panza is a

[28] *1 Henry IV*, I, ii, 118.

sort of make-weight to Don Quixote. . . . Servants are, in some sense, as things are, the hands of their employers, &, as such, wait on them as on their heads.—It is one moral of the relation of servants, attested by their parts in dramas & novels, that busybodyism in the affairs of others is generally in proportion to the plane & range of occupation. (J, VIII, 144)

January 31, 1866

Everyday's experience teaches men to be duly patient with each other's waywardnesses in mood & thought. People are prone to feel & think inconsiderately & immaturely. The odd man of today may be the even man of tomorrow: the unbeliever of today, the believer of tomorrow. The tenure of most people is the same in some faults & in some virtues: they start off at first impressions: they do not wait for the full notes, but follow discords or concords at random, according as they first enter their heads. Men may sometimes be taken, not at their words, but at their general motives. Benedict would have been rightly designated as flippant & headstrong, but not, as his professions, abstractly regarded, might have warranted, as yet radically unmasculine & selfish: he entered at last the very state which he & others thought that he disrelished or contemned in his heart, or at which he rudely scoffed; & he became "a married man." He crudely & wantonly made celibacy a hobby for a while: he did not think that a woman could suggest his own manhood to him. (J, VIII, 165)

February 2, 1866

Men sometimes fail to learn the most central lesson from their experience because they are prone to see the evils in others, rather than in themselves, which thwarted them. They learn, indeed, their own crudity & folly in not knowing evil in others, & in being imposed upon: but they do not learn the initial wrong of their own first standpoint. Timon is astounded at the discovery of human depravity; but he does not discover his own. It is notable, & characteristic, that he lavishes gold in an ecstacy of malevolence as prodigally as he lavished it in an ecstacy of benevolence. He throws away the capital of his life as wantonly & verdantly as he threw away the capital of his estate. (J, VIII, 175-176)

February 2, 1866

Unprincipled or inferior women resort to the artifices of coquetry to develop or insure the positiveness in a man, which they know their mere characters will not suffice to foster & attract. "Yet hold I off"[29] is the policy which, in itself, stamps boldly the difference between a Cressida & a Juliet. . . . (J, VIII, 180)

February 5, 1866

The hymns of one age serve in the hymnology of another age according to the identity of the experience of both ages with moral principles. The Puritans knew the meaning of the 136th Psalm, & felt a special interest in it, such as no other party in their nation . . . knew & felt in the same degree. They had fought against monopolising monarchy in old England & against monopolising savages in New England. They had dethroned & decapitated a crowned tyrant in the one land & they had slain some, & subdued other, crowned chiefs in the other land. . . . This Psalm could not have been more generically appropriate to their experience if it had been first written for their occasion. . . . "To him [*sic*] that stretched out the earth above the waters. . . . To him that smote Egypt in their first born. . . . And brought out Israel from among them. . . . To him which smote great kings. . . . And gave them lands for a heritage . . . for his mercy endureth for ever." . . . (J, VIII, 188-189)

. . .

Illustrating truths by Shakspear, & illustrating Shakspear by truths, are the performances of different motives. Exemplifying humanity by Shakspear, & collating Shakspear with humanity, are different kinds of diversions. A man who even disdains Shakspear could find interest & profit by finding humanity & himself in the dramas of Shakspear. A man may use Shakspear as Shakspear used the books which gave him his themes, plots, & models. (J, VIII, 191)

February 20, 1866

. . . The other prominent personages in Shakspear's tragedies have

[29] *Troilus and Cressida,* I, ii, 312.

something more or less exceptional to tempt them: Hamlet is tempted mainly through general waywardness. . . . (J, VIII, 257)

March 6, 1866

Adjectives impart roundness & fulness to language. They give names when nouns give things. Men of thought are addicted to the use of them in the degree that they are men of sentiment & emotion. They combine pithiness with brevity. Shakspear's addiction to adjectives is a matter-of-course. There is, perhaps, scarcely a paragraph not replete with them, in any of his writings. . . . (J, VIII, 304)

March 30, 1866

Poetry is, in some respects, a fugue-like refrain in the general tenor of sentiment. It is collated like the performance of a dance at a social meeting, or like an interlude of charades, or like a piece of music. It is not only marred but violated, when it is detached from the general occasion, as from the full theme or melody, & made an end in itself. It would be a poor feast where the tables were loaded with flowers & nothing more: &, more, it would be a deadly feast where flowers were served up as food. Poetry is, in some sense, a play of sentiment: & prose is the labor of sense. The mind sometimes uses poetry as a relief to thought &, at the same time, as a diversion of thought. It is sometimes a refuge of thought in sentiment. Persons, at some times, poetise in vague condition as at other times they generalise in vague condition. They indulge their impulsive sentiments in poetry, as they indulge their more thoughtful sentiments in generalisation. Some men evade reflection by poetising, as other men evade action by reflection. . . . (J, IX, 39-40)

April 11, 1866

Order is a part of loyalty to life. A disorderly man precludes himself from appeal against disorderly persons to the rights & requirements of order, so long as he is a denizen of disorder. Troilus could not relevantly & consistently censure Cressida for untruthfulness to him, inasmuch as, however heedlessly, he was, by his relation to her, untruthful to morality. So traitors to country cannot becomingly reproach one another for treachery to their own confederacy. (J, IX, 84)

April 16, 1866

All conduct that runs counter to society is, so far, divergent, eccentric & tragic; all conduct that conforms to society is, so far, convergent, regular, & merry. Whenever men are unhappy or impracticable, they are unsocial in method, principle, relation, or in point of fact; whenever they are happy & practicable, they are social in character, motive, & in fact. This truth is graphically, in some kind & degree illustrated by the contrast of the experience of the principal personages in the tragedies & comedies of Shakspear, to whose dramas a man of thought is prone to go for illustrations, rather than for suggestions, of principle. . . . The men after whom the tragedies are named, become wretched & demoralised through some violence or antagonism to social laws, order, & relation. Hamlet sets himself against society & society against him, by playing an arbitrary, idiosyncratic, mysterious, wild, & vaguely discordant part in it. Timon moodily spurns alike society & civilisation. Lear first defies the praccial tenure of conventional systems, & finally leaves the social spheres. Othello usurps the social right of judicature to his bitter cost. Macbeth loses society, by madly & illicitly seeking it. . . . Romeo & Juliet do not consider the signs of their times enough to be prudent & practicable.—In the comedies the principal personages become normal & happy in the kind & degree that they conform to the law & order of society. Valentine & Benedict correct the tragic scope of their celibacy by recognising & adopting love. . . . The triumph of social justice at once deposes Angelo & gives to him a wife; & it also redeems the Duke from nomadism & Isabella from a cell.—Society is the motive of comedy: isolation is the motive of tragedy. (J, IX, 104-105)

April 21, 1866

Principle is so essentially & intrinsically the oversoul of all relation, that all men instinctively, as it were, look up & recognise, in some kind & degree, its congenial & palpable presence. Even evil persons, in their rapture of low pleasures, evince a perverted action of this, so to call it, instinctive trait, by either personifying the principles that sway their evil scope, or by enthusiastically borrowing & using the generalisations & nomenclature of good scopes. The invocation of Macbeth to night, & those of Lady Macbeth to Hell, are instances of the former relation of evil persons to their scopes. . . . Cleopatra dresses her false love in the dress of true love & puts a wedding garment on her paramour, that she may the more enjoy her passion & her partner.—Thus, also, many men notwithstanding their addiction to falsities & vices, persistently use the name & enact the ceremonies of truth & virtue. (J, IX, 127-128)

May 7, 1866

Isabella's loss of temper & reason at Claudio's unmanly & unbrotherly abjectness is in fine verisimilitude with her general imperfection & onesidedness of thought & feeling. Her crude immolation of herself at the Juggernaut of conventualism would not have justified the assignment to her of a steady part at the sacrifice of Claudio to principle. . . . (J, IX, 207-208)

May 18, 1866

The rake who does not reform becomes a cynic. Jacques, in As You Like It, is such a man. The filth of his previous career incrusts upon him, & makes him hard, impervious, & odious. (J, IX, 235)

July 27, 1866[30]

Art in nature desires to be generalised, not imitated, by men. It furnishes materials & suggestions, but it seeks to be embodied in new forms. It sets the lesson in architectural writing, but, these once learned, it expects its scholars to do their own compositions. Its beauty is vitiated when it is shorn, & not sacrificed. The tree hints broadly at the pillar, but the tree itself makes an unwieldy & ungraceful pillar. . . . (J, X, 13)

September 12, 1866

It does not follow that a man is, in the common sense of the word,

[30] Newcomb took up residence in Philadelphia around July 14, 1866.

literary, because he sometimes writes, or even keeps a diary. On occasion, a man may express by letters as by speech; all men have done this more or less, whatever were their tendencies or occupations. A man who thinks may have cause to record his thoughts, as a man who does mercantile business may have cause to record his transactions. . . . The writings of a manly man differ from those of a so called literary man, in that the former contain what would be pertinent & discreet, in kind & degree . . . as the thought & utterances of a man of affairs, whilst the latter contain abstruse, redundant, irrelevant, far sought, & fond studies. . . . (J, X, 185)

September 15, 1866

There is a plaintiveness, a tenderness, a downrightness, a mourning, & an aspiration in the psalms ascribed to David, which peculiarly characterise them, & which distinguish them from the psalms ascribed to others. I am always glad to come to them in my calendar, much as I like the others; as, at this time, to the 86th Psalm.—How comprehensive is the 11th verse, for instance: "Teach me thy way, O Lord; I will walk in thy truth: unite my heart to fear thy name." Aspiration for truth, determination of conformity to it, & desire for an harmonious condition according to the order & nature of Providence, are highly expressed in it. . . . (J, X, 199)

October 9, 1866

Polonius is a character of much significance. It is of frequent occurrence in a world of Hamlets. . . . In all social circles there are pragmatical, conceited, sententious, officious, & loquacious men who are like him. He is rightly associated with Hamlet; for he is a sort of cross between Hamlet & other men. He is somewhat as a shadow of Hamlet &, spite of his persecution by that impractible man, seeks the company of Hamlet, if only to stand on the train of his robes & give him advice from the rear. . . . (J, X, 299)

October 13, 1866

Polonius was written Polonious in the play-bill at the theater last night: the blunder suggested an adjective. (J, X, 323)

October 16, 1866

The exquisite art, in its kind, of Shakspear makes his plays as interesting, instructive, & suggestive on the stage as in the book. Last evening, at the theater, where I went to see Edwin Booth as Iago, the moral of the play & Shakspear's qualities were the prominent & main interests of the performance. At first, the imperfection of the acting was annoying, & the evening promised tediousness; but the theme & the dramatist redeemed the time.—Booth is little like his father. When he came on the stage, I could not think it was he, now so famous, though the part was Iago's; his person, excepting his large head, was ordinary; his voice husky; & his acting second rate, though distinguished by earnestness, sentiment, & genius of a kind. I noted in picking him out amongst a group of other actors, that the mien of genius is marked boldly: this man could hardly be the son of his father & not have some genius. . . . One could easily see why girls were wild about him; he was too pensive & isolated for Iago; too much like Hamlet, in reflectiveness; & too much like Mephistopheles, in abstruseness & idiosyncracy of relation & posture; he was not accurate in his memory, like Charles Kean; he seems to have an organisation affected by his father's eccentricities. Othello was dressed, & acted somewhat, like an Indian; but the text was almost if not quite as well, pronounced by the actor of this part as by Booth. (J, X, 329-330)

October 23, 1866

As I stood amongst a miscellaneous crowd outside the ball-ground yesterday afternoon, witnessing a match-game within, deterred from entrance by the probability of losing the large admission fee by the breaking up of the game through an impending rain, the aspect of the people reminded me that Shakspear had grasped one main cause of abnormalism in the lower classes by merely designating & delineating it as plebianism. There was human nature running to weeds through want of culture. There were vulgarity & imbecility as creatures, vermin-like, of ill-breeding. . . . (J, XI, 2)

October 23, 1866

Eccentricity in dress rightly displeases people more than even foppery, because it shows a dangerous disregard of relations to society, whilst foppery shows, however crude, a regard for them. A woman intuitively knows that she can sooner depend on a pliant conformist to fashion than on a theorising & independent costumer. The personages in Twelfth Night are tempted to make a but[t] of Malvolio in costume, by his eccentric tendency of general sentiment. (J, XI, 4)

October 25, 1866

Undue concentration of thought or feeling gives abnormal & mischievous compactness & hardness to the character. A man whose traits are tightly compressed together has a stony energy in him, as a ball of closely twisted yarn has a leaden heaviness in it. Timon, the Misanthrope, is thus, somewhat, as different from Timon, the Prodigal, as a crude mass of wool is different from a cricket ball. Timon's last scope makes him a violent implement, as well as an idle plaything, of evil. (J, XI, 11)

November 1, 1866

To advertise the play of Richard 3ᵈ, as produced last night at the Walnut, as Shakspear's Play, was an act of forgery & fraud. No high toned actor[31] could lend himself to such a snare & perversion. It was probably the usual stage-version: a blended medley of Shakspear & of Colman. Henry 6th is the hero of the 1ˢᵗ act; an allotment of which Shakspear was incapable. (J, XI, 44-45)

. . .

The part of Furies is rightly assigned to females, because logical recrimination is consonant with the perverted relation of their sex to thought & feeling, & because talkativeness is more in the line of the general frailty of women than of men. Where angry men would use the fist, angry women use the tongue. Outraged women talk the more,

[31] The actor was Edwin Booth.

because they then feel assured that they talk rationally, so far as argument goes. The entanglement of Richard 3ᵈ in the group of women whom he has wronged, one of whom is his mother, is a masterly scene of dramatisation. It suggests & illustrates the relation of Orestes to the Furies. (J, XI, 45)

November 3, 1866

Hamlet's words in designation of a book, "words, words, words,"[32] indicate & mean that, like most thoughtful men, he knew that thought was not substance. He sickened at the fulsome & vapid taste of husks of action. The presence of the pragmatic Polonius added force to Hamlet's impatience with the satiating banquet of abstract reason. (J, XI, 55)

November 10, 1866

The naturalness of theatrical representations is attested by the propensity of children to play at dramas of dolls, horses, & society; & invites the normal adaptation & uses of the theater for practical purposes in the training of all ages of life in experience.—Was reminded of this, at the Chestnut Street last evening, where I sat beside two little boys, absurdly misplaced indeed, at their age; but there they were. At first, I thought they would see no more in the stage-scenes than scenes, similar in kind to those they saw everyday & that they would wonder at the reproduction of life in what would seem to them unreality, & something like mimicry: but I remembered the fondness of children for playing social parts, & so was in their secret & also thought better of the theater than before. (J, XI, 81-82)

November 12, 1866

A wit might say that Shakspear meant to indirectly compliment Hamlet by calling him "fat," so obvious is his aversion to leanness. . . . (J, XI, 88)

November 15, 1866

Conjoint artlessness, energy & sensibility are principle ingredients in the effective & pervasive power of what is called genius. Men

---

[32] *Hamlet,* II, ii, 194.

who feel warmly & act determinately tend to make impressions on other people in favor of both themselves & their cause. Edwin Booth's performance of Hamlet, which I went to see at the Walnut last eve'g, was an illustration of this fact. Although not a first rate actor, he threw himself so diligently, sympathetically, & artlessly into the part, that he was something, in kind, positive, whatever it was, & drew the rapt attention of a miscellaneous house. He gave to Hamlet too mobile & demonstrative an impatience & restlessness, but his exaggeration served as an emphasis on the reading of the character. His husky voice, which was suited to Richard 3ᵈ, gave to Hamlet the effect of a cold in the lungs, but did not prevent what impression he produced. I doubt if any delineation of Hamlet ever before so much interested an audience: & the cause was the greater zeal & simplicity of the actor.—As I looked around once at the audience, understanding the attractive nature of Booth's standpoint too well to be surprised at its effect, I was filled with admiration at the engagedness of the spectators in the performance. Here were people of all ranks drinking in with their eyes the type of men of all ranks. Shopmen, stockbrokers, lawyers, apprentices, news-boys, sailors, loafers, scholars, & hod-carriers were listening to a problem which all the ingenuity & mythology of Greece & Egypt had not presented to their schoolmen & kings. (J, XI, 105-106)

November 30, 1866

The drama has an advantage over history, in that it generalisingly reveals, or hypothetises motives. It gives history in the masks of the personages who made it. Marlborough may well have studied English history in Shakspear, for there was more of the main fact of human history, doubtless, in Shakspear than in Hollingshed.—Most histories are poems, without being dramas. (J, XI, 179)

December 7, 1866

Fallstaff, as in his analysis of honor[33] . . . denies principle from predilection to feverish sensualism: Iago, as in his definition of virtue[34] . . . from predilection to cold malignity. Fallstaff is parboiled in vice; Iago is frozen in it. (J, XI, 213)

[33] *1 Henry the Fourth*, V, i, 130 ff.
[34] *Othello*, I, iii, 322 ff.

December 20, 1866

The contrast of an Italian to an American or English actor, in the part of Macbeth, reminds one of the greater predominance of consideration & composure in the Anglo-Saxon race. The Italian made a good & interesting Macbeth, of its kind; but it was, on the one hand, too arbitrary, as before the Witches, &, on the other hand, too ecstatic, as in his remorse. Scotch witches would have never answered so domineering a man; & a Scotch Lady Macbeth would have been disgusted with such maniacal morbidness. (J, XI, 268)

December 22, 1866

A superfine man is never a sound man. He who cannot see, use, or characterise coarse things cannot see, use, or characterise fine things. Bran is known to be an essential part of the nourishment in wheat, yet an effete civilisation discards it; so an effete literature discards, what is called homeliness in scene, though it is an essential part of all relations. . . . (J, XI, 282)

January 23, 1867

Greek literature stands against modern literature, somewhat as the pale & waning, but still glowing & resplendent, moon stands, at dawn of day, against the crescent sunrise. The light in Shakspear is warmer & more tinted than the light in Homer: yet Homer shines; & Homer must, in his place, always shine, because what light he has is reflected from the same orb which illumined, in other, though also incomplete, kind, Shakspear, in his place. (J, XII, 85)

February 6, 1867

It is of natural justice that Gertrude should, at last, however unintentionally, be killed by the same hand that, for incest with her, killed her husband. The very blunders of evil men are mortal crimes: their softest touches are paralysing blows. (J, XII, 171)

February 9, 1867

The French aphorist, who made it a maxim that virtue was selfishness,[35] might have found an, on its surface, as he would wrongly

---

[35] La Rochefoucauld.

see it, pertinent & exquisite motto for his treatise in the dialogue of Speed & Launcelot: *Speed,* "Here follow her vices." *Laun.,* "Close at the heels of her virtues"[36]. . . . The interpretation, evinced by his selection, of this motto would have been in keeping with the sophistry & superficialness which he evinced in his interpretation of morality & immorality in the world. Yet he would have, therein, introduced a Trojan-horse of wit into his discourse, out of which would come a force that would rout & confuse the speaker. Vices are near virtues, because virtue is disciplined by contiguity to vice. Good men are tempted, bad men are led, by the devil. (J, XII, 191)

February 16, 1867

If a man makes a sponge of himself, he must expect to be regarded, used, & treated . . . as a sponge. To some intents & purposes, he is metamorphosed, in his scope as author, into a sponge. Accordingly, a Shakspear, whose soft brain sucked up seas of humanity, must expect to be met, sucked, squeezed, wrung, & turned inside out, whilst anything of what he so largely absorbed can be got out of him. . . . (J, XII, 249-250)

March 1, 1867

. . . If anybody ever reads this diary they may think that the criticisms & moralisations on Shakspear are so many successive attempts to study & illustrate the passages in his plays; whereas, in great part, they are the record of references suggested by thoughts & sentiments that were initiated in the world & only collated or connected with Shakspear, or referred to him, or hung upon him. . . .[37] (J, XII, 324)

March 4, 1867

Pope's translation of Homer is a graphic attest of the facility of men of talent at second hand. Pope was incited by Homer's genius, not to appreciation & invention, but to artifice & imitation. Pope spawned in Homer's sea.—But this is only a partial, though not an ugly, statement. It is to Pope's credit, so far, that he took fire from Homer's heat; that he generalised, appropriated, & modernised, as it

---

[36] *Two Gentlemen of Verona*, III, i, 325.
[37] This passage may be taken as a key to Newcomb's approach to the criticism of Shakspere.

were; & that he was not a servile copyist: as it is to Homer's credit, that he served as a prompter & model to a man who stood on a lower plane, in some respects, & on a higher plane, in other respects. (J, XII, 341-342)

March 8, 1867

George Herbert said that the sun, arising in the east, brings his own sweets along with him: he might have said, also, that he brings his own broom along with him. He no sooner rises than the dust-like vapors in the air show that he is cleansing & cleaning the ground of the refuse of the last night and of the yesterday's clouds. (J, XIII, 15-16)

. . .

Hamlet is Hamlet, because of all men; & more or less like all men, of whom he is thus a representative, he is an impractibilist.—Hamlet is one of the myriad race of humans, who,—from infancy, sucking candy, & bawling because they have sucked it up, to old men morbidly mourning over the cup of past life which they have drained to the dregs,[38]—desire some or other sort of good, & will not take it as they can get it, nor comply with its terms. . . . (J, XIII, 23)

March 11, 1867

. . . Perhaps one of the motives of the forest-like significance, if not mystery, of the Gothic style is that Europeans had worshipped in woods & in the pine woods of the north, before they received letters; while the Greeks had neither forests, nor much mythology, before they had letters.—The Goths had more art than the Greeks, in the respect that they had more nature. (J, XIII, 35)

March 27, 1867

It is Shakspear's readiness & summariness of eye which makes him so apprehensive & adept an observer of men & things, that every craft claims him as a graduate of its guild. (J. XIII, 115)

---

[38] The confusion of construction in this section is typical of Newcomb's style at its worst.

March 28, 1867

That excess of the sentiment of prowess in a man is not only unmanly but effeminate, in that it is not only sentimental but also mongrel, is illustrated in the fact that Coriolanus resembled a masculine woman, in the person of his mother, more than a masculine man in proper person. Coriolanus' colloquy with Volumnia, at the beginning of the 4th Act, evinces the consciousness, which he had, of more resemblance between his mother & himself than there should have been, for her as a woman & for him as a man. He was too much like her in the sentiment of valor; she was too much like him in the temper of valor. (J, XIII, 119)

March 29, 1867

Shakspear's handling of Hamlet is very different from his handling of merely intellectual abstractionists. Hamlet is, in some sort, an elegaic discussion on an experience compounded of many goods & evils, of sore sorrows, & outcropping hopes, in which Shakspear shared more complacently & patiently than he regarded the condition of sheer scholarship. It is his book of Lamentations. (J, XIII, 123)

April 3, 1867

The anxiety of the sentinels before Elsinore Castle to have the ghost speak to them, & the incapacity & indisposition of the ghost to speak to them, illustrates the normal order which precludes the address of deceased people even to the eyes of men. (J. XIII, 135-136)

. . .

Noticed that Murdoch,[39] who played Hamlet last evening, very well,—being a better elocutionist . . . but less of a man of genius, than Edwin Booth—prudishly substituted "trull" for "whore" in Hamlet's soliloquy, "ay, so";[40] that, amongst a few other mistakes, he left out, probably in a momentary embarrassment of memory, the word "What" in the address to the ghost, "say, why is this? where-

[39] Probably James E. Murdock.
[40] *Hamlet*, II, ii, 614.

fore? what should we do?"[41] . . . that he put "the" before "fardels" in Hamlet's "To be";[42] & that—I think, like Booth—he repeated the word "play" in the line, "the play's the thing."[43] . . . (J, XIII, 138)

April 11, 1867

Amidst all the heat of Lear's affliction & affection, Goneril & Regan coldly unite against him like pieces of ice freezing together in scalding water. (J, XIII, 171)

April 20, 1867

It is touching & rich that Benedick should declare himself to Beatrice & that these creatures should betroth themselves, at the time & place of Hero's blighted nuptials. These two remained, after the others had scattered, to good purpose. They made more than friends at the wrongs of another, whom they would support & avenge: they were, in part, brought together, & revealed to each other, at this occasion, by their similar charities, practivenesses, loyalties, & general sentiments: they swore love, over a championship of innocence & over an antagonism to guilt: they consecrated the hour & the catastrophe: they were the glittering & effective rays of sunlight in a shadowed room.—Benedick felt emboldened toward Beatrice, as a lover, by his purpose toward Hero, as a knight. (J, XIII, 199)

April 27, 1867

If poetry was not natural & did not pervade all conditions of men, why should the hucksters along the streets, as now under my window, cry "Fresh shad O!" instead of "Fresh shad"? . . . (J. XIII, 225)

May 2, 1867

The scene of Don Quixote's hallucination is, probably, elucidative of his condition. A barren, flat, monotonous, & untilled landscape favors abstraction & exaltation of mind.[44] What part the desert of

---

[41] *Ibid.,* I, iv, 57.   [42] *Ibid.,* III, i, 56.   [43] *Ibid.,* II, ii, 633-634.
[44] Newcomb felt little sympathy with nature that was not cultivated and settled by man.

Arabia had in nursing the superstitious, egotistical, moody madness of Mohammed, the prairie of Le Manche had in nursing that of Don Quixote. . . . (J, XIII, 240-241)

May 9, 1867

Noted in Dante, yesterday, a nice touch pertinent to my recent commemoration of the requisiteness of fear as a trait of character & relation. He makes Francesca say that they read Launcelot together "without fear." This void of fear was prelude to their fall. (J, XIII, 263)

• • •

The proneness of the sectarian & personal followers of Swedenborgh to accept his wild & deluded claim at supernaturalism of function,[45] because of their regard for the patent truths in his teachings, is in curious apposition to that of many sectarians at large, to accept truths because of their abstract regard for the supernaturalism with which they are historically connected. Swedenborgh's hallucinations as a seer are, singularly enough, most easily demonstrable even from his own statements of the origin of his dementia in an overloaded stomach. . . . (J, XIII, 266)

May 10, 1867

The adeptness of genius in verisimilitude is a sequence of the affinity of genius for fact & form. Genius is honest because it is genial. It loves a firm base, because it loves the flowers & fruits that grow only in sure ground. It hates masks & cosmetics, because it seeks shapes & hearts. Longfellow's translation of Dante[46] does credit to him, because of the genius which he shows in his regard for simplicity, preciseness, & reproduction. The few faults probably to be found in it are, so far as I can see by specimens in newspapers, deviations, however slight, from his scholarly & faithful standpoint; not, as the critics absurdly say, from too rigid conformity to it.— Longfellow seems to be just poet enough to make a nice translator.

[45] Compare November 17, 1858, 97.
[46] Published in 1867.

He puts American scholarship at the head of the class of translators. (J, XIII, 271)

May 11, 1867

. . . . every man feels poetical, & as if he was a poet, when he sees nature; as every man feels harmonious & buoyant when he hears music. I was reminded of this in looking into Emerson's new poems,[47] which reached me from his long hand yesterday, & noting, as I wrote him, that everybody who was anybody, who had walked along the beach on the meadows, would see, from the lines on the sea-shore[48] & two rivers,[49] that a poet had been there after, or before, them, & would acknowledge that the waters had not sounded all this long time into hollow ears nor shone into vacant eyes. . . . (J, XIII, 275)

May 20, 1867

It would be a good point for an actor, as I felt at reciting the passage on Saturday, to burst into tears at Hamlet's adjuration of his father, "Do you not come your tardy son to chide."[50] . . . The pathetic currents of extraordinary & harassing relation to two parents meet at that point & overwhelms him with, at least, emotion & tenderness. (J, XIII, 299)

May 22, 1867

The Germans run Shakspear to the death.[51] They are like spinsters, who, once taking hold of a fashion for embroidery, do not cease embroidering until they have embroidered something for everything & everybody. They mean that nobody shall ever have anything to say about Shakspear that they have not said. Whoever imagines that he can say much, if anything, new in the way of criticism on Shakspear, should read his German expounders. . . . (J, XIII, 308)

---

[47] A volume entitled *May-Day*, which was published in 1867.
[48] "Seashore," 1839.
[49] "Two Rivers," 1858.
[50] *Hamlet*, III, iv, 106.
[51] Newcomb says that this train of thought was brought on by his looking into Ulrici at a friend's house.

June 1, 1867

Mozart's music, when I formerly heard it played, by loved hands,[52] on the piano, pleased me for its cheeriness, flutiness, & childlikeness. Recently I heard the Italians perform Don Giovanni, &, last night, the Germans perform Figaro, & I was not interested at either occasion. The contrast of Fidelio to Figaro suggests that there is not sorrow & thought enough in Mozart's music to give due accompaniment to the plots of his pieces; whilst, also, an orchestra does not seem to suit his bent, because violins do not seem to be the best instruments for his motive. . . . (J, XIII, 342-343)

June 22, 1867

The fretfulness & fury of a child, at irksome, unwonted, & uncongenial tasks, stamping with the feet, striking with the arm, screaming with blended rage & sorrow, destroying prized toys with indiscriminate malignancy, seared with feverish wrath, soaked with tears, & frantic with irritability, is the crude image & presage of a malady to which, under other conditions of development, in degree &, perhaps, in kind, most grown up people are prone. What the child sometimes shows in a comparatively mild, temporary, & exceptional form, the man often shows in a severe, chronic, & confirmed form.—Iago's malady is the child's malady become virulent & rank; what is somewhat of childishness in Cordelia, is more of fiendishness in Goneril & Regan. (J, XIV, 52)

July 1, 1867

The main place for dirt is on the ground; yet dirt flies up at the least commotion of wind or contact of tread as if it was winged: so, the main seat for evil is hell though it infests & befouls, for a while, the air of heaven upon earth. Othello & Iago aptly separate at their deaths. If Othello may rejoin Desdemona he is forever beyond the farther reach of Iago. . . . (J, XIV, 81)

October 4, 1867

The facility with which men who are addicted to sententiousness

[52] Probably his mother's.

& to saws are diverted from principles & ends is exemplified in the ductility of Polonius in Hamlet's hands, through sheer wit. Although he is studying the sanity of Hamlet, he . . . forgets the main issue in observation & commendation of Hamlet's sententiousness; "Will you walk out of the air, my lord?" *Ham.* "Into my grave." *Pol.* "Indeed, that's out of the air. How pregnant sometimes his replies are!"[53] . . . Polonius is somewhat of a Sancho Panza turned scholar. (J, XV, 26)

October 26, 1867

Art, like sunshine, works everywhere, according as it is received, for weal or for woe.—Ristori, as Medea, leading her children, robed in draperies of red & of green, burst, at the theater on the audience, from the top of the precipice down which she descends to the stage, like an apoclypse of some Grecian myth. . . . (J, XV, 116)

November 13, 1867

Violence is the cause & the condition of hell. To say that a thing is evil is to say that it is violent. Shakspear makes Suffolk, in Henry Sixth, go a little way toward the recognition & application of this fact, in his admirable line, "for what is wedlock forced, but a hell."[54] . . . There is no peace to the wicked, because the tenure of wickedness is violence. (J, XV, 192)

November 14, 1867

Stoicism changes the shape, not the soul, of selfishness. It conserves, as well as hardens, a man's abstraction of himself, just as cold conserves, as well as hardens, water by condensing it into ice. It is notable that Brutus, who is a professed stoic, refers to himself more frequently & persistently, than anybody else in Shakspear's play of Julius Caesar. . . . (J, XV, 196)

January 1, 1868

A recent French criticism, spurning Hamlet as an uninteresting savage & specifying [?] Gertrude as an interesting star, reminds one

[53] *Hamlet,* II, ii, 208 ff.
[54] *1 Henry the Sixth,* V, v, 62.

that such a reflective character as Hamlet must be a marvel & a mystery to such very demonstrative characters as the Frenchmen. . . . An Englishman is more like corn, simultaneously boiling with the water that cracks it; a Frenchman is more like corn popping on the red hot pan which explodes it. The one retains his juiciness in form, like boiled corn; the other, is turned into a dry outside, like popped corn. . . . (J, XVI, 53-54)

January 3, 1868

There is something isolated & individual in the column of Greek,— something social & reciprocal in the pillar of Gothic architecture. The former reminds one of the palm, flowering at the top, & almost rigidly personal; the latter, of the pine foliating at the top & interlacing with its fellows. The inventors of Greek architecture had evidently been accustomed to groves, gardens, & plains,—whether in Arcadia or in Egypt; of Gothic, to vast forests of odorous pines & somber hemlocks. (J, XVI, 64)

January 24, 1868

Reiteration in speech, by means of tautologies & synonymes, is often a groping of the speaker's wit for the most meet & telling amongst several & similar words. It handles many until it gets the best. It is, also a symptomatic endeavour at self-balance on the part of an unsteady & overflowing sentiment which is too vague & swift to summarily & squarely fit one form. It is, also, a play of orators at definition for others as well as for self. Marc Antony's pleonastic sentence, "For I have neither wit, nor words, nor worth, Action, nor utterance, not the power of speech, To stir mens blood"[55] . . . illustrates this fact. (J, XVI, 158)

February 6, 1868

Possibly, alliteration may serve as a systematisation, if not as a simplification, of language. It helps to assort; also, to assist memory; also, to emphasise. But I do not, on the whole, approve it; I seldom relish it in others, & never relish it, after it is expressed, in myself. (J, XVI, 228)

[55] *Julius Caesar,* III, ii, 225-227. Properly ". . . nor the power of speech."

February 18, 1868

Coldness of character, in its own greater & arbitrary semblance, hides &, in some respect, even hinders, but not supersedes, filth of soul, just as frost varnishes, not eradicates, dirt on the windows. Lady Macbeth would find herself in a slough of moral mire, of whose depth & degradation she had not dreamed, if she suffered her heart to soften some of her hardened traits; just as a traveller in winter-time on frozen ground & on frozen water might find himself, in spring-time, surprized in a vast morass or sinking through rotten ice into a bottomless lake. (J, XVI, 289)

March 13, 1868

Telling P. R.,[56] yesterday, of Emerson's remark to me—during my last stroll with him in his meadow, at my mention of Cervantes, or of Coleridge—that it was strange no one before Coleridge had thought of Don Quixote as a type of pure reason; he asked me if I thought Cervantes meant this, & if Shakspear meant what the critics make him mean; to which I replied, "of course not," yet, that a man's cerebral, like his corporal, progeny is to be taken as it is in itself, & in our own eye, not as it is, or was, in its parent & in its parent's eye. Behind the motive & matter of a man is the motive & the matter of humanity in man. A fire is none the less a blaze in an audience because it is only a spark in an orator. What nature means in Romeo, in Hamlet, or in Don Quixote, is of far more moment than what Shakspear or Cervantes meant in them.[57] A reader takes, at will, Falstaff or Shakspear, & Sancho Panza, or Cervantes, from the mask of the stage-actor & from the mouth of the tale-teller. A man may portray what he does not fully think of, or care for, or complete,

[56] Philip Randolph was the grandson of the surgeon, Philip Syng Physick. Emerson described him as "a reading & thinking man, with great tenacity of purpose." *Letters,* ed., Rusk, V, 538. In a letter to Newcomb, written on July 25, 1858, Emerson said: "I wish I could make you acquainted with Philip Randolph of Philadelphia, who has bought a farm in the Narraganset country, & spends a part of every summer there. He is an upright sincere gentleman, with a love of truth,—working truth." *Ibid.,* 115.

[57] Compare Emerson's poem, "The Problem," where, speaking of the architect of St. Peter's in Rome, he says:

"Himself from God he could not free;
He builded better than he knew;—
The conscious stone to beauty grew." *Works,* IX, 7.

or, in general, mean—just as he may profess what he does not fully regard or believe. As the landscape means what the providence of it, not what the painter of it, means: so literature means what the subject of it, not what the scribbler of it, means. (J, XVII, 58-59)

March 17, 1868

Shylock's strength of wit & even of character, as a man—such as it is—is in sequence with his force of imagination & conduct as a miser. More or less mind is implied in the generalising regard, in the abstract, of riches; & more or less caliber is implied in the resolute endurance of privation for the sake of an abstracted principle. Misers are, somewhat, poets in the sense [i.e., "setting up"][58] of images: &, somewhat, heroes in the service of them. (J, XVII, 73)

March 21, 1868

The contrary & chilly atmosphere of the court of King Lear is, at the opening scene of the drama, thick with the conspiring elements of a horrible storm. Lear's fitful heat; Cordelia's sullen temperateness; Goneril & Regan's vigorous heartlessness; Kent's impetuous indignation; Gloster's stagnant sentiment; the suitors' hushed expectations; the tacit amazement, & surprised [—][59] of the courtiers, prepare & prelude a violent outbreak. Preparation serves a promise &, thence, a forcast, in that it procures the presence of active forces. (J, XVII, 90)

April 8, 1868

Whatever fault may be diagnosed from a predilection for alliteration, it cannot be want of mind or of matter,—as I am daily reminded by the offset of my own alliterativeness, hitherto an offhand dainty to me, which no disgust at previous alliteration has been able, until recently, to begin to nauseate.[60] . . . If Shakspear is not a mere fool or a mere fantasist, or a mere trifler, because he alliterates . . . in such a solemn tragedy as Macbeth, & in such a solemn tem-

[58] "Setting up" is one of the deleted phrases for which Newcomb substituted "sense."
[59] A word is omitted after "surprised."
[60] Compare with February 6, 1868, *133*.

per—"so well thy words become thee as thy wounds"[61] . . . "two truths are told".[62] . . . Why should I . . . be charged with witlessness & vacuity, for the same—whatever it is—vice or virtue? (J, XVII, 178)

April 10, 1868

Coriolanus is one of those crude personages who, ignorant of the law of reciprocity, wish to confer, but not to receive, favors. He does not consider that the very principle of action, which he emulates is cognate to that of the alms, which he spurns.—I once knew a noble sort of woman[63] who was lavish in lending, but not in borrowing, books, not considering, as I frequently told her, that she should give to others as well as to self the pleasure of generosity & the priviledge of good-doing. (J, XVII, 187)

April 11, 1868

In architecture, the principle would be developed & the piquancy would be favored, if architects would apprehend & apply the geometry of nature as it is in beauty, instead of . . . books. . . . The Gothic genius, which generalised the trunks & the traceries of trees into colomns & ceilings, does not seem to have ever observed, much less to have generalised, the informal grouping of the trees. The gawky talent, which fondly packs wooden rosettes by the cord, as carefully as eggs, at equilateral distance on the vaults of their edifices, seem to have as little considered the splendid scattering broadcast of the stars . . . as even the round shapes & easy setting of the roses in the fields. In default of other device, it would be better to trust to the chance of the hands, in the placing of pillars & in the frescoing of ceilings, than to the yard-stick.—I do not remember anything of what I read of Ruskin's architectural criticism . . . better than . . . his commendation of some Italian, I think, for irregularly placing the columns in some portico, & his own fancy for straight towers, for recesses in windows, & for rough to hewn stone. . . . The art is false to itself which, without regard to occasion, makes men turn for art itself from the pretended reproduction of nature in works of art to

---

[61] *Macbeth*, I, ii, 43.   [62] *Ibid.*, iii, 127.   [63] Newcomb's mother.

the original art that is in the works of nature itself. Casuality—so to call it,—is a better artist than conceit. . . . (J, XVII, 189-190)

May 11, 1868

The diaries of some men illustrate their daily sentiment & speech not, in a technical sense of the word—like those of other men— their daily studies. For instance, anybody who sees this diary & infers from the frequent mention of authors that its writer is much of a reader, will blunder. He scarcely reads at all, even Shakspear; what he records is the thoughts which come fresh out of his experience at his systematical recitation of Shakspear in memory, or out of colla- tions of his experience, at other times, with Shakspear,[64] Dante, Cervantes, & others once, in part, read. It is a progress of scope, not of study, which this diary records. It has more like talking than of thinking, in its purport & plane. (J, XVII, 320)

May 25, 1868

Biron is a sort of Benedick touched in the head rather than in the heart; he is not, as yet, so completely, & so positively, converted as Benedick is. (J, XVIII, 44)

June 4, 1868

Morbidness is a moral malady in which the simple relations & responsibilities of life seem intricate, doubtful, & impossible, just as in physical malady the least movement in one's chamber seems long, & the ordinary amount of diet on one's plate seems monstrous.—In an invalid condition of general morale, Hamlet reflects upon, magnifies, & is horrified at, his peculiar & exceptional plane & part. (J, XVIII, 87)

June 15, 1868

To poets Shakspear gives whole surloins of solid meat: to philoso- phers he gives rarest & unexpected delicacies. What a wholesale poem, for instance, is his description of Cleopatra's sail on the

---

[64] On February 10, 1871, Newcomb wrote: "Terence is the first book which I have read verbatim & seriatim for many years." (J, XXVII, 8)

Cydnus:[65] yet, what a titbit to metaphysical symbolists he throws out in one of the lines of it, "being barbar'd ten times o'er.[66] . . . (J, XVIII, 121-122)

July 3, 1868

. . . I noticed, a day or two since; in an English editorial on Longfellow's ruddy face in white hairs, an allusion to some one of Hawthorne's unpublished, or last published, writings in which, in almost the very spirit of my long & persistent pleadings for old age, he says, in effect, that old men need youth as if it was something which was their right, & without which they feel awkward. Just as I saw at once, in the latter case, my own sympathy of sentiment with Hawthorne in some such things, as I knew long since from a summer with him when I was a youth & we walked like two boys together,[67] though he was much older; so I see, at once, in the former case, identities, not imitations, of intellectual condition—Hawthorne would smile with me, in incessantly renewed wonder, on finding our senses reflected where 'we never thought of seeing them in any shape. . . . (J, XVIII, 172)

August 1, 1868

Death has a future on these terms that it has a present, & on the terms that life has a present & a future: that is, through the law of sequences, of similars, & of developments. That which leads to hell now, leads to hell always, & never to heaven; & vice versa. This is the secret moral & meaning of the Clown's Song in Twelfth Night: "What is love? 'tis not hereafter: Present mirth hath present laughter."[68] . . . Wherever there is principle & plane there is a here & no hereafter of them. (J, XVIII, 269)

August 22, 1868

Taking advantage, last eve'g, of the shelter of a long awning at 11th & Chestnut, under which I waited during a heavy shower, & of the isolation & darkness, to recite some of the witches' songs in

---

[65] *Antony and Cleopatra,* II, ii, 195 ff.   [66] *Ibid.,* 229.
[67] Evidently while they both were at Brook Farm.
[68] *Twelfth Night,* II, iii, 48-49.

Macbeth,—which were in my course,[69] through apt coincidence—I found that sympathetic [?] & stormy . . . as the songs themselves were to my sentiment. I could not, without a forced & wild change of mood & mind, tune them to the storm & to the night as the witches themselves fondly, fanatically, & freely chaunted them.—The thunder was too musical & pure for such morbid & foul discord; the lightning was too vital & vivid for such deadly & dark benightedness; the rain was too sweet & too soft for such sourness & harshness; the night was too kindly for such hostility. (J, XVIII, 334)

October 5, 1868

Romeo may be said to have groped for the truth, before the good, of love; & thence to have played with the form & fact of love in Rosaline before he lived love with Juliet. Troilus may be said to have groped for the good before the truth of love; & thus to have fastened upon Cressida for the sake of experience before principle. (J, XIX, 106-107)

November 13, 1868

Few men of genius, of any sort, ever thought & felt, who had such little apparent positiveness of thought & feeling as Hawthorne. He may be called a loafer in the ways of genius.—He had something of childlike virtue, & something of childish vice. (J, XIX, 251)

December 31, 1868

Noted in the mien of an English company of Actors at the Academy of Music, last night, that the English especially in contrast with the Americans, have marked aplomb, but, also, marked unripeness. . . . I noticed also, that Mrs Scott-Siddons[70] carried an English nature to

---

[69] Newcomb spent part of every day in committing passages of Shakspere to memory and in reciting lines which he already knew. On February 21 of 1867 he wrote, "On this stormy day, when I cannot walk, I devote some of the afternoon, always set apart for exercise, to learning Ulysses' long address to Ajax. . . . I walk & gymnasticise, while I learn, & recite, the text, &, also, discipline my impatient temper . . . so I, at once, cultivate memory, muscles, lungs, & amiability." (J, XII, 285). He also memorized the *Psalms*. In January of 1869 he began his third committing of the *Psalms* to memory. See Section IV, January 4, 1869, 277.

[70] Mrs. Scott-Siddons made her debut in 1866, as Lady Macbeth.

the part of Lady Macbeth, which served toward the reproduction of a Lady Macbeth, in her own account, whether or no on Shakspear's account. In some points, she was remarkable as, in herself, such as she then was, a powerful & influential woman. In the first act, she was splendidly suggestive; & I could at once comprehend that Mrs Siddons, her namesake & kinswoman, merited contemporary & national fame in the part. In the other acts she was not much anyways: excepting once or twice, when she threw herself especially upon herself—like a person who takes deep breaths—in such a way as to revive the semblance which she wore in the first act, & as to explain why she had appeared so differently at first than afterwards. The dress assisted her abnormal prestige of power. It, together with her mien, gave her the aspect of a Scotch Medea. As an exceptional, rather than ordinary & somewhat feminine Lady Macbeth she was more impressive & picturesque than Ristori; but she did not hold out. She did not keep to the same key . . . throughout the play, that she pitched herself by at first. Little Mary McVickars[71] was, in American style, more intense & interesting, as a whole, but Mrs Siddons was, in English style, more mechanical & substantial. (J, XX, 80-81)

January 28, 1869

Malvolio, well impersonated, is, on the stage, one of the most marked & graphic personages in Shakspear's plays. He is a diluted & damaged first class sort of Shakspearian personage. He is a cross of Hamlet & of Romeo, of Polonius & of Jaques. Barton Hill did it well, excepting in the cross-gartered scene which was superficial & flat. Mrs Drew,[72] the enterprising manageress, took the part of Viola, instead of assigning it to a young actress: but though she was corporally too old for full verisimilitude she played it with a character which, in part, justified her ambition & persistency; soul, after all, is the life of sense . . . Sir Andrew, who is a sly-witted, flat-headed, knight, was shown up as a wholly soft nimcompoop & coward. Caricature spoils an actor, as farcicality spoils comedy. (J. XX, 207)

[71] Mary McVicker played leading roles in Edwin Booth's company.

[72] Mrs. John Drew, in 1861, became manager of the Arch Street Theatre in Philadelphia.

April 10, 1869

I was pleased, at the performance of Don Giovanni last night, to note the genius shown in Mozart's reserve of composition, in his subornation of accompaniment to action, in the sobriety & steadiness of his regard, in the moral gravity of his motive, & in the discreet sweetness of his own sensation. As soon as the opera began, I saw we were going to be treated to something as sober & as individual as Shakspear's, & so far as it went, it was more determined, because more definite, in standpoint, than Shakspear.—In Mozart & Beethoven, the music, just as in Shakspear the text, is notable even if the acting is not. It would be opera, indeed—at least, speaking comparatively—if we could have the German, instead of the Italian, composers to cater to us. The orchestral accompaniment of the ghost scene was remarkable, in a kind, as is the scenic accompaniment of King Lear. It was solemn & significant.—It was almost the first time that Mozart music interested me much when played by an orchestra.— The play was well done by La Grange, Kellogg, & McCulloch, three prima donnas, as should be, in one opera. I wanted them to rejoice in the successes of each other, & perhaps they had genius & goodness enough to do so. . . . (J, XXI, 56)

May 10, 1869

Orestes, Don Quixote, & Hamlet are types of men of disordered thoughts & feelings amongst the better class of morbid &, more or less, mad persons. Orestes is the representative of remorse; Don Quixote, of romanticism; Hamlet, of moody impractiveness. (J, XXI, 131)

June 10, 1869

If art would be art, it must toe the mark. Jefferson's[73] make up in Rip Van Winkle, especially in the first part, was admirable; but he seemed afraid of disshevelledness & woke up from his twenty year's sleep with tattered clothes, a disjointed gun, & a long, nicely combed, white beard. (J, XXI, 230)

[73] The Philadelphia-born actor, Joseph Jefferson, collaborated with Boucicault in a stage-version of *Rip Van Winkle*.

New York, July 31, 1869

The Greek classics were, for centuries, the only remarkable blooms of literature. In the middle ages they were like evergreens in a winter's landscape: now, in a more summer-like scene, they are like evergreens amongst other & fresher greens. (J, XXII, 1)

September 24, 1869

Booth made a tolerable point, the other night, by sitting down after pronouncing Hamlet's invective against Claudius, "lecherous, treacherous, kindless villain,"[74]—& then, after a pause,—as if, either . . . stopping to regret his impulsive indulgences in mere words, or remembering & renewing himself—continuing, "Why, what an ass am I,"[75]—But, Hamlet is so swift in thought & emotion that he needs little self-recollection so far as mere thought & emotion in his kind & degree, is concerned. This invective against Claudius, & his invective against himself, were part & parcel of the same surcharged & general mind & mood. His wits are ahead of his words, always. I make no break & no pause in reciting that, or any, soliloquy of Hamlet's, & so do not think Booth's point a strong one.

Booth said, "bawd," for "whore," in the words, "& like a whore."[76] He put "heel" before "sequel," in the line, "But is there no sequel at the heels of this monster's admiration,"[77] but soon corrected himself. . . . (J, XXII, 152)

October 1, 1869

. . . If they [scholars] took time for their thoughts to settle into their senses, they would be more clearly & summarilly perceptive & more succinctly & briefly expressive; than most of them are. They aim at declaration before they have aimed at digestion. If Ruskin had waited a year or two before writing his Modern Painters,[78] he might not have felt like writing at all, but if he had then felt like it, he would have been much less diffuse, excited, & elaborate, & wordy than, intelligent & suggestive as his book is, he was at first flash & time when he wrote it. (J, XXII, 180)

---

[74] *Hamlet*, II, ii, 609.   [75] *Ibid.*, 611.   [76] *Ibid.*, 614.
[77] *Ibid.*, III, ii, 341-342.   [78] Published 1843-1860.

October 10, 1869

Dickens, perhaps, specially represents the emasculated, super-refined, & abstract tenure & tendency of the times in respect of manly sentiment & scope. He caters to the age, & he is in many respects, doubtless, a man of the age; & love is, if I remember right, scarcely thought of, & introduced, amongst his viands. The modern play of superfine & prudish intellectualism in the direction of negation & effeminacy of thought & taste is attested in the contrast of Dickens &, also, of Scott, with Fielding & Smollett. The fact that fully discreet virtue has much less to do with the, so called, delicacy of his romances, as compared with those of some others, is suggested by his congenial, as well as professional, treatment of drinking, intoxication, & social, apart from sexual, scrapes. He is coarse in those departments of verisimilitude which he elects. (J, XXII, 217)

October 28, 1869

On the terms that Bertram[79] is deceived by himself he is deceived by Parolles. . . . (J, XXII, 289)

November 16, 1869

The comparative flatness of Forrest's Lear,[80] at the Walnut last night, suggested, at first thought, whether literal & mere verisimilitude to a part, in either actor or author, were sufficient to procure large & telling interest for it; but I soon saw that the cause of the deficiency in the tone of the whole piece, as then played, was a lack of a sort of leading consciousness & generalisation,—such as almost every active-minded & active-willed man has during the enactment of daily experience on the part of the actor. Forrest threw himself, as it were, point blank,—when he was at all remarkable & effective in the personation of Lear—into his part, without maintaining a free range & conduct of general relation to it. He was, as it were, an abjected Lear . . . he neither maintained his mere assumption of the part, throughout, nor gave it at any time the buoyant rampancy of its

---

[79] In *All's Well That Ends Well.*
[80] Edwin Forrest was by many critics thought to be at his best in the part of Lear.

intellectually moral motive. Part of it was very tedious; & I doubted if it was not the tediousness of the morbid old Lear himself; but Forrest's self-recovery of dramatical standpoint, & flashes of strength, revived the interest of Lear himself & showed that the fault was mostly the actor's. . . . (J, XXIII, 13)

December 6, 1869

My theme of contexts reminds me that Swedenborgh owes what practical sagacity & subtlety he had to, probably, the scientific base & preparation of his studies. Unlike most moralists, he made the body of man a foundation of his moral metaphysics. He was a sort of moral Baconian in method: for, as Bacon depended on fact & experiment for truth, so Swedenborgh depended on form & fact for truth. Nobody who wisely & generalisingly studies the body of man can miss the doctrines of relation to general principle—which is similar in operation, to relation to general providence—of use, & of marriage, which are Swedenborghs formost specialties. Although these great truths are . . . matter-of-fact commonplaces & matters of ordinary common-sense in the world, yet they were never before thought by schoolmen & sectarians, worthy of, or wisely regarded as, matters for dogmatical morality & theological science. . . . (J, XXIII, 108)

December 25, 1869

Wherever there is genius, there is as well vivacity as hilarity. I was reminded of this by the lugubriousness of a once renowned old Mass which I went to hear at St. Augustine's, whose gravity made it especially inappropriate for the day; Mozart would have composed more merrily for a requiem. (J, XXIII, 176)

January 8, 1870

That Byron should not have liked Shakspear, is sign that his wit was unsound, arbitrary, & unmetyphisical. That Goethe should have liked Byron, is sign that his wit wanted the impulse & the fluency which he indiscriminately admired in Byron. Byron was not moral enough for a just regard of Shakspear. Goethe was too mechanical for an impartial regard of Byron.—Byron would have been much insaner than he was, if he had not been so intellectual as he was. . . . (J, XXIII, 216)

February 6, 1870

One use, if not object, of farce is to make comedy seem sober, proper, & dignified; & of caricature, to make the person or thing caricatured, seem decent & seemly. Excess & contrast not only offset, but recommend, the original which is unjustly, or partially, or playfully, treated of. . . . (J, XXIII, 309)

February 7, 1870

As is love, so is faith. They who love much, question little, & profess less. The contrast between the leaves-takings of Romeo & Juliet with those of Troilus & Cressida are illustrative of this truth. The former pair would as soon think of doubting each other's love, as of making professions of constancy to each other. Troilus wishes he had the love of Cressida, because he wishes to be loved by such a woman as he thinks she is; but the very facts of the case makes him consider concerning pledges & vows, diversions & losses, whilst they make Cressida almost exhaust the eloquent rhetoric of [lovers] in her attempt at make-weights for her superficial sentiment. (J, XXIII, 314)

February 18, 1870

Shakspear commonly has a sort of series of personages, in which the lesser virtues of some foil the greater virtues of others, & the greater [sic] vices of some foil the greater vices of others. The grades of character & conduct in Love's Labor's Lost show this in specially bold relief. Biron, Amado, & Costard offset each other in amatoriness & in wit; & they are but parts of a long line of homogeneous & various impersonisation in the same play. Amado makes Biron seem much less conceited & much more refined than he might seem by himself. So, in Hamlet, amongst the others, Osric, Polonius, Laertes, Horatio, & Hamlet illustrate each other. So, Lady Capulet, the Nurse, & Juliet, show something of gradationalism. (J, XXIV, 3-4)

February 20, 1870

Music may be said to be part of the saccharine matter of morality, & be expressed by artificial instrumentation, as sugar is artificially expressed out of reeds, & perfume out of flowers. (J, XXIV, 12)

February 27, 1870

. . . Malvolio's character is exquisitely drawn by Shakspear; &, on the stage, is admirably effective & suggestive. Barton Hill[81] played it well; but Cathcart, last night,[82] was better. Cathcart's somewhat stilted & monotonous, but industrious & telling style of acting especially befitted the part. . . . (J, XXIV, 35)

March 4, 1870

Shakspear takes to rhetoric, when he has meaning for it; his wealth of matter keeps him from mere verbiage. It may be proposed that his love of resonance assisted & incited thoughts themselves in him. Where most other playwrights were led to sentimentalism & mouthing, through predisposition for practical sensation & effect, he was led to general wit & verisimilitude. As the handling of toys meant more to a Newton & to a Watts than to more trifling & less generalising players with toys, so the handling of words meant more to Shakspear than to less ready minds. . . . (J, XXIV, 55)

March 5, 1870

Shakspear's historical plays are better history, because better human history, than most of the more professed & precise histories are. They are illustrative & suggestive, if not descriptive, of Greeks, Romans, &, especially, of Englishmen. Even as a historian, apart from a dramatist, he may be proposed as having as much right to his theory & poetry of events as Grote, Hume, Clarendon, or Froude, here. (J, XXIV, 61)

March 6, 1870

What Cervantes gives of character is peculiarly suggestive of outline & picture; what Shakspear gives of outline & picture is peculiarly

---

[81] See Newcomb's entry for January 28, 1869, *140*.
[82] Newcomb saw Cathcart play at the Arch Street Theatre.

suggestive of character. Accordingly, Cervantes is, after a given degree, better read in the portraits which he suggests than in the experiences he draws; whilst Shakspear is, almost always, better read in the experiences, than in the portraits, which he draws.—One cause of this distinction, which I did not think of when I noted it, is that Cervantes saw, as it were, a scene in his mind's eye, & then turned it & interpreted it into a sort of dramatic romance; & that Shakspear wrote deeds & words for the actors who were, in one, to reproduce & to incarnate them in full. Cervantes had graphicness behind him in the world; Shakspear had it before him on the stage. (J, XXIV, 62-63)

March 8, 1870

Fechter[83] is an extraordinary actor without being, on the whole, a great one. I do not wonder that he was made much of by those to whom, before he was famous, he was a surprise, as perhaps he was to Dickens, who advertised & recommended him to the Americans. . . . He has a feverish energy, which would have made the part of Hamlet in actual life an impossibility to him. Such determination & vigor as he showed, was inconsistent with the feeble conclusions to which the part constrained him to come. He did not suborn his energy to his role, & was thus inconsistent & untrue as an actor. His acting was, in some respects, a cross between fine & coarse . . . it was questionable whether he was very effective, or extremely ridiculous. He was too external to identify himself with Hamlet. . . . There is a pathos & plaintiveness in his voice which would become the part of Hamlet, if he knew the part better, or if he cared for it more. The soliloquies of Hamlet were never recited on the stage with such aplomb as he gave them. . . . I never before saw Hamlet so effectively played in respect of distinctness . . . positiveness, & pronouncement. . . . His yellow wig was becoming to the play & to himself. He reminded me of a man of sentiment of the times of Sir Horace Walpole. He omitted the soliloquy on Claudius at prayer, & the lines on his killing of Polonius, "but heaven hath pleased it so," which are two important key notes of the play. . . . (J, XXIV, 75-76)

[83] Charles Fechter, a French actor, first appeared in the United States in 1870. The critics did not approve of his Hamlet.

March 13, 1870

A second hearing of Fechter's Hamlet would have made me wonder why I, or anyone, had cared to be so critically interested about him, if I had not considered the interesting points of a stranger to an American in the part, at his first appearance, conjoined with the interest of deciding on the disputed question of his fame—& so on . . . whether he had become discouraged by the preponderating verdict of our press against him, or whether to please the critics, he had toned down his performance so as to divest it of what remarkability in some way of energy it had; he seemed scarcely worth special attention, excepting in way of incidentalisms, last night. His voice was thick, so that I wondered if he had not taken wine at dinner; the performance was remarkably mediocer, at first, until, in the third act, he apparently got more into the part as he plays it, through the acting of it, & became somewhat peculiarly interesting again. . . . (J, XXIV, 102-103)

March 24, 1870

The relation of Sam Weller to Pickwick is a suggestion of, although not—at least consciously—a suggestion from, that of Sancho Panza to Don Quixote.—The squire of the Spanish Knight sunk downwards towards the part of servant; the servant of the English esquire buoyed upwards towards the part of squire. In some conditions amenities are commonly in reverse ratio to exigencies. (J, XXIV, 141)

March 27, 1870

One of the apparent puzzles of Shakspear's plays is his representation that Hamlet is fat. Only a predetermined & arbitrary wit could say that [the fact that] Hamlet was slower is accounted for by his fatness. Hamlet's temperament was sanguine & nervous, not lymphatic. It was, possibly, a waywardly Hamletian stroke of art on Shakspear's own part: or, he may have had some obese, excitable, furious, overscrupulous, & impracticable Englishman, in his mind, as his prototype of Hamlet, &, while writing the part, he [may] have transcended & indued him, as he transcended & indued the personages whom he chose from history.—It is not unlikely, however, that . . . Shakspear took a certain degree of corpulency in a man of Hamlet's age for granted, without meaning any derogation of spiritedness & swiftness by it, or anything more than mere contingency of habit & constitution: & this is a good enough solution of the seeming puzzle. (J, XXIV, 154)

April 20, 1870

Hamlet's quick & abandoned response, "Hillo, ho, ho, boy! come, bird, come."[84] in answer to Horatio's "Illo, ho, ho, my lord!"[85] is in keeping with his responsive impressibility . . . to men & things. (J, XXIV, 232)

June 2, 1870

Hawthorne, to judge from what I knew of him & from what little I have read of him, was a hermaphroditical sort of thinker & artist. He was unmasculine & unpositive. What masculinity he had came from following some [?] of the courses of Nature. He was a sort of humanitarian monk, so to speak, at least before he married. He was a dawdler of thought, & was redeemed, perhaps, from acute morbidness only through what genius he had. He had some of the virtues, but also, & especially, some of the indiscriminateness & other imperfections of a child. His aim in thought & art was, so to speak, dilettantism. To have a thought of some sort, for its own sake, was almost his only occupation & pleasure. He was much of a sensationalist, in a simple sort, in sentiment & sense. He had genius of a kind; but, not as a whole, the genius of a manly, & therein masterly, mind. He was a sort of Timon, in somewhat reversed positions. He was rather amiable on his own terms, & on his own plane. It may be proposed that he had some reserves—perhaps [a] suppressed & partly overcome, or, otherwise, more or less superseded, malice or ill-nature. He was very shy, because he was very moody.—His novels are unreadable because of his blended aimlessness & morbidness. His diary will be his best production, I think, because it is more of himself under natural & social influences, than are his elaborate romances. I did not care to read Blithedale,[86] though I was with

[84] *Hamlet,* I, v, 116.
[85] *Ibid.,* 115. This line is spoken not by Horatio, but by Marcellus.
[86] Published in 1852.

him, & rather, though a boy, intimate with him, then,[87] after which I never met him, that I remember, save once, at tea, at George Hilliards, in Boston, where, I think, he boarded.—His wife[88] illustrated some of his stories with engravings, & that, probably, brought about an acquaintance, which I doubt not happily, at least under the circumstances, for him & for her, resulted in marriage. I know not, of fact, &, thus, certain; but I doubt if he would have married unless he had been encouraged by the special interest shown in him by her; this is all conjectural on my part, yet, if it was the case, it is one of a few proofs of the good resulting, in some exceptional cases, of the courtship of a man by a woman, as of Bertram by Helena.—I erase all this,[89] because I do not like to write of an acquaintance, much less of, in part, a friend, by name, with anything like public exposure of private & social affairs, lest . . . it be a sort of betrayal of personal honor & an abuse of privileged facility. Still, the truth does no harm in the long run—if it is the truth—& even the heedless & unamiable way, not altogether unfounded, indeed, but incomprehensive, if not captious, in which Hawthorne speaks of our 3 [?] friends in his diary,[90] is of no essential disservice, but, perhaps, the contrary, to all parties. But I prefer—at least, as yet—reserve. (J, XXV, 47-48)

June 4, 1870

The extracts from Hawthorne's diary in today's Tribune—in their way, sweet &, everyway very like him—were opportune to my recent thought of him, as well as to the renewal, in thought, of my former personal acquaintance with him. He was so chronically & chiefly self-conscious that every thing he thinks & writes is a reflex of the personal man himself. He tends somewhat to discriminateness of a general sort, in cases where men differ from him; but he sees others only as he sees himself when he conditionally puts them on his own personal standpoint. He says scarcely a word that is downrightly moral & masculine. I noted eagerly & gladly his own tribute to marriage & family, such as it is, & his wife's fond, but vague, tribute to

---

[87] At Brook Farm, the scene of the *Blithedale Romance*.
[88] Sophia Peabody.
[89] This whole passage about Hawthorne was cancelled by Newcomb.
[90] Possibly Emerson, Margaret Fuller, and W. E. Channing.

him in the household.—Unlike Shakspear, Hawthorne could say nothing which was not strongly tinctured with his own correspondingly & commensurately active experience. Truth, art, beauty, morals, observation of all sort, are reproduced through, rather than by, him. They are acted on & affected by him somewhat as a landscape is by its reflection in a plate-glass—the landscape, not only being incompletely rendered by the glass, but also—being less vivid & distinct in presentment & show than is the quality, function, transparency, & opaqueness, of the glass itself. He was such an exclusively, introvertively, & isolately reflective person, that he reflected mostly himself, & was scarcely anything more than a self-centered, self-reproductive, & soliloquial person. He thought of things to think of & to say, not of things to do. His thought of things to say was not, indeed, so far abstractly intellectual as to be sundered from his own peculiar standpoint, such as it was, of pleasure & convenience; but it was, such as it was, predominant, however much it was qualified by its concomitance with his sort of feeling, sentiment, & experience. He sought thoughts somewhat as ladies seek patterns, for the sake of working them out in fancy work.—He was a sort of school-boy, who loved some of the exercises of school so well as to become a truant in order to play his own plan of scholarship, & to follow study on his own terms. He was not literary in the common sense of the word; but he made thought his occupation & his preoccupation. He was a reverist of thought. He was passively, rather than positively, social. He assented, responded, & conspired, during social intercourse, in a given kind & degree, but more or less reservedly & shyly. He had, in kind, the familiarity, frailty, accessibility, sympatheticalness, & reciprocity of an humane genius. He was so little in, & of, the world, & yet, withal, so partially & sentimentally diligent, that his activity of thought & of feeling was somewhat like that of a bed-ridden but, in a way, active-minded, person. His impositiveness kept him in the back-ground, whilst his humaness kept in within the bounds, of what society he resorted to. (J, XXV, 59-61)

September 21, 1870

Shakspear took what falsetto there was in the pitch & tone of classic art—as in conventional attenuation, exclusiveness, & formalism—that had become associated with classical themes, by downrightly humanising & boldly rationalising them in his own treatment & reproduction of them. But there was much less, especially in spirit, of this reputed precision & abstraction in classical art than the ceremonious & theatrical French assumed there was &, hence, imaginarily imitated.—Racine, in some respects, caricatured, rather than copied, Greek style; & Goethe—if I do not speak from imaginative memory—was less fundamentally successful in his Greek plays than he would have been if, like Shakspear, he had thought more of Greek matter than of Greek manner, & had entered his classical theme, as Shakspear did, through the headquarters of art in nature. The Greeks had a rigid standard of dramatical propriety somewhat as the medievalists had of chivalrical propriety; &, accordingly, the one more or less assumed to separate the dignified from the undignified in subject-matters, as the other did the dignified from the undignified in social manners. Their purism of bent, however, did not preclude what ordinariness & commonness of life their genius commended to them; &, herein, Homer is more Anglican, than French, in catholicity, liberality, & breadth of treatment.—Eschylus is no more of a martinet in art than is Michelangelo [?]; Sophocles, indeed, is the formalest of the Greeks, & puts on more of the airs of abstractly & peculiarly Greek idealism of art than the others do, whilst . . . Euripides is, in some respects, licentiously informal. Art would be unverisimilar in morality, as well as in reproduction, if it was arbitrarily eclectic & expurgative in its regard & treatment of men & things.—The commoner in life requires the juxtaposition of the uncommon if only on the terms of reciprocity, balance, & complement. Fallowness is the field of husbandry; even chaos, itself, invites & besuits [?] shaping orderliness. An orator must address all sorts of audiences. . . . (J, XXV, 357-358)

September 24, 1870

The length of the play, the lateness of the hour,—it was after twelve when I got home from the Walnut St. last night,—& the blasted, & literally blasting, atmosphere of unventilated theaters, commonly make Hamlet, after the third act, a tedious performance;[91]

[91] At this period Newcomb makes several references to the tediousness of Shakspere in general and of *Hamlet* in particular. His impression is not surprising

& to these causes of fatigue must be added the lack,—especially as the motive of the play is commonly taken & played,—of positive & heroical action in the piece itself. In the first parts, last night, I thought that Forrest, because of his prestige, & the reserves of his stronger physique, made, or would make, the acting less tedious than Booth made it; it suggested, at least, the rough, but solid, scaffolding & underflowing of the histrionic edifice; & even near the last I thought the performance more tedious in itself than Forrest was in himself; but his voice was not up to the promise of such a big chest & frame, not only having the huskiness, or what not,—something as Booth has it,—which seems peculiar to actors, but, becoming lower than was agreable, & even the burley & ambitious Forrest fell flat toward the end. The brisk & clear voice of Chapman, as first grave-digger, relieved the whole house, &, which is uncommon, made the principal actor, under the circumstances, insignificant in comparison. Still, Hamlet is a play to be performed,—not only for sake of the unlettered, who would otherwise never see it, but of the lettered who are served by the palpableness of the action, by the suggestion of the performance, by their scenic readings of the text, & by the impressions of, even, the fatigue of the last act. . . . (J, XXVI, 7)

November 6, 1870

The tragedies of Shakspear, excepting as studies & as artistical performances, are tedious on the stage for the same cause that the experiences which they depict were tedious to the personages in them; on the terms that Hamlet & Macbeth were tired of themselves, their spectators get tired of them. Nevertheless, they are, in part, best studied when seen on the stage; [for] what of poetical, philosophical significance is in them when well acted. The comedies of Shakspear, on the other hand, are altogether agreable, in kind, on the stage. The tragedies are tedious to the same moods [minds?] in the theater that they are tedious to in the closet. (J, XXVI, 105-106)

November 7, 1870

There was, in the long run, a sort of oriental exclusion in Lady

---

when one remembers that he knew long passages of *Hamlet* by heart and had seen it on the stage at least a dozen times. Compare, however, with December 13, 1870, *155.*

Macbeth's country castle &, whether or no, a sort of solitude through
her seeming superiority, under her conduct of it, to those about her,
which tended to give her a vehement, preoccupied, & fatuous hold
of what special themes of incitement & sentiment occurred to her.
So, doubtless, eastern women shut up in Harems, are easily trans-
ported with violent emotions or with petty concerns. Fanny Janaus
chek's rendition of Lady Macbeth was remarkable in this aspect of
the part. (J, XXVI, 108)

December 9, 1870

. . . Shakspear never speaks of the human eye without showing his
sense of the significance of its use. Hamlet recalled with filial pride
& manly interest his fathers look, in which was prominent, "an eye
like Mars, to threaten & command."[92] . . . Henry Fifth's own martial
semblance is hinted in his counsel to his army,—"then lend the eye
a terrible aspect; let it pry through the portage of the head, like the
brass cannon."[93] . . . The Tamed Shrew exhorts her fellow wives "&
dart not scornful glances from thine eyes, To wound thy lord, thy
king, thy governor."[94] Iachimo is made to speak of the contrast of
a virtuous to a vicious womans eye, by saying, "Then lie peeping in
an eye, Base & unlustrous as the smoking light That's fed with stinking tallow"[95] . . . & the last instance which I now verbally recal, &
the one which reminded me, today, of this theme, is in Florizel's
protest of liege love to Perdita, "—were I the fairest youth That ever
made eye swerve"[96] . . . (J, XXVI, 186)

December 10, 1870

. . . Pickwick is a commonplace simpleton, however sweet in sort,
compared with Don Quixote: in that he has less of any kind & degree
of manly ambition & activity. Dickens,—& this does not gainsay his
merit, such as it is,—as if goes to a museum,—& to a hot-heated
museum at that,—for the portraits of personages. The Ibernian Don
Quixote has something of the sturdy heroicism of old Scandinavia
about him; &, therein, Cervantes' touch of genius shows the whole

[92] *Hamlet,* III, iv, 57.   [93] *Henry the Fifth,* III, i, 9-11.
[94] *Taming of the Shrew,* V, ii, 137-138.   [95] *Cymbeline,* I, vii, 108-110.
[96] *Winter's Tale,* IV, iv, 383-384.

world kin.—It may be proposed in favor of Don Quixote that there is more of sanity than of insanity in him; & that his experience is valuable & salutary as a . . . conditional process of redemption from ordinary, commonplace, conventional, & unmasculine causes of life, in part deliberately, & in part compulsively, taking place on his part. (J, XXVI, 189)

December 13, 1870

The Play of Hamlet was never before such a sustained & rich treat to me as it was last night at the Walnut St. Sometimes I thought I was getting tired of such a profuse feast of meats & wines,—& if I had tired, it were not to the discredit of the play, for one cannot, at one sitting, eat up the whole of a feast; but, as a whole, my interest lasted to the end. Edwin Booth was at his best, & won the attention of the audience by his earnestness. He took the part to himself, instead of on himself: yet the text, not the actor, was almost the only & not merely the chief, cynosure of the evening. His unaffectedness & zeal were admirable, but he lacks particular power as a person, being neither stately, vigorous, or loud-voiced. He was too scholar-likely rapt, moreover, in his part, for Hamlet himself. His expostulation with his mother was sweetly done, & his rudeness to Ophelia was tactive & self-explained. . . . Shakspear is a standing repast of human & intellectual significance to one who, as I have learned to do, takes in every word as it is uttered or read. (J, XXVI, 192-193)

January 14, 1871

Mythologism may be said to be romanticism of metaphysics; & ritualism, a romanticism of morality.—I was reminded of this by Richard Wagner's Tanhauser, at the Academy last night.[97] I went to see an opera of that new school, & sat it out, as it was my first & last seance. It reminds one of Walter Scott & of tractarianism. It is a piece of Bavarian renaissance, or rather, in part, of revived medievalism. It is ritualistical drama. It was Verdi sublimated & refined. There is a respectable earnestness in the music & conduct, as there is, always, even in sentimental & ritualistical mediocrity. It was no more wonder that the young king of Bavaria was infatuated by

[97] This was one of the earliest productions of Wagner in Philadelphia.

such music than that some of the young nobles of England were by Puseyism. (Note: this was written before I knew that Wagner was a liberalist, & under the idea that he was a sort of popish dilettanti: I must hear "the music of the future" again. May 7.) (J, XXVI, 276)

January 15. 1871

After noting at the Chestnut St. last night, that the Lady of Lyons was evidently written by a man of intellect, I thought afterwards, suggestively enough, that I had not noted it as written by a man of genius.—On terms, also, that it was not specially preeminent in genius, it was deficient in the fine taste & tact which, always, at least in spirit, characterises preeminent genius. The improbabilities in Shakspear's plays are of another sort from those in Bulwer's play.— Bulwer showed some aspect of genius, however, in the moral— which was the republican—motive of the piece. He has written an effective play, on this ground, for the cultivation of self-respect in the audiences. There is some French forwardness & abstraction in his treatment of it.—Shakspear was not, on all sides, theoretically democratical, as a person, apart from the inevitable tendency of his wit in efficient action, because he looked to social good & order rather as it was than as it should be. Yet though he was, herein, so far of a theorist in favor of aristocratical regime, it would not have required much to have made a democrat of him through his English individualism & self-respect.—On the terms that Shakspear found his genius by means of professional use of his wit, he, neither, applied or kept it, in all of his daily condition & conduct as a man.— This after-life somewhat re-submerged it, as his for-life had, apart from his occupation as a dramatist, submerged it. Democracy of spirit is very creditable bating crudity in pliance of it,—to one of Bulwer's patrician antecedents. (J, XXVI, 279-280)

February 3, 1871

In some sense, & in the literal sense of the word, there is more body in the Latin drama[98] than there is in the English, & other modern, drama. The cause of this is that, such as it was, there was more balance & proportion between the mind & body, the inward &

[98] Newcomb had started reading Terence and Plautus.

the outward, amongst them than with us. There was a greater reserve of power in waiting on present conduct, amongst the Ancients; whilst amongst the moderns there is more idealism & development, but less proportional, staid, & equal incarnation & operation. The Romans thought, felt, & acted, & wanted to know, be, & act more; the moderns think & feel more already than they act, & so, need more action than they need apprehension. It is on corresponding terms that a country boy has more physical presence than a city boy has.... (J, XXVI, 347-348)

February 12, 1871

Though I do not prefer & like the pliance of an intellectual avocation, as a profession, by women,[99] yet I do value & enjoy what of a woman's fine sense, observation, comprehension, & general faculty & nature is shown in the work of such an artist as Jane Austen unpretentiously was.—What this creature saw, she saw, whether or no she should have elaborated & published it. Moreover, she is still so far feminine as to reproduce by means of suggestion & intimation, rather than of complete art. A man catches her meaning instantly from her faintest outlines, as especially from those of most of her men. I doubt if more men than women do not relish her novels, & because of the operation of this latent complementariness on her part which would especially induce a male mind to understand, accompany, & complete her graphic references. Miss Austen was as quietly & sympathetically, in her way, a drawer, as she was an observer, of others; she demeaned herself, other things being equal, & under her intellectual condition, as sweetly as she regarded them. No female artist is, so far as she was developed &, for the while, intellectualised, so feminine as she in grace & manner. . . . (J, XXVII, 17)

February 17, 1871

. . . It seems as if Ruskin had got into the habit of incontinently proclaiming & printing whatever he thought;[100] this is, partly, a bias & tendency of most enthusiastical thinkers. Good wit like good

[99] Newcomb once warned his mother that too much reading and writing would make her too masculine.
[100] Compare with entry for October 1, 1869, *142*.

wine will, for the sake of ripening & reserve, bear keeping; in fact, due keeping & reserve are conditions of the due using, of wit; but, still, if crude wit is forwardly imparted by some hasty, but intelligent, thinkers, it may serve the better reserve, digestion, & keeping in hearers than it serves in speakers. Many a man is irritable & impatient until he has spoken or written something, who, presently, will be indignant & vexed because he has spoken & written it. (J, XXVII, 32-33)

February 20, 1871

Holmes' book[101] written to prove that Bacon was Shakspear,—instead of, rather, that both were, in part, on terms of common humanity & intellect, each other,—& which I first saw at the Library, today,—serves the double purpose of showing, first, by its special pleading & digest of evidence, what a lawyer can do in way of deceiving himself as well as others, &, second, by its running away as well with science as with the case in hand, how easily scientists can let their theories of nature run away with their common sense & scope. . . . Some of the coincidences of thoughts, but especially of words & metaphors,—& the author had only to read Bacon, & then look into a concordance of Shakspear,—between Shakspear & Bacon, are rather remarkable: but, in the first place, even the styles are different; Shakspear's having more poetry, variety, rhythm, & figurativeness, &, second, the dramatic art itself of Shakspear being, virtually, left out of the question. Every man finds his own thoughts in Shakspear; therefore,—if such argument were possible, on Holmes' terms,—every man is Shakspear. . . . (J, XXVII, 48)

February 27, 1871

In some sort of spirit & scope of life, Fallstaff comes nearer to the Parasite of the Roman Comedies than most other characters in the modern dramas. So far as he can be called parasite to Henry, his other companions can be called parasites to him.—The old parasites, cunningly enough for themselves, break the shamefacedness of their gluttonous & timeserving dependence by frankly confessing it & playing upon their conduct.—The comedians, however, may have

[101] Nathaniel Holmes, *The Authorship of Shakespeare,* 1866.

meant to caricature & expose them by making them talk as they acted, instead of as they really talked. . . . (J, XXVII, 73)

March 7, 1871

A difference between men of more, & of less, genius is that the former,—as Shakspear,—have to choose words & plots for their sentiments, whilst the latter,—as Ben Jonson,—have to choose sentiments for their words & plots. (J, XXVII, 101)

March 16, 1871

Horace is notable for being willing & desirous to say well whatever, & however little, he has to say. He reminds one of a genteel sort of person in society, who does even little things either with grace, or with grace in the will. He would cut the pettiest gem as nicely as he could.—Nevertheless, his dilettanteism, as well as his limit of genius & thought, is a draw-back on him. He seems to be in briefer latin, somewhat, in some respects, what Pope is in diffuser English. He is more of an artist, & less of a philosopher, than is Pope; he is more sententious & less generalising. He would be lost, as a poet & thinker, in more abandon, on his own ground. (J, XXVII, 131)

March 21, 1871

Hawthorne was deficient in heroical sentiment & scope. Hence, the themes of his tales are exclusively what they are: & hence his life of Franklin Pierce. He had something of it in him,—or he would have had no genius,—& this his sketch of Lincoln,[102]—in which glumness, in sense, of possible, & partly active, sensibility to heroicality,—shows.—Lincoln was something of the traditional & caricatured Yankee in the leanness & length of his person, in his humor, industry, alertness, & readiness: but he had a natural gentility & repose which kept him from that peculiar obtuseness, sharpness, restlessness, & acquisitiveness, which especially characterises the conventionally typical Yankee, & which distinguishes him from those, as

[102] Hawthorne's sketch of Lincoln was originally part of his article, "Chiefly About War Matters," *Atlantic Monthly,* July 1862, X, pp. 43-61. The paragraphs concerning Lincoln were omitted by the editor of the *Atlantic* because they lacked reverence. They were first published in James T. Fields, "Our Whispering Gallery," in the *Atlantic* for April, 1871, pp. 510-512.

Lincoln, in whom his other traits are more or less common through common virtue. (J, XXVII, 147)

March 28, 1871

. . . Dr Furness' son painted a portrait,[103]—which he left unfinished at his death,—of Emerson, which gives some of Emerson's express & characteristic entity & mien, though I do not say that it is thoroughly like him. It is Emerson as Emerson, commonly, is heard, seen, & thought of, & as Emerson, commonly, is to himself. It is strong in some individual characterisation. It is an incarnation of Emersonianism, as Clio is of Clionism. (J, XXVII, 171)

April 30, 1871

Dickens infuses his personages with so much of his own congenial humanity as, in one, to secure their verisimilearity in some respects of however partial & excessive humanity, as in a caricature, as it were, through excessive development of a good thing, & their nonverisimilearity in some respects of precise impersonisation. His personages are all framed out [of] his own predisposition, so that his Uriah Heap & Fagin are, in some sense, villains made out of sugar, & seem to be but superficial villainy. . . . (J, XXVII, 281)

May 22, 1871

Goethe showed his essentiality of genius by his persistent alliance of art with externalism, as in his symbolisation of ideas, & in his induction from forms. All true genius is intrinsically realistical in its main bias, however romantic it may be partially & collaterally. Goethe seems to me to have been onesidedly realistical, that is, to have thought, in some aspect, more of shape than of soul, or, to speak more graphically, of forms than of ideas, & hence more of what has been done than of what might & should have been done. He resorted to the body of nature more than to the mind of nature, & to the his-

---

[103] This portrait, by William Furness, was painted about 1865. F. B. Sanborn writes: "It seemed to me a good likeness of Emerson in his quiet and domestic character. . . . it preserves the expression of those few years following the Civil War, when none but Emerson himself noted the approach of old age. . . ." "The Portraits of Emerson," in *The New England Magazine*, December, 1896, p. 451.

tory of man more than to the ideal of man. Shakspear, with genius' own subtle relish & life-grasp, so far as he went, for forms & facts, yet, not only took them, in a kind & degree, in great part for granted,—somewhat as a man of society takes due ceremonies & due conduct for granted, whilst carefully complying with them, but also compounded & enlarged the truths & principles on which they were based—if, indeed, he may not be said to have gone so far as, in some effect, & have even, more or less, submerged forms in their original truths through excess of inward activity, not, however, through excess, because, on the whole, of predeterminately inward exclusiveness or predilection, on his part. (J, XXVII, 353-354)

SECTION II. NATURE

August 24, 1855

Saw a remarkable sunset the other night, on the railway, beyond Baker's landing. The horizon was round; the sky was low, thick & heavy with masses of colored cloud, & was like the painted covering of a tent.—The clouds are remarkable in a special way, by the water. They lie in strata, heaped distinctly apart,—but compact, like things in amber. Moisture diffuses the colors, & spreads them all around, making the most of the rich paint. The Eastern sky is beautiful also at sunset. Its glories are older & graver than those of the Western sky flushed with the later smiles of the sun. The eastern prospect, in a landscape, is also fine. The light is quiet & equable.—To-day noticed that the clouds were thick & involved as in engravings of Turner.[1] (J, I, 53-54)

August 16. 1856

The lower parts of clouds sometimes are so shaded off as to look like vases, or frames, for the bright upper part. Saw a grand one coming up from New-Port yesterday in a sloop. It was piled up like peaks over peaks, full & soft as fleece within fleece. . . . What spectacles of wondrous art constantly abound in all nature.

---

[1] Compare March 24, 1854 (J, I, 31), where Newcomb describes Turner's engravings: "The clouds are extravagantly given. I doubt if one could tell what they were if the landscape was covered by the hand, reminding one of a map of the moon."

Yet the divine love is more beautiful in them than the divine power, for all these exquisitely finished objects are for uses. In use they live and move & for use they were formed. The wise love of Providence has kept the sky from being monotonous by making it a place of constant change. The grandest spectacle of cloud or sunset is changing even while we look at it, & never again is repeated. The stars continually move. Thus all things work with one another for man. Man must look upon what is called Nature as the constant work of Providence that is ever going on. . . . (J, I, 63)

September 5, 1856

How much color there is in all nature. Yet it is so grandly employed, with such divine ends & such divine power. The sky is not variously colored in the day, but at dawn & eve when men are making their morning or evening prayers as if in a temple of divine glory. . . . The quiet colors of the ocean are magnificent. The other day at Narragansett beach,[2] which in some respect excels New-Port, I saw the blue water with its round lines boldly drawn against the delicate sky, the green of the breakers bursting into purest white which lines the strand as if truth was the end of the ocean. (J, I, 70-71)

March 18, 1859

Spring has come again. Up springs all life to germinate & fructify in its genial sweet warmth & in that of Summer, which is spring's noon, as autumn is its sunset, & winter, perhaps, its night. The ground is springy with moisture, swolen with conceiving embryos. The brooks run in noisy animation down the banks, like schoolboys getting out of doors. . . . (J, I, 142)

March 29, 1859

The lakes are tossing up their thousand hands in play with the sweet vernal winds: the waves, lively & merry as children, make faithful reflection to the faithful sun. So the lower should ever reflect the higher & be resplendent from it. (J, I, 144)

[2] Probably "Atlantic" Beach in Westerly, R.I.

June 25, 1859

Riding along the beautiful valley of the Blackstone[3] to pleasant Woonsocket, the other day, after the late rains, noticed the fatness of the exuberant foliage. The river, almost concealed by the meadow it watered & the trees it cherished made me think of the wisdom of the good, which shows itself in the richness of their dress & the abundance of their fruit; as this stream was almost hid by the fertility it promoted, so the life of the good is the chief evidence of their wisdom. (J, I, 154)

July 1, 1859

. . . I think there must be a depressing influence from this great prairie of water [the ocean][4], & from the western land prairies on persons. I would not like to look on this great lidless eye much. The rural country, not the sea shore, is the place for homes. (J, I, 163)

July 1 [?]. 1859

The Narragansett Bay, in the early afternoon sunlight & a brisk breeze, on the passage up, was a mass of porphyry frosted with silver light. Besides the great plates of silver, there were silver dots. I do not love the old sea, but one misses, at first, leaving it, its mighty mass & movements, & the Newport ranges of walk.—Have not the dwellers by the sea a weir [d] look, & is there not an influence about the ocean, which as men are & as they receive it, is as a spell to them? (J, I, 164)

August 27, 1859

. . . Today, a very dark cloud covered the north: before it, in the narrow wooded road, a silver leaved ash stood, illuminating the darkness like a candle-labra. . . . (J, I, 178)

---

[3] The Blackstone river flows from Worcester southwards through Woonsocket as far as Pawtucket where it is called the Seekonk River.
[4] While yet a boy Newcomb longed for the day when he could become a sailor. By the 1850's, however, his attitude toward the sea seems to have become one of mixed fascination and repulsion.

December 29, 1859

The cracking of the ice, today, at Mashapaug Pond,[5] after the severe cold, reminded me of the sounds in all nature. It sounded at first like the tuning of violencellos:[6] as I listened I was surprised at the continuity & variety of the sounds. It made a natural symphony. Drums, cannon, stringed instruments were in it. . . . (J, I, 201)

January 10, 1860

The snow limns the trees with white, illuminating them like light; as the hues of autumn, even in a cloudy day, make a prism of the rays of the hidden sun, so the snow-covered trees make a kind of sunshine in the thick storm. . . . (J, I, 204)

February 13, 1860

As the sea is green near a sandy beach, so the ice is amber, sometimes, near the gravelly shore of the lake; & the other day autumnal leaves were inlaid in the ice as in amber. Medallions, round, palmleaf-like, & of divers shapes, are set in the ice, beneath the crystallised transparency, & the air bubbles on the surface are like little pearls. Indeed the ice is an orebed of pearls & diamonds. How real are the wonders of the divine Providence. The ice is no dream, no romance, yet oriental fancy could suggest nothing so apparently improbable as that water could harden like glass & that one could walk on it as on marble. It will come in a night, & a warm sun will dissolve it into molten snow in an hour. The very cracks in the ice add to its beauty & strength, seaming it like a carpet, bracing it as with crystal beams. They are the strings of the music which they sounded in breaking. The snow ice is soft & thick as cream, as white & consistent as the best of marble. (J, I, 208-209)

June 17, 1860

. . . The earth sends up trees as the water sends up fountains. (J, I, 228)

[5] A pond in southwest Providence.

[6] Compare with Thoreau's description of the breaking of the ice on Walden. This sketch may possibly indicate a reading of *Walden,* which was published in 1854.

June 19, 1860

The trees look, at a little distance, in the night, as if they were the shelter of darkness. . . . The shadows which sit under them in the day seem to have mounted into them in the night. . . . (J, I, 229a⁷)

May 23, 1861

Last eveᵍ the moonlight rested on the little haze-like leaves of the tall elms like clouds. The lower leaves stood out as if they were pencilled. A bright star broke from behind a bough as from a cloud. The beauty was magical. An avenue of elms in a moonlight, in the middle of May, is a scene of almost fanciful imaginativeness. (J, I, 323)

November 22, 1862

In my walk yesterday, after a week of wet weather, & whilst it was yet raining, the golden tufts of grasses illuminated the side of the rail way with dark carroty gold: the purple of the bare trees was a richer brown, the green of the pines amongst them a softer green; the dead leaves that were yet unfallen from some trees, hung in their autumnal hues as if only wilted by the rain. The fields & all things looked deepened in tint, like colored stones in water. (J, II, 103)

December 8, 1862

Mountains, like a new earth coming down out of heaven, attest the divine origin of the earth. There is a freshness, an innocence, an interestingness, around them as around infancy.—Providence, in some degree, works alone in them as in the clouds. Their beauty is indigenous like that of the sky & sea.—Mountains connect the two worlds of heaven & earth. Their tops, worn by the tread of stars, by the sweep of clouds, by the weight of atmospheres, by the rush of winds, rise into heaven; their bases pour down trees & waters as out of their high stores, into the earth on which they stand, & blend with it in a common garment. Their sides are decked with the uprising vegetation of the earth that climb up them but

---

⁷ There are two pages numbered 229. This paragraph is from the first.

keeps, like the sea, in its limits.—Mountains stand, like the aged good, partly divested of their earthly body, as if about entering the next world to which they are near. Mountains are beacons of eternal joys & hopes. (J, II, 109)

December 26, 1862

The pine wood is the garden of winter. Its green leaves & yellow floor bring to mind the verdant summer & the golden autumn. It is as changeless as the sea, & resounds incessantly like the waves. The bark of the pine is shaggy like the skin of the polar bear. It is knobbed like a coat of mail. In all seasons it asperges the air with purifying & salutary odors, tossing them off from its broomlike branches. (J, II, 123)

March 23, 1863

The shadows of trees, lying on the ground, look like divestments of the trees at transfiguration. They are like bareing for the sunshine. They are the confession of nothingness in self, of entity only in central influences. They are uncoverings of the trees in high presence. (J, II, 239)

April 25, 1863

The April showers have augmented into heavy rains, as if they had grown by what they fed on. They beat out, as with a mallet, the twigs into leavelets, & the buds into blossoms. . . . (J, II, 287)

June 22, 1863

In my walk, day before yesterday, to Quidnic,[8] in all about 27 miles, the working aspect of nature suggested that the hospitalities of nature were regulated & graded by industry. The fields & woods were as truly, in their kind, busy as the operatives in the factories which lined the Pawtuxet valley through which I walked, or as the farmers who were tilling the ground by the wayside. They were not cold or indifferent, but were responsive & sympathetic to the man who was at sympathy with them. The romantic youth

[8] Quidnick is a village in Coventry, R.I., on the South Branch of the Pawtuxet River. This is probably the "Quidnic" mentioned by Newcomb.

must learn this fact to counteract in him disappointment & heart-sickness. There is no place for an idler in nature, as there is no place for an idler in a workshop. Nature cannot, if it would, stop to entertain the aimless stroller, any more than can the working husbandman or mechanic stop to entertain him. He goes pleased through nature who has sympathy with its action & ends; as he goes pleased through a mill who has a common interest in the productiveness of the industrial laborers. I walked along amid the busy trees & fields, as respectfully, unselfishly, & undemandingly as I would have walked through a machine shop. . . . Groups of children lined the way laden with green whortleberries, impatient of ripeness in vegetation as youth & men are in humanity. The chestnut trees showed the marks of annual rough handlings in the fall. (J, II, 346)

June 30, 1863

The sunset sky last evening was of the hue of gold at white heat. The mass of the trees before it stood dark against the brightness like fuel just thrown into a fiery furnace. At the edges of the mass, delicate long pendent leaves of the locust hung in full relief, cut like embroidery. The beauty was as simple as it was splendid. It was as the common & practical beauty of a baker's oven. It was the fiery significance of life. It was the burnish & incandescence of experience. (J, III, 1)

July 22, 1863

Wachusett House, Princeton, Mass.[9] Storms have in them some thing of the chaos precedent to creation, & their clearing off has something of the development subsequent to their creative agency. Last evening, after a day of heavy rain, the clouds rolled away like a curtain, & there was inaugurated, as it were, a new aspect of nature. The new moon, like a bow of promise, &, on a lower line with it, the evening star like a cumulating dash of fresh pigment, hung & shone in the blue sky. Long lines of clouds, like megatherion stood stranded in the dried up firmament of waters. A haze was

[9] Newcomb spent five weeks at Wachusett House in the summer of 1863.

in the atmosphere, like the gloss of a new picture. The wind remained, a passive agent in the storm, nurturing the new landscape, yet brisk as if it was in the first exercise of its office. (J, III, 22-23)

August 29, 1863

As the farmer spots the trees on his estate in token that he is to cut them down, so the earth sprinkles the trees with mould, even before their prime, to convert them in due time into loam. The pure white trunks of the delicate beeches are marked & variegated with a mould which has something of the picturesque effect of knots on the columns of pine trees. (J, III, 63)

October 19, 1863

In my walk to Cumberland Hill,[10] of about 26 miles, day before yesterday, noticed that the tinted foliage was dimmed by the rain of the previous day. Autumnal foliage basks in the light, & wilts under rain as under fire. As I walked home along the valley of the Blackstone, on the railway, thought if high color was not, in some relations, a symptom of decadence. Colors are superb, sensuous, & suggestive, in their place, especially as moral symbols, but to the everyday, working world perhaps they are not germane. Positive colors are too prominent, emphatic, unreserved, perhaps, for everyday dress in general. (J, III, 121)

November 24, 1863

Last evening, clouds in the livery of the sunset, went about scattering new clouds, like spiders weaving webs out of themselves. They rolled toward the sun like sun-tinted seas ebbing & leaving behind them colorless & bleak sands, as for the night. One cloud, shaped like a dolphin, plunged toward the sun, dissolving itself in smoke-like vapor. . . . The difference of the sky in the water from its primary aspect, reminded me of the difference of art & nature. The reflection was polished, flattened &, in some respects, more facile in a limited degree of impression, because it gave color &

[10] In Providence County, R.I.

form divested of the deep significance of the simple substantiality of the full sky. It brought near & concentrated on an even plane. (J, III, 176)

November 30, 1863

. . . Noticed, also, the touching significance of the bare trees. They stand in the very attitude of outstretched arms with which they poured fruit & foliage upon the earth, arrested by the winter like mountain streams glaciered by the frost. (J, III, 185)

December 7, 1863

The sun gilds the bare trees of winter with a foliage-like hue of warm color. The delicate sprays of some trees hang down like flowers. (J, III, 196)

December 8, 1863

The long brown trunks & branches streak the clear amber of the air like veins in agate. (J, III, 196)

December 9, 1863

There is nothing of mere fancy in nature, yet nature is so comprehensive that its reality sometimes has, apparently, a semblance of fancy. Thus the clouds assume fantastic shapes, the frosts scribble art on the windows, & air bubbles group in figures on the ice. The pond, on which I skated yesterday, was like an aquarium of curiosities. The ground was covered with green & grassy moss. Lily stems radiated in every direction, like simulation of lines, bent beneath the water like limbs of trees beneath snow. Leaves, finely cut as in summer, were preserved beneath the ice as in amber. The water itself was contained in the ice as in a crystal vase. A large yellow lily plant held up the floor of the ice with its broad palms like brackets or columnar entablatures, & played at architecture. The dust of the skate-tracks, elongated into needle-shaped forms, was piled in heaps like corded wood. The plants dug their roots, like heads, into the ground, with their flat leaves uppermost like the web-feet of diving ducks. (J, III, 200)

December 28, 1863

In the sunset, night before last, there was a crude, soft yellow, different from gold, such as I never noticed previously. It was such a pigment as children use: the melted & refined yellow of a lily.— The moon, last night, shone from behind a film of clouds. It was cased like the face of a statue draped in a marble veil. (J, III, 243)

March 10, 1864

The azure water, rippled with plumage of liquid softness, bounds & sings in the vernal air before the birds return. (J, IV, 15)

March 29, 1864

There is much grandeur, of a kind, in a storm of the air. The ear hears a great tumult as of the sea, though the eye does not see it so fully. The atmosphere is swept through with a force which dims the lustrous sparkle of still air as if it riled it, & which turns aslant the quick sun-beams as if it dulled them. A steady & central power, of which a rough sea is only an effect, rages, re-sounds, & splurges in the landscape. . . . (J, IV, 60)

April 25, 1864

Little buds come out on the candelabra-like trees like the first dim flames of newly-lighted tapers. (J, IV, 120)

April 30, 1864

Looking at the bright horizon below dark blue clouds, yesterday aft^n. by the bay-side, the treble of some frogs in my ear as the silver of the sky was in my eye. I felt the harmony & analogy of the notes of the treble of the frogs & of the tenor of the sky, &, for the first time, thought of the intrinsic music of the landscape & nature. Farther on, the gushing sound of the gently plashing surf of the dark water on the shore seemed in accord with the silent notes of the dark blue clouds above the illuminated horizon. . . . (J, IV, 141)

May 13, 1864

Yesterday aft^{n}. the vertical rays of the sunbeams in the misty air, finely set off the steep pitch of the dome of the sky. They were like illuminated dust in a vast dome, of which the thick array of white edged clouds were the frescoes. (J, IV, 168)

July 2, 1864

There is a range of seasons even in one season. The first month of summer does not close before a harvest has been gathered of hay, dandelions, strawberries, & peas. The ripe grasses are sheaves of seeds & stand like wheat & rhye, their brown grain dotting their golden coverings with films of shadow.—Doubtless, all climates show the same series on other scales. (J, IV, 262)

July 28, 1864

The earth fattens in these mountain woods[11] like a flock sent out to pasture. A tree does not fall but vegetation seizes hold of it like a worm, & covers it with loam & moss, as with spittle before it absorbs it. The mountain soil is porous as the snow, & soft & tremulous as a bog. The moss is ferny in its luxuriance. Rocks are decked like vases. Trees are plucked up, like weeds, & thrown into the bed of verdure as into a compost heap. (J, IV, 294)

August 1, 1864

Inquiring of a countryman in these Mountains[12] if it was not dangerous to walk about in the woods as I do, on account of the bears, & bob-cats, as lynxes are called, who are seen along the road, even near the hotel, & why it was that so powerful an animal should not be as dangerous to meet loose as he is when chained, he replied that the wild animal did not know man as the tamed ones do, or that he had not become used to him. This was a counterpart motto of a rustic to the maxim of the Frenchman, 'that no man is a hero to his valet-de-chambre'. . . . (J, IV, 300)

[11] At this time Newcomb was spending a few days at Profile House, Franconia, N.H.

[12] The White Mountains.

August 3, 1864

. . . The mountains are backgrounds & reliefs to mists that rise from the plain & lower hills & form clouds. . . . A mist stood before the broad mass of Mt Clinton today, delicate, transparent, but perceptible, as an immense pane of plate-glass in which the clouds were as flaws. The woods were clearly defined on the hills as through a lens.—The large clouds stoop low from the sky to take up the little clouds rising up, like young creatures, from the ground.— The earth crouches at the mountains to spring down upon the plains. Its wooded back arches like the tawny back of a lion about to jump. (J, IV, 302)

September 9, 1864

. . . The ocean fell upon my senses, in the morning, as calmly as an old shoe, as I first saw it after a summer amongst mountains & orchards. It lay sparkling with gems of light, like a desert of broken crystals. . . . (J, IV, 352-353)

September 29, 1864

The division of day & night is indicated in trees, as in animals & in space. The transition from the fields or from a grove of oaks to a grove of hemlocks & spruces, is like the change from sunlight to night. Shadow seems in its nest amongst spruces, & has in them some of its darkest affinities. . . . (J, V, 53)

October 27, 1864

Nature is redundant with moral suggestion & analogy. As I walked along the riverside yesterday aft^n., the black water, between the dark hemlock grove on one side & the yellow & russet grove of chestnuts & oaks on the other side, was as a river Styx between two spheres. The hemlocks fell on the polished surface like a deeper shadow of a shade, on the one shore; the chestnuts & oaks painted the surface, on the other shore, like a far shining glory. On the hill over the hemlocks, the golden chestnuts shone like singing birds. (J, V, 112)

November 12, 1864

After a storm of four days, the clouds rolled away, day before yesterday, like a veil or scaffolding; & the dome of the sky & the floor of the earth appeared as if they had been retouched & cleansed, like a vast temple repainted & reopened. . . . Yellow tints exuded from the ridges of the clouds like stalactites of color decolating through a bed of gold; & overflowed at the leeward like sheets of water brushed out of shape by the winds.—Yesterday, as I walked homeward. . . . In the east, the white moon hung resplendent in a sky of bridal purity of tint, like a pearl in a delicate & open shell. . . . Later in the evening, the bright stars glimmered in the fair hase of cloudy blue, like sparks in a white smoke from the sun hovering below the horizon. The earth sent up trees & the city sent up spires, like shadows, into the air; & the air sent down shadows from trees & spires on the ground, which one walked on as on ice, delicate but firm in texture. (J, V, 155-156)

November 15, 1864

The rising sun sends its rays before it like couriers to announce its coming & to clear its way. The western hills are lit in the dawn like beacons in the night. It treads over the earth on a golden floor of its own light, like a hero marching amid his own glory. It shoots out its beams, like arrows, in advance, to mark the distance it will make good. (J, V, 164)

November 30, 1864

The winter forms of the trees . . . tread the earth like elephants, & brush the sky like clouds. . . . The limbs of some of the trees are as boldly muscular as they are finely linear. The hickory is hard & vigorous as iron in its flow & grip of line. The big elms claw the ground with such firm hold that their roots outcrop in the trunks like distended muscles along the arm of a grasping hand, & throw out protrusions like butresses. (J, V, 208-209)

December 1, 1864

The tapering forms of the trees indicate the effective vitality of their lines of motion. Their arch & flow of outline attenuate as if they sprang into the fine sphere of the empyrean. They suggest relations of the finite to the infinite, of the mortal to the immortal. This attenuation is part of their symmetry. It is their completion, not their exhaustion. It points, not dissipates. It vaults, but arches. The delicate twigs are as fibrous as are the stout trunks. They suck the refined air, as the roots suck the coarse ground. They flow toward the earth like the hills, & the trees dome earthwards like the sky. (J, V, 212)

December 24, 1864

If the beauty of the winter is, in some respects, as bright, it is, in other respects, as barren, as a gem. Beauty must be correlative to be opportune. The husbandmen would be starved if the soil of his farm turned to crystals & garnets, & none of it to apples & turnips. . . . (J, V, 290)

December 27, 1864

Winter is something like an hollow shell, cold, hard, polished, holding instead of meat a crude pearl. (J, V, 302)

February 24, 1865

The broom-like trees brush the air, as if they would sweep away all traces of the frosts before they lay their verdure out. They toss heat into their buds with the same motion that they toss cold out of the atmosphere. They wrestle with the elements for scope. (J, VI, 100)

March 1, 1865

The March snow comes down as if the clouds of ice were breaking up. The flakes fall lightly, & hover in the air, as if they knew they were driven from the relentless sky to an unrelenting earth. (J, VI, 115)

March 8, 1865

The liquid & waving sea leaves its mark in the rounded stones & on the traced sands of its shores; but the liquid & waving air leaves its mark in the curved limbs & cut direction of the trees. The pencilled rocks show that the tossing billows have moved over them: the moulded trees show that they have moved on the billows of the swaying air. The sea beats the unresisting stone to dust; the air beats the sympathetic wood to its likeness. . . . The trees crouch, curve, & sing under the congenial touch of the winds, like tigers arching their backs & purring under the riding Bacchus. . . . (J, VI, 136)

March 9, 1865

The graceful & rounded trees stand before the farmhouses & on the roadside like wooden flowers. No roses or lilies are finer in form, softer in flow, or delicater in bearing: no plants are so muscular or so elaborate. . . . (J, VI, 142)

March 14, 1865

Winter is, in many respects, a conserving season. It is not without more significance than seems on the surface of their act, that men borrow the ice of December to preserve the fruits of August. Was reminded of this yesterday in hearing the peculiar notes of a bird in the warm afternoon. They sounded as if the bird was drawing up with its tongue, as with a bucket, the vernal music out of its winter depositary. (J, VI, 157)

March 15, 1865

There is something in the consummate finish of a flower which suggests a special repose to the eye. It satisfies like a work that is done & that asks no more labor upon it. It is complete in its kind. Its time is short, & it wilts while it is looked at, like a sunset cloud sobering into the sleepiness of night. Other vegetation is more vigorous & more enduring, & suggests more vigorous & more enduring scope. Yet the flower, like woman whom it most resembles, works in its field; but its kind of work is simpler than that of the vegetable as the work of women is simpler than that of men, & as the work of the Sabbath is milder than the work of the week-day. The nature of the flower makes it a peculiarly appropriate ornament for festivals & for ladies' gardens. It is the type of holidays. It is the rainbow of beauty in the seething farm-yard. (J, VI, 161)

March 21, 1865.

The whole moral of nature is life. As I rested in the warm afternoon yesterday near the Pocasset[13] river, long which my walk took me, the soul of nature pulsated with life as the conscious-ness felt its vitality. The white haze nourished rain; the ringing notes of the birds awoke love; the antlered trees pricked the juicy air for blood; the singing river nursed the soil as it meandered along like an almoner; the buoyant wind incited movement as it cleared the way for breath. (J, VI, 180)

April 28, 1865

A hot day in April is a freshet of heat. The leaves are forced out, like soils opened by freshets of water. The summer seems to brood in it before it has wholly built its nest. The flowerets open their tiny eyes as in a broad glare of mid-day. (J, VI, 311)

June 8, 1865

A walk by the bayside is a great contrast to a walk in the meadows. The sea is restless & eager like a thing whose nature is not, by its laws, preoccupied with, so to speak, self-centered relations. It moves rather like an animal demonstratively following a man, than like the fields stilly growing by the side of man. The crops & grasses surge almost as inaudibly as dancing women: the waves chatter aloud like uneasy & gossiping sparrows. The sea shows its joy in sympathy with the teeming earth. It jumps about like boys on festive days of which they do not know the full significance. . . . The earth produces here & there a veiled diamond or opal: the sea is a molten fire of porphyry, silver, emerald, & ruby. Its work is incessant & serious like that of a watchman. It is a seething laboratory of clouds. It is a never ceasing mill that grinds stones into soil, & weaves lime into stones.—Yesterday, as I walked down the Narraganset Bay, the winds of heaven drew myriads of white waves out of the purple plain, like the trumpet of resurrection rousing spirits from their beds in the

[13] A river that runs through Johnston and Cranston, R.I.

graves. Sea birds find it a garden of fish, as land birds find the earth a garden of worms. (J, VII, 54)

June 19, 1865

The beauty of nature is terrible & even deadly to a man out of due relation to it. Was reminded of this as I walked day before yesterday, on one of the hottest days of the year, to & from Rocky Point,[14] about 24 miles. The last outward, & first homeward, 4 or 5 miles were over a shadeless & sandy road. The prairie-like meadows were beautiful; the bay rested on its cool bed like a beast in a pasture; the woods painted one side of the wide fields with shadow, & the light gilt the other side with sunshine: but it was not the time for such a walk. The landscape was fair, & the air was even cool, as I reclined on, or rose from, the wayside: but the walk gave a wrong & perveted focus to beauty for that time. A walk in such a brilliant day, on such a road, was innopportune like a walk in a dark night. (J, VII, 73)

August 8, 1865

The aspect of nature follows the observer like the eye of a portrait. The landscape pivots with the traveller. The sunset clouds loomed over Long Island Sound, yesterday afternoon, on my passage home,[15] like lines of long beaches. (J, VII, 120)

August 26, 1865

It may be in the mood of the observer, but it sometimes seems as if there was a sort of moral vacuum in the air & landscape at the first coming of autumn. The summer is almost ebbed; the winter has not inflowed though its scent is in the winds which hurry on its cold tide. The atmosphere is at equipoise: the sunshine is warm; the shade is cool; the ground gives out heat; the clouds give out cold. The foliage is mostly green as in summer, but it wilts when the summer declines, as sea-weeds wilt out of water; some of it is bloody at the hard grip of the advancing frost. . . . (J, VII, 169)

[14] In Warwick, R.I.
[15] From New York, by boat.

September 6, 1865

The summer sun so deeply stained the ground that a sort of sunshine beams from the wet fields during the September rain which cannot remove it. Only the sun itself can change the dye. This it will do in spring. . . . (J, VII, 190)

September 11, 1865

Summer has left a scorched trail behind it. The fields are yellow with heat & dusty with ashes. The trees are dismantled, like untenanted houses after a conflagration. Fruits are thrown down from them like treasures that should be saved & moved. (J, VII, 199)

September 15, 1865

A drought robs the sky as well as the land. The dry earth has less & less moisture to give to the atmosphere. The clouds look dry & hard like clouds in a picture. The sun strikes on a bald & hot ground like water on an empty & heated iron. There is no lubrication to temper its force. Dust flaunts up in the face of the heaven like smoke from a burning earth. (J, VII, 213)

November 10, 1865

The leaves fly away, like birds, before the snow comes. The landscape looks like a deserted nest. (J, VII, 351)

November 15, 1865

Hills are touchingly domestic features in the landscape. They rise like warm pulses, or like uplifted limbs of the earth. They are like prolonged cadences of the ground. They are like waves of active & aspiring movement transfixed at the beck of Providence for significant purport to man. (J, VIII, 5)

January 1, 1866

The trees rise from the earth like rockets, & go out in the fruits, leaves, & shadows which they drop upon the ground. Their motion is centrifugal & centripetal: they grow upwards, they hang downwards: they form columns & arches: they break out from the soil like waves from the sea, & spread themselves along the air like breakers across the water. The earth uses them so thoroughly & pervasively that they turn into earth. (J, VIII, 89)

January 5, 1866

There is no beauty in nature so splendid as beauty in man: neither is there any deformity in nature so repulsive as deformity in man. (J, VIII, 99)

February 2, 1866

The beauty of a winter's afternoon seems like a crystalisation of a portion of that of a summer's afternoon. It is fair but cold, pure but congealed, lustrous but not radiative, ripe but not mellow.— The dark trees stand in the white landscape like shadows that have survived the wreck of warm verdure. The snow invests the ground as with a mantle of unassimilated clouds, & gives it the monotonous & barren monotony more dreary than that of the monotonous sea. Clouds of smoke stream out of closed houses, & clouds of snow stream out of frozen oceans: the former attests that man is at work, & the latter that nature is at work. (J, VIII, 179)

February 12, 1866

There is something peculiarly & especially feminine in the nature of mountains. They are earth of earth in their relations to the skies. They are drawn out, held up, & enfolded, as it were. They are s[t]rongarched & big ground. They are nearer the heart of heaven. They are dilated with elevating fires. They are more given to the quickening sun than are the less ardent valleys. They are first & last to catch & hold the light. They are above the plains. They have more of the distinguishing appositeness of the earth as toward heaven. (J, VIII, 220)

April 3, 1866

As a lovely day in springtime, when the mild & lambent air is especially sensuous & refreshing in contrast to the stern & fettered weather of winter; when the earth flowers, & the trees bud, & the birds sing, & the blood of men & beasts runs in their veins like red fire; followed by a wintry day of relentless storm, when the earth is ashed with frost, & the buds are nipped, & the birds hide their heads in their wings in vain from the killing cold: so the play of Romeo & Juliet opens & closes. (J, IX, 51)

April 23, 1866

The beauty of nature, like the beauty of man, is patent: undue consciousness of one is as demoralising as is that of the other. Nature is, in respect of beauty, an accomplished fact, where its development & culture under man is not involved. It tells, as, for, & in itself. Its processes are complete. The simple rustics, who make no ado about the beauty of nature, are, so far, wiser in their relation to it than are the sentimental abstractionists, who make too much ado about it. Like exquisitely tinted nectar, it is made for more purpose than to be looked at & admired. (J, IX, 132)

April 25, 1866

The sun sucks up vegetation through the trees as through syphons. It lets it fall again, as in suspended movement, toward the mother earth. . . . (J, IX, 144)

May 2, 1866

A man has a faint idea of what the earth is to vegetation & animals until he has lain on it & risen from it refreshed, during a weary walk. The sun burns into him as if he had got nearer its hearth; the earth communicates its precious & tempered dampness to his parched pores; his body recuperates at the touch of its native element. (J, IX, 182)

May 4, 1866

The heat of spring is just cool enough to be called sober in its ardor. The season is like a young parent, who cannot be all smiles to its offspring. It is duly reserved & moderate. Its nurture strengthens as well as develops. It prunes & sacrifices. It is rough as well as gentle. Parents can learn many lessons from its method. (J, IX, 191-192)

September 10, 1866

The summer air gradually tones down in temperature, like a long standing drink of spiced wine. One can feel both its warmth & its chill at the same touch. (J, X, 180)

September 28, 1866

The mellow glow of the air in autumn suggests the fancy that the summer ripened the atmosphere as well as the fields. It stands out by itself like a fair & luscious fruit. It will soon fall, like the leaves, into the maw of winter; but its soul will have passed into the soul of man, as the harvest will have passed into the body of man. (J, X, 256)

February 11, 1867

It is the full beauty that absorbs & appropriates, assigns & blends, lesser beauties. The eastern sky, tinted with yellow of pansies, & red of roses, & white of lilies, as I came along Filbert Street[16] just about sunrise today, afforded the dim sort of beauty of a half-closed eye; the flash, as well as the presence, of the iris-like sun was as yet in reserve. The white of noonday is made up of a full tide of splendors & colors of which the hues & flares of dawn & twilight are only low tides, even refuse & settlings.—The sunrise may be compared to an empty shell on a beach, whose gay color is dimmed by the incoming tide of the sea which bears the crab that appropriates it: the sunset may be compared to the same shell, lustrous with the fresh & dry color of the crab which leaves it, as if it goes away with the ebb of day.—Noon day is the eye of the giant in his strength. (J, XII, 202)

February 13, 1867

The shrewd & vigilant movements of some crows, in my walk yesterday, reminded me that animals were intelligent, because Providence was intelligent, & because Providence ordered & used them, not because there was any intrinsic intelligence in them. The crow that stood alone, like a sentinel mounted on a tree, warned his fellows,

---

[16] In Philadelphia.

& gave a cry at my approach, fired off his caw as pertly, as if a puppet's tongue had been pulled, & made to squeak, by the showman of
it. (J, XII, 223)

September 14, 1867

The clouds are, perhaps, broken into strata & into groups by
the motion of the earth. They are aligned as by settling in the air.
It is curious that dirt, settling in water, settles in ridges & heaps
like the sand on a sea-washed beech: as if water had a predetermined
method & purpose.[17] (J, XIV, 316)

September 26, 1867

When nature strikes, its aspect is stormy: but in the very antecedent
of striking, it is exquisitely beauteous, as if it smiled with the love
that was the motive of its severity. While crossing the Delaware,
yesterday afternoon, the delicate poise of a ragged [?] & soft end of
a cloud, on the verge of what fair sky was uncovered, provoked my
exclamation of "how beautiful"; but, presently, down poured from
the northward [?] northwest, out of the center of this cloud, as
out of a battery, a furious fire of hail stones, which beat like
cannon balls on the boat, & broke, I guess, about a million of
panes of glass in the city. (J, XIV, 357)

October 18, 1867

. . . Big, but dry, verdure treads the air of October, with resounding tread, as athletes, swollen with muscle, & spent with
achievement, walk heavily after a campaign in the arena; little, but
juicy, verdure hangs buoyantly & facilely in the air of April, as
children, cheerlily & agilely toss & spring about in the arms of
their smiling parents.—It never came into my head, until the other
day, that the soughing sound of autumnal winds was owing to the
stiff age of the foliage. It reminds one of the creaking of an old
vessel, laboring in a storm, on the tossing ocean which is about to
engulph it. (J, XV, 81)

[17] Newcomb was "reminded of this by the way in which some dirt had settled
in my wash-basin." This sentence was later cancelled.

November 14, 1867

Again, today, I rejoiced in the good of early rising; on my way to breakfast, the eastern sky was decked with saffron, as with the leaf of a great golden flower, whose coronal center was the sun; in the western sky, the moon shone like a pure lily; along the sidewalks the graceful trees stood, in their unvested forms, like empty vases, waiting for a share of the blooming beauty. The heaven seemed like a splendid plant spread on the surface of a sea of air in which it growed, & on the ground of which we walked. (J, XV, 195)

November 21, 1867

The sky wears, almost every day, a different attire from that worn on the previous day, as if it adjusted its cloths & colors by a ritualistic rubric. The meaning of changes in the semblances & shows of nature is, not millinery, not mannerism, but variousness, development, renovation, augmentation, compositeness, usufruct.— Ecclesiasticism, although it learnt what it has of falsity from immoral & artificial men, learnt, what it has of beauty in its symbols, from the morale of art in nature. It took the hint of incense from the perfumes of pines & of roses; of genuflection, from the bowing of boughs & of reeds; of altars, from rocks; of altar cloths, from clouds; of holy water, from the aspersion of the earth by wave-tossed spray; of flowers, from the fields.—Who so would see ritualism, unsentimental, unsuperstitious, & unaffected, let him look at nature. (J, XV, 225-226)

December 19, 1867

The sun evinces a balance of constructive & of destructive forces. It ripens & it rots. It distils perfumes from pines, & miasma from morasses. It is uniform in its method. It disintegrates, impartially, stones in the quarry & in the edifice. It dissolves, to-day, the exquisite traceries of frost on my window just as it has, hitherto, faded the exquisite tints of painters on canvass. (J, XV, 288)

December 21, 1867

The grey tints of mists & clouds are thickened, as if condensed like milk, by the cold of winter. The atmosphere becomes as graphic in frost as the rain becomes in snow. (J, XV, 299)

February 4, 1868

The spring is seen in the air before it is seen on the ground. It hovers before it nestles. The trees resume their pliability under the tension of its tread. As I skated up the Schuylkil yesterday af[n]. from Greyferry's Bridge to Chestnut Bridge, the vernal alembic which had made the air fine had made the trees feathery. The trees were less woodeny, as the atmosphere was less wintry. The sap had burst the bark, before the water had burst the ice. It had an inside ladder wherewith to mount, & meet its coming lord.—In many things, rigidity kept pace with frigidity. (J, XVI, 212)

.   .   .

The frost bites the flesh as if it were a parasitical animal. It stings me today in my cold chamber, as with a thousand fangs.[18] It gets through my shoes & through my coat as if it had the reach of a sunbeam. Very likely, it is stamping my blood as it has stamped my windows with arctic semblances. It lurked yesterday, in the track of the south wind; & when the southwind had retreated, it reappeared, with a vengeance. But the strength of winter is broken: it can do no more, now, than skirmish. (J, XVI, 213)

February 13, 1868

Beauty in nature, like beauty in women, becomes its attire. The fair earth tells in coarse stones as well as in fine stones, just as handsome faces tell in calico as well as in silk. Granite is a gem, though it is not recognised as a gew-gaw by lapidaries or costumers. The rail-way bridge at Schuylkill-falls stopped my skating excursion from Fairmont Park, near the dam, yesterday af[n]., as if it had been a breast-work of beauty in a foray of pleasure. Its rough-hewn stones set in it like cut jewels in an ephod. They were not limited in size like amethysts or opals; & they reflected shadows as diamonds do not. They were not transparent like crystals: neither is milk transparent like water. (J, XVI, 263)

[18] Newcomb for a time preferred to write in an unheated room.

March 9, 1868

The saffron of the sunrise, in todays early springtime, was as the yellow of flowers, not, as in mid-winter, of metals. The caw of the crows was softened by the beating of the bursting rivers against their shells of ice. The song of the robbins broke out of the vernal air over the muddy landscape, like the first rippling of an incoming tide over a miry strand. (J, XVII, 38)

March 20, 1868

The chilliness of spring, despite the genial intercourse of the sky & earth, reminds one of the apparent indifference of a newly married couple to everybody but themselves. (J, XVII, 85)

August 5, 1868

Art in nature seeks uniformity without evenness. Where it uses one mould, as in the casting the leaves of one species of trees, it varies the position of the counter pattern on either side of the leaf. It seeks general accord without angularity. If it wrote poetry it would not make the lines of the same precise length. It aims at symmetry without sameness of outline, as is patent in the shapes of mountains & of waves. It sets the stars at uneven distances. As if to vary its liberalism of uniformity, it occasionally practises greater precision of style, as in the cut of some flowers.—This is the daily lesson to me of a tree near my window. (J, XVIII, 280)

October 13, 1868

Blossoms are the swaddling clothes of young fruits. (J, XIX, 136)

October 17, 1868

The summer, before it evacuates for the winter—which drives it away from its sweet place & possession—lays the train of a fire in its rear which shall, of itself, consume the vegetation before it falls into the cold & uncongenial hands of the invader. The conqueror comes over a track of blasing verdure. Summer leaves nothing fresh, juicy & green for a prey to its successor: after the tinted flames amongst the verdure are spent, only wilted & ash-colored remains are visible. (J, XIX, 150)

October 29, 1868

The earth is such a goodly & beauteous object, that men wish & need to see much of it around them & to see it in various forms. Accordingly, in their senses & sentiments, mountains are agreable & . . . necessary, like meadows. Men ask for more of the society of nature than the monotonous & vast expanses of prairies. . . . They are grateful for hills as for woods.—I am always, as yesterday, reminded of this in my walk, along the flat lands of Broad Street. . . .[19] A landscape without hills is somewhat like an eye without lids, like a tree without shade, & like an interview with a prostrate person. (J, XIX, 188)

March 9, 1869

A scene at Fairmont[20] *. . . Poems, No 3.*

The icicles hung on the hillside,
Like udders from a cow;
The creature, that the god did ride,
Stood confessed now.
Water exuded at the hot touch
Of the fond & forming snow;
Drop by drop it formed much,
And heaped the river's basin.

A little bird in the drippings dashed,
Like a baby in a bath;
Near it, its partner watched
Its turn in the pool's path.
Not honey to the humble bee,
Nor milk to the raven-like fly,
Gave e'er such sweet hilarity,
As, to these birds, this lakelet high.

A statue, carved in marble white,
Amidst the white icicles rose;
It answered the vault like a stalagmite,
And did the mastership of man disclose.
However the cold frostwork of nature showed
Instinct & skill in portraying vegetation;
The cold limestone work of mankind proved
That only men could play at higher creation.[21] (J, XX, 320)

[19] In Philadelphia.
[20] Fairmont was one of the parks where Newcomb skated.
[21] This is no cruder in form than are most of Newcomb's verses.

March 26, 1869

. . . People must admire icebergs on the terms that they admire crystals. Yet no . . . blinded creature wishes to live near icebergs.— The art of nature is like an accomplished cook, who cooks all his dishes well, whether they are healthy or unhealthy, & like an expert dramatist, who portrays all of his personages well, whether they are virtuous or vicious. (J, XXI, 15-16)

November 30, 1869

If a plant could rebel, as a man rebels, against the order & leadership of normal rule, the results of its vicious license would be palpably obvious. The plant would be seen, without gloss, palliation, or relief, to wither & die, if it chose night, instead of day, for its forthputting; yet, the fatal results upon man . . . of reversal & perversion of the plans of nature are similarly pronounced. . . . (J, XXIII, 86-87)

December 9, 1869

The brown hue of the trees of winter, when stripped of verdure, is similar to the brown hue of the earth when stripped of vegetation. Foliage is the vegetation of trees; trees are the vegetation of the earth. (J, XXIII, 122)

February 25, 1870

The world builds galleries for the display of reproduced & imitated art & yet constrains the concealment of the highest forms of living art. It exhibits a simulated man in cold & dead marble, & hides a real man of warm flesh & blood, in dull & graceless haberdashery.—While I was skating on the meadow yesterday af^n. two men broke in; & one of them, taking off his pantaloons & wringing them out on the bank, showed limbs which were revelations of human beauty. The bare trees all around were beautiful in their bold outlines; but they were as nothing in beauty & significance to even the bare legs of a man. (J, XXIV, 29)

May 25, 1870

While taking a delicious saunter on the western side of Fairmont over the locks, at the dam this af^n. among the tall grasses, who flung out sweet odors at every stroke of my umbrella, a naked boy, who was running about in the river below, straddled a brown rock, & instantly assumed a significance & suggestiveness which his crude & thin person had not previously had. His legs were lost sight of in the river, & his figure assumed dignity & expression in very contrast to the less shapely & graceful stone. Instantly, I saw the meaning of the Greek Tritons & nymphs. The loss of part of the body of the boy, through its sensuous immersion, was such, as of old, gave rise to symbols of a blended human & animal shape in the person of marine deities. (J, XXV, 15)

May 26, 1870

The vast vault of the aerial heaven is a meed of the vast proportional power & need of the little chest of man. The atmosphere is required for man's lungs, as the earth is required for his mouth. (J, XXV, 16)

June 2, 1870

The animals live in some respects a nobler & happier life in nature than many men live in society, such as it now is. The life of the victims of the present system of society may be compared more aptly, for some purposes to that of the animals who are their fellow victims than to those who are at liberty in the forests & on the plains. . . . (J, XXV, 44)

June 26, 1870

. . . At my first treading of Coney Island beach,[22] today, after the gradual breaking of the sea, to me, by the bay through which we approached it, & during a low surf on the shore itself, I thought, at first, that the ocean was too old a story to me, especially in my present mood, to be very interesting or very pronunciative to me. But soon the incessancy of the action, & the urgency of the sound, of the great element impressed me; & presently I found that the more of an old story, the more, for that very cause, of a new—because of . . . a comprehended & a repeated story—it was to me. It was as vast, powerful, persistent, & fresh as ever. I quaffed a little of it as of a

[22] Newcomb spent part of the summer of 1870 in New York.

mineral water.—The sturdy forms of men reclined on the margin, & gave to the ocean an expression which it could not have without the show, or suggestion, of man. They are its masters in form as well as in fact. (J, XXV, 229-230)

October 27, 1870

. . . For the last two nights but one,—the white stars have been deliciously mingled with red auroras, like pieces of ice in rosy wine. . . . (J, XXVI, 87)

SECTION III. SOCIETY AND GOVERNMENT

June 9, 1858

I have wished to put on record the remarkable interest in religion which has prevailed over the whole country during the last winter & spring. I think it began in a prayer meeting of men in the business part of the city of New York, at business hours. The time was highly favorable for this great revival: being the season after the extraordinary failures in business, when the entire mercantile community was passing through an unprecented state of bankruptcy or loss & depression of business. . . . Men were thus led to reflect on the true nature of worldly relations, & to see the connection of the latter to spiritual things. All over the country prayer meetings, characterised—as even the worldly observer acknowledged—by great earnestness & simplicity of feeling, & an absence of unhealthy excitement . . . in which the laity took equal part with the clergy . . . were held in innumerable places over the country, many times every day. . . . I have attended the Methodist conference meetings at the Mathewson St. Church[1] with great interest, & have often felt that the house of prayer was indeed the Gate of Heaven. . . . (J, I, 107-108)

October 13, 1860

. . . I noticed this[2] with great pleasure at the reception here[3] of the Prince of Wales. His refined & modest bearing, his fresh, earnest, youthful interest in what is before him, his unpretension, his ac-

---

[1] A Methodist church in Providence.
[2] Newcomb had been noticing the enthusiasm with which the general public was doing honor to heroes "distinguished for morale."
[3] New York City.

complishment, his gentleness, joined to our gladness of hospitable greeting of our English Cousin, the descendant & heir of the monarchs of our forfathers, take & hold the eye. . . . I saw him several times, & the last time it occurred to me—perhaps it was only an imaginary reading—that he had something of the coldness which springs from royal isolation. He looks like his mother's portraits, has George 3ᵈs profile, is slender, has a dignity of a kind. He is not English in robustness, & suggests whether royal blood will not also end in this, as in the Spanish race, in puny form & character. He inherits much of his mother, does not seem very manly, has a sort of feminine dignity, is rather plain but full of expression in the face. (J, I, 255)

December 22, 1860

We are in strange times. We see what an abyss we walk on, without having had due consciousness of it. Yet the thread that upholds man in Gods heaven is strong, though fine. Has the time come for the North to propose a last & just compromise,—that slavery shall be no longer recognised in any way by the constitution, & that this blot, left by the fathers in fond confidence of a quiet erasure, be forever effaced by decided act & the nation thus be strong in consistent principle? Or does good . . . enjoin the prudence, under the circumstances of not yet amending the constitution, of confiding at large in the government. . . ? Man is bound to the state by all the ties of order & the penalties of anarchy. Secession is an absurdity. Man is born into the Government. (J, I, 278)

October 19, 1861

The removal of the portraits of past rulers from public halls, who have turned traitors or who sympathise with traitors, & the ready approval of loyal people of the measures, remind one of the imprecation in the psalm, "let them be clothed with shame & dishonor that magnify themselves against me."[4] (J, II, 21)

February 17, 1862

Slang phrases are illustrative of the facility & readiness of men to dodge the sober forms of expression. They blend the trifling & the

[4] Psalm 35, 26.

playful. They impoverish language, because they give substitutes for it. . . . The phrases, less common now, were formerly, "seen the elephant," "who struck Billy Patterson," "over the left," "gave them Jesse," "or any other man," "No, siree." Now the phrases are, "I don't see it," "a big thing," "played out," "Is that so"; "bully" is now substituted for "first rate"; as "bully skates" & "bully for you," meaning, "you have done well" . . . a Western phrase for running away, "skedaddle," is coming into vogue. (J, II, 63)

October 27, 1862

It is due to a soldier's health & general morale that he be well exercised in camp.[5] A soldier contracts a sort of phobia for exertion which is a sign of unhealthy inertia. . . . This is partly engendered by the condition of his system produced by change of climate, food, water, habits, & associations; partly by laziness; partly by listlessness, produced by his habit of reclining when not on duty or at meals, a bad habit which benches might avert. . . . Exact & regular & brisk exercise at drill, or otherwise, will call out his energies, circulate his blood, & brace his system against physical & moral disease. . . .

Sergeants & corporals & chiefs of messes, should be required to attend to the morale of the men. They should discountenance laziness, & forbid & punish profane & indecent conduct & expressions. No eating should be allowed in tents; it is uncleanly, & the crumbs attract insects. A soldier suffers from want of sleep, & I am glad to see that the 11th Reg[t] are required to have taps at 7 ½ P.M. We found it hard & a bore to have to wait for the nine o'clock roll-call before we could go to bed; & this was in summer. We had to rise at reveille at 4 ½, & did not get enough sleep. . . . (J, II, 85-86)

November 7, 1862

The President should long ago have arrested such men as Fernando Wood. He did not do that which justice required; & now this disreputable man is elected in New York to Congress. So want of vigor sows plagues for the feeble government. So justice is the ally of mercy. In like manner, the impotence of the administration has perhaps involved the country in meshes of party complications which

---

[5] This entry is one of the first made after a break of three months during which Newcomb served as a private in the Tenth R.I. Volunteers.

may thwart the effective prosecution of the war, & threatens agitators of compromises, by the return to power of the party which has been the accomplice of slavery.[6]—It may be that the absence of the soldiers who are voters accounts for the apparent reverses at the polls; & they should be allowed to vote, for service of the country at the seat of war should not be allowed to endanger the safety of the country. . . . But vigor in the administration would have cherished a unity of patriotic sentiment, or held faction in the background. (J, II, 94)

November 27, 1862

The constitution should provide for inefficiency & incompetency in the executive, & for disloyalty or imbecility in it, & thus spare the future the evils of Lincoln as well as of Buchanan. The latter could have suppressed it in its fountain; the former long before its flood. (J, II, 105)

February 23, 1863

. . . At the commencement of the war, all parties rallied to the support of the administration: but its conduct was so incapable, so prodigal, so ineffective, that ambitious & selfish partisans, & disloyal men, gained a ground for organisation of parties & sects which only the good sense & reliable principles of the people prevented from seriously embarassing the progress of the war. . . . (J, II, 204)

May 1, 1863

. . . The American Congress & the British Parliament of today probably contain a much higher average of character than could have been collected a century ago, but they do not contain a man of marked ability in his day. America has no Washington, no Adams, no Jefferson, no Hamilton, no Marshall. England has no Pitt, no Burke, no Fox, no Mansfield. . . . (J, II, 295)

July 8, 1863

. . . A draft is taking place in this state,[7] & the people receive what

[6] Newcomb was slow to acquire confidence in Lincoln's administration. He was impatient for immediate, even ruthless, action on the part of the government. Compare November 27, 1862; February 23, 1863; May 1, 1863; August 21, 1863, *192, 193.*
[7] Rhode Island.

it has done, & await what it is yet to do, with equanimity. Europe is much more excited & perturbed about the war than are any portion of the Americans excepting the factionists of the north whose hearts are with their southern allies or with their party alone. . . . (J, III, 8)

August 7, 1863

I was glad & amused to see by a Richmond newspaper, The Examiner of Aug. 1, that there is some appreciation of New England men in the south. It says, in substance, that "the true Yankee" fights, after all, better than the Northwestern "brutel hords." This is at the same time giving credit to New England valor & making a distinction between Yankeeism at headquarters & elsewhere. It is an instance of a truth uttered in anger. . . . (J, III, 37)

.　　.　　.

In time of war, the medical inspection of men volunteering for soldiers should not be rigid. The strict examination, which enhances the effect of drill & can be afforded by the paucity of men required in time of peace, is absurd & impracticable in time of war. Invalids & infirm persons, of course, will hinder an army, & must be exempt from field service; but that nearsightedness, or stammering, or loss of teeth, & many other infirmities of like degree should be cause for exemption—especially in a conscription; when every man on some accounts is needed, who is drafted—is irrational. A nearsighted man can fire his musket in the same direction as his comrads & can do service in camp like them. . . . Besides, he can wear glasses. . . . Many men are lost to the service not because they cannot be of great use, but because they may not be of so much use as if they were, in some respects sounder. Too rigid exemptions set a premium on diseases & infirmities. (J, III, 38)

August 21, 1863

It is to be said to the credit of the American nation, that, during the whole war of the rebellion, it maintained its loyalty & effectiveness, its enthusiasm & earnestness, without the stimulus, guidance, example, encouragement, of a leader. The President was a man honest & upright in disposition, but singularly devoid of the char-

acteristics of a leader & even, apparently, of the desire to be one. His
moderate conduct; his deliberateness; his want of eloquence, of
ardor, of enthusiasm of resonant energies; his professional techni-
calities in his messages & proclamations at a time when the heart of
millions were open for the highest & earnest rhetoric; his reticent &
rather reserved demeanor, keeping, as it were in the background;
threw the people upon the cause itself. Abnormal, perplexing, dangerous, as this trait was, in some respects, it served the purpose of
trying & manifesting the real temper & caliber of the nation. . . .
(J, III, 53)

September 1, 1863

Providence. A great thing is made greater by its elevating contact
with the lowly. . . . I thought of this as I saw today, for the first
time, the negroes drill in their camp. I have not liked to have our
national uniform worn by this class, nor to have them enlisted in
our army, because the races are distinct, & the white man should fight
the battles of what is the white man's country & of which country
only the white men should be citizens. . . . But it gave me great
pleasure to see the Africans under the manly influences of the military
drill, because it promised to give them character. The drill was not
humiliated but ennobled by its effective good. . . . A race once accomplished in martial matters will never allow themselves to be enslaved. (J, III, 64)

October 27, 1863

The difference in the style of writing between President Lincoln
& the arch-traitor Davis is illustrative, somewhat, not only of the
difference of the two men but of the two causes, & of the two systems
of society under which they were brought up. Lincoln, who got his
education mostly as he got his living; who rose to his present station
by character & energy; who is as upright, as far as he goes, as he is
sturdy: who writes rather roughly & plainly, but with a downrightness,
freshness, & simplicity which beget confidence in the general motives
of the man as well as conviction in the general soundness of his argument. Davis is what would be superficially called a fine writer. His

style is plausible & hollow, specious & false. One might almost say a man seldom acts like a man who writes in that style. . . . (J, III, 135-136)

November 2, 1863

It often occurs in states, especially in republics, that the very rich & the very poor are in factious alliance with each other. The one class feel a sort of independence because they have an abundance of money; the other class, because they have none. One class is licentious through wealth; the other class, through poverty.—The state should bind both classes to the common weal, by a heavy proportional tax of the rich, & by circumspection about the industrial interests of every class. (J, III, 139)

November 3, 1863

Perhaps the President carries into his office something of the habits of the lawyer: a tendency to decide from an obvious or gross array of facts, rather than from a fine sympathy with a cause that induces impressions which assist the mind to a subtle & rapid judgment, & predispose it, generally, in a right direction & to right bias. . . . He is too lenient, too confiding, too deliberate, too judgmatical. The character of a statesman is a balance between that of the judge & the general. (J, III, 142)

November 20, 1863

The newspapers of today contain two speeches, respectively characteristic of the countries in which they were made & of the rulers who made them: the address of President Lincoln at the dedication of the Gettysburgh Cemetry & the speech of Napoleon 3ᵈ to the French legislature. The one, prompted by practical patriotism, the other by impractical ambition: the one addressed to the consciences & hearts of a nation, the other to the vanity & selfishness of a nation. The one effective through its truth, the other ineffective through its hypocrisy. . . . (J, III, 170)

November 23, 1863

The rhetoric of Lincoln is a model of what speech should be, in some essential respects. . . . Lincoln is, doubtless, the greatest orator of the age: a point not now seen generally[8]. . . . (J, III, 173)

December 7, 1863

Britain, as a country, is somewhat like a rocket: small in the stick but large in the expansion of discharge. (J, III, 195)

January 5, 1864

There is a limit in social intercourse which is required by convenience & is thus the good of all classes. What seems exclusiveness is merely economy. Too large a circle of society is an overtask for all. Selection is part of adaptation. As too many in a game is an encumbrance to all engaged in it, so too large an acquaintance is a general burthen.—Was reminded of this by our ignoring the volunteered presence of others in tagger[9] whilst skating yesterday. To have admitted them would have made the game too large for their convenience as well as for ours. (J, III, 261)

February 4, 1864

Wise principle is part of decorum & refined conduct. An unwise act shows, always, both a need of principle & of social tact. Amidst the general honor accorded to President Lincoln for his political tact, far as it goes, & in some respects, & amidst the tender respect in which he is, on the whole, held, it was painful to hear that he demeaned his manhood as well as his high office, by attending recently the lecture of a female orator in the Hall of the Representatives. The laws of sex should be rigidly conserved by all. The more manly a man is, the more manly will be his notions of sexual propriety. About the same time, his wife showed a want of moral sensibility by sending flowers & music to an entertainment, given by the notorious Fernando Wood[10] of N.Y., at Washington, & invitations to which most republican officials patriotically returned to him unanswered. It is said,

[8] J. B. McMaster points out that "The short address by Lincoln has become a classic of the English language. It was not then so considered by the crowd that heard it, nor by the newspapers that published it." *A History of the People of the United States during Lincoln's Administration,* New York, 1927, 400.

[9] Evidently some game, perhaps tag.

[10] Congressman from New York.

since, that Mrs Wood asked for the flowers of Mrs Lincoln: but the wife of the President could & should have refused them. (J, III, 309)

February 11, 1864

The English Parliament has done almost nothing for the improvement & advance of the people in general. What it has granted in civil franchise has been wrung from it by the pressure of the people. It would read like a cruel & exaggerated burlesque, in fiction, if it had not been lately reported of some English Corporations, that the deposit of money in the Savings Banks by laborers was discountenanced & made the reason for reduction of wages. It is the policy of employers in the American republic to encourage the saving of wages. Respect for man as man is impaired & almost ignored, in an oligarchy. (J, III, 322)

June 9, 1864

The re-nomination of Lincoln to the Presidency by the Baltimore Convention is a pleasing mark of good sense & steadiness on the part of the people. It shows that they are thoughtful, judicious, & grateful. The splendid glare & tumult of battle do not dazzle them from cognisance of civic virtue. . . . He is a man both for, & of, the people. . . . He is renominated because he is known & esteemed. Admiration of Grant cannot displace regard for Lincoln.—Lincoln is much of a natural statesman in many respects, as far as he goes because he identifies his official conduct with natural practiveness. . . . (J, IV, 221-222)

July 6, 1864

A conservative in the right & best sense of the word is a man who possesses the principle of organisation under all forms, in all continents, & sees to it that [it] is securely kept or that it is transmitted safely, & for the best in every way, to enlarged form or continent, if such change be necessary. He conforms to the law while it is law. He is neither doggedly tenacious of the past or vaguely considerate of the future. . . . He does not force things to the measure of the abstract ideal, but adapts the ideal to things as they are. . . . As a statesman he regards the civil code as precisely & dutifully, as, as a

soldier, he regards the military code. He looks to the good of the
people under law, as law is. . . . (J, IV, 268)

September 24, 1864

The Presidential election of the eve of the fifth year of the war,
shows the remarkable aspect of a nation so true, in that degree, to
the main need of public affairs as to be ready to elect to the highest
office in the republic a man for whom they not only have a qualified
enthusiasm as an official, but whom they do not wholly esteem, or
approve, as an executive. They vote for him because, under the circumstances, he is representative of the cause & safety of the country.
The republicans cast aside personal considerations in voting for him,
as do the war democrats. Lincoln is deeply seated, in a great degree,
as an individual, & in some degree, as a President, in the heart of
the nation: but few regard him as the best man for the Presidency.
Few of the parts of the country will vote for him with the hearty &
enthusiastic sentiment with which they would vote for some other
men; but all of them will vote for him because he is the candidate
of the patriotic party, & because the election of his only rival candidate[11] would grossly humiliate & endanger the country. (J, V, 36-37)

October 18, 1864

The allowing of soldiers in the field to vote at their posts was a
republican & just measure. It not only continues to citizens, who are
in arms for their country, the right of suffrage which they had at
home, but continues this right to the citizen who would be likely to
vote the most intelligently through the wisdom & energy of action.[12]
It would be cruel, impolitic, & foolish to allow the soldiers' state or
town or district to be injured by the predominance in numbers at
home of inactive & perhaps disloyal citizens, merely because the
soldiers were prevented, by their service to their country on the field,
from doing service to their country at the polls. . . . Pennsylvania was
secured, beyond doubt to the administration, at the October election,

---

[11] McClellan.

[12] One must remember that Newcomb assumed that a man of "action" would, as
a matter of course, make sounder decisions, and cast a wiser vote, than would a
man of thought.

by the votes of the soldiers, & the constitution which made Maryland a free state was carried by their votes against an opposition majority on the home vote. (J, V, 86)

November 3, 1864

The moral significance of rank divests it of its personal & petty evil: thus a manly & industrious poor man does not feel himself belittled by his seclusion from the parlors of the rich any more than a manly & patriotic soldier in the ranks feels himself belittled by being precluded from the tent of his superior officers. He knows that he has exclusive relations, of a kind, in his cottage, as the so styled & perhaps, in points, really richer man has his in his bigger house; & that if their positions were reversed, the order of relation would be reversed. . . .[13] (J, V, 124)

November 7, 1864

. . . War is intrinsic to the antagonism between right & wrong, good & evil. Right force is moral in its very nature. A man must use force over himself; a state must use force over men. War is not against peace, but is for it. It is not its opposite, but it is its counter-part; not its antagonist, but its minister: not its rival, but its fellow: not its obverse, but its double. The interrelation of war & peace is attested by the fact that an unjust peace partakes in its character of the evils, & of the most perverted quality, of the war which was crudely & weakly refused or deferred in the name of Peace. Peace is not only insecure, but onesided, without the resource of War as its complement. . . . (J, V, 135)

November 8, 1864

The Presidential election, in the fourth year of the war of the rebellion was especially remarkable in many respects. A great & free nation then performed its office of determining the policy of the government for the next four years, in the matter of its own existence, safety, & unity. . . . It had in 1860 elected to the Presidency Abraham Lincoln, as the representative of just principles of government, un-

[13] Compare January 5, 1864, *196.*

der threats of rebellion. It proceeded in 1864 to reelect him to the same office, as the representative of government itself, under a war of rebellion. . . . The election was further remarkable in the character & circumstances of the Candidates proposed to the nation. Lincoln was a man known to be upright, prudent, sagacious, & trustworthy, in his kind & degree. He could be said to be unknown as a statesman only in the respect that his character was progressive, & that his policy kept pace with his character: but his character was known to be based on principle in kind & he was thus confided in for upright measures in the future as upright in kind as were his measures in the past. There was little prestige of either brilliant success in his particular department, or of downright energy in his will, to, for the while, impart eager enthusiasm & direct personal relation towards him as an official, on the part of the people. Many voted for him merely because they had no alternative; perhaps few voted for him as their last choice in other circumstances. . . . He was voted for, not only in the main, but almost entirely, on the whole, as the candidate of the only party whose character, position, & professions of principle were upright & patriotic. . . . Men . . . went to the polls as to a battle-field. They went in a sovereign, as well as in a militant, capacity. They expressed their wills as citizen-rulers, by consentaneous choice of their officials & by indication of their policy through them. I voted to day, for Lincoln, grateful for the privilege of thus upholding my country, as, when I voted for him at his first election, I was grateful for the privilege of restoring my country to the policy of the forfathers in the matter of slavery, & for the putting into office of a party of principle. (J, V, 137-141)

March 1, 1865

Spurious magnanimity to the enemies of the country is a sort of sentimental treachery to country. Men who proffer forgiveness, without condition of repentance, to murderous traitors & who hasten to take by the hand those whose unwashed hands are reaking with the blood of patricide & of martyred patriots, compound with damnable sin. Between men who call themselves patriots, yet run to greet merely outwardly subdued rebels, & men who call themselves conquered rebels but who are unchanged at heart, & only compulsively succumb to national power, the country is lost sight of. . . . (J, VI, 115)

March 14, 1865

. . . Recrimation, slander, defamation, & false witness are committed in the name of virtue & right. Iago recognises the virtue of chastity whilst he maligns Desdemona, though he ignores it whilst he dogmatises upon it in the abstract. During the civil war of the rebellion, the factious opposition to the administration, clamored in the name of respect to the constitution & laws on the conduct of the government, whilst they were dumb in regard of the violation of the constitution and laws in the conduct of the rebels. These factious democrats expatiated on the disgrace which the alledged intoxication of the new Republican . . . Vice President had, at his inauguration, inflicted on the country: yet they had never spoken of the habitual drunkenness of Senators of their own party. They ignored the manly services which Andrew Johnson had done to his country by his unflinching truth to it, in a border state, at great personal sacrifice;[14] whilst they commended their own candidate for Vice President, Pendleton, who had not only done nothing for his country but had hindered it & proved himself a cowardly sneak as well as a craven factionist. . . . (J, VI, 156)

March 15, 1865

Napoleon was a sort of natural man on an artificial plane. . . . (J, VI, 162)

April 14, 1865

The national success in suppressing the rebellion is so great that it silences all opposition: it is so joyous that it silences all discontent. The grand . . . triumph includes all. Never was there such a harvest to a war; never was there such joy in any harvest. The happiness of the people is as great as their work.—Was reminded of this last evening, as, during a torchlight procession by a military company, & a college[15] illumination in honor of the times, I saw the faces of women

---

[14] This statement is in great contrast to Newcomb's later opinion of Johnson during the period of reconstruction.
[15] Brown University.

in their open houses. Happiness welled out in them. There is no
note or sign of petty or personal exultation in the whole land: nothing
is to be heard but the voice of noble joy; nothing is to be seen but
the expressions of noble commemoration. (J, VI, 260)

April 15, 1865

By the death of President Lincoln a nation is stricken in the midst
of its joy. The cannon that announced in quick voice the vitality of
the country now announce in measured voice the death of its leader.
The bells that pealed in triumph now toll in resignation. The flags
that could not be raised high enough to reflect the pomp of heroic
success, now droop at half mast in sympathy with a people's sorrows. . . . (J, VI, 264)

. . .

. . . Poor Lincoln's facility, which the country has had some cause
to mourn in its consequences to public good, seems to have had something to do with his assassination. It is said that he went to the
theater against his inclination, because he shrank from disappointing
the audience which had been drawn by a previous announcement of
his presence. A man of bold energy would not have felt constrained
to make that sacrifice—especially a man in his position. The presence
of General Grant had been announced, like that of the President, but
he did not go, & probably did not consider himself obliged to go.
The murderer might have preferred him for a victim, if he had been
present. The death of Lincoln could not have been, in kind, more
heartily felt: but it might have been more fully felt as a larger loss,
if men had felt as sure of his energy as of his amiableness. (J, VI,
265-266)

June 1, 1865

The summer begins with a national fast for the evil in the nation
which fostered assassination. The country must not only clear its
skirts from the stain of evil blood, by the administration of justice to
criminals, but, also, its heart from the pollution of bloody evil, by
the application of moral scrutiny, contrition & repentance to itself.
. . . The closed shops, the suspension of business, & the open churches,

give deep tone to the shadow of the dreadful wrong commemorated in this fast: & clearly indicate the usefulness of ceremonies, forms, & seasons. (J, VII, 37-38)

September 28, 1865

The stern & hearty dislike which the Puritans had for the pageantry of the Romish & English churches was not based in mere associations of it with priestcraft, superstition, & tyranny, though these had much to do with it. It was mainly based on a desire & determination that a man should not be hid in his office; that paraphernalia should not veil character; that the insignia of office should not divert either the official or the layman from the purport & tenure of office; that the eye should not beguile the energy. There was something of the principles of democracy in their antipathy to gilded & tinselled trappings. . . . They also knew & dreaded the tendency of pageantry not only to mere formalism but to abstract & deadly doctrinalism. They saw that undue ritualism both precluded morality & favored monstrous heresies. That they were right in this apprehension & fear is attested by the notorious proclivities of formalists in ritualism to the debased & pernicious institutions & creeds of the medieval ages. . . . (J, VII, 239)

October 20, 1865

The Puritans were not model men, but, as the world went, they were the most heroic men, that is, the manliest men, of their day & of all previous history. They combined more moral principle with more sturdy energy than men before them. They applied their truths to character & to action. They were sober, earnest, determined, active, combative, constructive, & effective in their scope. They knew more of the rights of men than did other parties in state & church, because their relations of principle & conduct confronted the matter, & identified rights with duties. So far as they were free, they recognised, desired, & claimed freedom. They showed their Saxon stock & English breeding by their slowness in generalising beyond their range of habit & occupation. Their faith & their belief were parts of their understanding. They had more judgment than sentiment, whilst the cavaliers had more sentiment than judgment. They were, probably, inferior to the churchmen in social culture & development, but they had better base for social virtues so far as some points of morality were concerned. Their inferiority in this respect was owing partly to their fewer advantages for the highest breeding; partly, to their association of social festivities & accomplishments with fashionable follies, dissipation, & inertness; partly to the grave influence of their adversities, adventures, & original thought; partly to the exceptional & temporary predominance of other moods & traits; partly to the crude tendencies of newly organised habits & institutions. The cavaliers had some of the natural virtues of children & youth: the puritans, of men whose childhood & youth had not become duly assimilated with their maturer age. But one speaks of the difference between the puritans themselves in social culture without exact knowledge. What virtue the Puritans had was more soundly grounded than was that of the cavaliers. They were masculine on a plane on which the latter were not masculine: what the latter were on another plane, which the former were not, is another matter. Social culture is indispensable & vital but it is unsubstantial & uncertain unless it is collateral with general moral culture, & confirmed by principle. Puritans & Cavaliers wanted, perhaps, the better traits or tendencies of each other.—The Puritans were, so far as they went, & such as they were, heroes on a new field of civil & economic life. They were sturdy pioneers of a new civilisation. (J, VII, 301-302)

February 28, 1866

. . . In the disagreement between Congress & President Johnson on the matter of reconstruction, both parties were injudicious & hasty: but Congress had the advantage of more discreet & earnest care against premature reconstruction, & accordingly had more of the confidence & sympathy of most loyal men. They wisely thought that the Constitution should be amended; Johnson even officiously harangued against amendments. They feared to endanger the results of the war for country, & of the conquest of rebellion by hasty measures; they wished to amend the constitution before the presence of representatives in congress from the late rebels should preclude the opportunity, a two thirds vote being necessary in each house: they manfully & patriotically, so far as they went, determined to hold the

advantages of triumphant order & conquest by consolidating & ce-
menting things. Johnson thought enough had been done; but his
thought lacked the heavier mettle of prudent patriotism. The unani-
mous & hearty sympathies of factions & disloyal persons & parties
all over the land accorded with his arbitrary & indiscreet haste. (J,
VIII, 279-280)

March 8, 1866

Red lines of cloud, like stripes in the flag of the country, have been
often, & especially, noticed in the sunset sky, since the war begun;
but tonight one distinct line of white, & another less distinct one,
alternated with the red; blue is always in plenty. Nature is richer in
suggestions & generalisation, than in specific depiction, of some
themes for human art. (J, VIII, 316)

April 30, 1866

If the Anglo-Saxon race is not virtuous because it is Protestant, it is
Protestant because it is virtuous.—The simplicity & substantiality, in
kind, of the Protestant ritual, contrasts as notably with the artificial-
ness & demonstrativeness of the Romish ritual,[16] as domestic worship
contrasts with a partly religious, partly mythological, operatic play
in a theater. (J, IX, 170)

July 31, 1866

Philadelphia is a net work of streamlets, which, if they were not
often discolored & odorous with the refuse of sinks, might be called
brooks. Out of every yard flows the waste of the Schuylkil water.
Pavements are broken into ravines for its accomodation. The effluvia
from the street below my window offensively attests the mixture of

[16] In the 1840's Newcomb was with some difficulty dissuaded from entering the
Catholic church. During his residence at Brook Farm, he hung a garlanded picture
of St. Francis Xavier on the wall of his room and nightly disturbed the other
inmates of the "Eyrie" by chanting the Catholic litany. In the 1860's he occasionally
stopped in at the Philadelphia cathedral to hear mass but seemed to wonder at the
"deluded congregation." In 1866 after a visit to a Roman Catholic church, he
wrote:
"He [the Bishop] invited the prayers of the vast congregation for the Pope:
there was at least one man, who prayed, then & there, that the power of popes &
priestcraft might be blasted." (J, XI, 297)

hydrants & sinks, or the evaporation of stagnant water which has been estopped ere it reached the central rivulet. The law against emptying garbage into the streets does not seem to be enforced. Such carelessness renders a city unhealthy & unpleasant: &, more than the heat, drives people away from it during the summer. (J, X, 27)

August 2, 1866

. . . I cannot look out of the window of my room down into a street on which it sides, without diversion & instruction: the swarms of women & children, & the few men who sit on the steps of groggeries, have the same scene & opportunity as I have. Groups of little children with bare arms & legs; the startling & musical cries of hucksters; boys playing; horses groomed on the sidewalks; the inevitable streamlet, with its branches, of running Schuylkill water, in the middle of the street; an innocent-hearted & lonely chamber-maid looking out of the windows, while doing her work, or, after changing her dress, sitting on the steps, doubtless with artless thought of a neighboring & friendly young barkeeper; cursing & resolute courtesans; the judicial-like visitation of robed policemen at intervals; the fair fruits of the rural districts . . . borne through the street as in procession of triumph, ready for the sacrifice of the table. . . . (J, X, 32-33)

August 17, 1866

One phrase for a left handed person, here, is "a south-pole man."[17] "Nobody there," is a general ejaculation, on the ball-ground, at the passage of a fly-ball in the part of the field where no player posts himself or hastens to catch it. . . . Games are occasionally played, painful to see, because, determinedly, made matters of jest by the spectators, by second nines. . . . (J, X, 92)

August 27, 1866

. . . The democratic party, for a long time before the rebellion, borrowed its creed, & most of its rhetoric, from their southern allies & leaders: the New York World, perhaps the leading organ of that

[17] It is hard to know whether Newcomb misunderstood the expression, "south-paw," or whether "south-paw" was derived from "south-pole."

party, now crudely, abjectly, & shamelessly calls the convention of southern loyalists, that meets here in September, a convention of "mean white men." (J, X, 124)

August 28, 1866

The ill-breeding & unmagnanimity of Johnson's accepting the hospitality of a republican community, accorded to him, merely as President, & taking advantage of it to make partisan speeches, obnoxious to the people, was somewhat southern, & in consonance with his blunt sense of honor. He looked to me, in the distance, at which I stood, clouded with anger & ugly predetermination. The group on the balcony of the Continental Hotel before he spoke was notable. Johnson lifted his hat in his hand up & down in salutation of the crowd, stiffly & angularly. Seward stood on his left in a sort of dilettanti, & lax attitude, beating time to the music on the railing, with one hand, & looking like a mere sciolist. Grant stood on his right with a larger & squarer brow than the pictures give him, & with tempered thoughtfulness & sweetness on his face. Perhaps Grant is a little ensnared by the logic of the Johnsonites; or, is perplexed about it. . . . His & Farragut's[18] were the honestest & most interesting faces there. (J, X, 130)

August 31, 1866

In the procession that escorted President Johnson at his visit to Philadelphia, an association of tailors who turned out in honor of his former occupation, or rather, as they perhaps imagined, of their present occupation, bore a banner, on which was depicted Adam & Eve, who were each attired merely in a narrow belt of leaves or flowers. The appropriateness of this device to the trade of clothiers could only be accounted for by the hypothesis that dress was a generalisation of the fig leaf, or that some people might think that nudity, to be eschewed need only to be exposed.[19] (J, X, 145)

September 1, 1866

President Johnson is so egotistical &, withal, so ill-at-ease, his speeches read, in parts, like soliloquies. . . . (J, X, 146)

[18] Admiral Farragut was a Southern officer who adhered to the Union.
[19] One of the few examples of humor in Newcomb.

September 7, 1866

. . . The popularity of patriotism in Philadelphia seems to be, in part, correlative with, &, in part, enhanced by, elegant & refined architecture & manners. . . . (J, X, 169)

October 19, 1866

. . . The eight hour movement ought to have the sympathy of all sober & kindly men. But most business men will oppose it, because they pervert the industrial system unto a mere scheme of money making & of fast money making. This movement promises, I hope, to be the beginning of a reformation in the whole system of labor.[20] Working men—under which noble title speculators & brokers are not, as a class, to be placed—hold not the mere balance of power but, in some essential respects, the power itself, in the matter of labor & profits, & should have long since procured a fairer & normaller system of labor.—The bar-keeper of the hotel, where I lodge, tells me that he is kept at work eighteen hours every day; & that he cannot get out excepting on Sundays. Yet men are glad, however reluctantly, to take such posts, rather than be set adrift or starve. The predecessor of this bar-keeper was anxious to retain the place, though he was confined in the same degree &, like this man, was especially fitted for properer, that is, for proper, business. . . . (J, X, 344-345)

· · ·

The use of saleratus & soda, in the households & culinaries of this country, has long made eating a matter of physical demoralisation & peril. One is surer of having poisoned bread, cake, & pastry proffered to him by his housekeepers, landladies, & hosts, than a traveller is of having rats served up to him in China, or an old John Bull of frogs served up to him in France. I remember, at a boarding-house table, in the country, once, of being informed that even the green peas before us, were probably cooked with saleratus to improve their color. Bread, now-a-days, generally tastes of alkalies as strongly as ices taste of perfumes. The stomach is eaten up by what it should eat, the teeth

[20] Although Newcomb lived on an income which he did not earn he often expressed the hearty wish that the laboring classes might have better working conditions.

are corroded, & indigestion caused by this pernicious & useless system of cookery. I have often thought if flour & meal could not be cooked in water alone: as Indians probably cook them. Physiologists begin to detect the fungi, which are the results of the decomposition & rottenness produced by fermentation, in the best of baker's, & of home-made bread; so that, obviously, people feed on corruption & malaria. Aerated bread is a move in the right direction. (J, X, 345-346)

October 27, 1866

Money cannot compensate for forced & unnatural labor; but large wages evince something of consideration on the part of the task-masters who take advantage of the urgent wants of men to impose bondage upon them. The bar-keeper of the hotel, where I lodge, whose incessant & almost unmitigated labors, from about six in the morning till twelve at night, have attracted my pity & protest, tells me that he receives only eight dollars a week as a salary; & that the young man, whose character interested me—his predecessor—received less. This sum is not large enough to clothe & feed him, yet he has wife & children whom, like slaves, he visits only on Sundays. The little boy, who waits at a restaurant in one of the markets, tells me that he gets up at three o'clock every day, sometimes, I infer, at one; & goes to bed, at nine or ten. Such practices make a bondage & a fatuity of industry. Although labor under such terms is better than idleness, it should be forbidden by law & public opinion, &, if at all licenced, should be largely remunerated. (J, XI, 17-18)

November 3, 1866

Prudery holds up its head so strainedly & backwardly, it cannot hit immodesty in the face, but aims at the air. . . . Was reminded of this, lately, at being told by the boy in charge, at my inquiry, after looking at the library of the Young Men's Christian Association in Chestnut Street, that a copy of Shakspear was not amongst the three thousand volumes which it contained. I can think of no reason, likely to occur to the cruder members of evangelistic sects, for excluding this dramatist, but alledged indecency in some passages, &, possibly, the mere connection between the drama & the theater. Histories of

England, & the works of such reverists as Coleridge & De Quincy, stood on the shelves, whilst the works of Shakspear were interdicted. (J, XI, 53)

November 7, 1866

. . . The investment of a bishop in his robes, which I saw today, reminded me of a parlor I once entered in the country, in which every article of furniture was covered with a tidy wrought specially for that purpose, during the rage for tidies by the old maid who presided over the room. (J, XI, 70)

November 17, 1866

Extraordinary &, what has been called, crowning performances in fine arts—as in monuments, temples, paintings, & literature—have, perhaps, been contemporary with the decline of the countries in which they occurred; partly because of the fact that they were correlatives of an abstract use of talents & energies in the people. They were, at once, exceptional & exhaustive. They evinced an impracticable addiction to onesided & exclusive relations. Egypt may well have fallen when the industry of its laborers was diverted to the construction of vast pyramids & porticoes. (J, XI, 121-122)

December 17, 1866

The fact that Mary, Queen of Scotts, an adultress, a murderess, & a papist, has engaged more of the interest of people, at large, than Queen Elisabeth, is pertinent to what of loveliness was associated with the more feminine range & bias, as woman, of the one, & to what unfeminine positiveness was associated with the range & bias of the other. Mary's softness, of a sort, veiled her vice, to many. Elisabeth's hardness veiled her virtue, such as it was, to many.— Notably enough, Mary was better known at home than abroad. The Protestant party there took, from life, the impression which only the careful researches of historians have since commended to the world, in place of the imaginary impression which papist refugees from reformed Scotland gave elsewhere. Some news-paper critic on Froude,[21] I noticed, aptly remarked, in effect, that England regarded

[21] Probably a discussion of Froude's *History of England,* the first volumes of which appeared in 1856.

Mary as Scotland did not.—The world is wise in preferring to honor & esteem a woman as a woman more than as a sovereign. The fact that it has done this, with intention rather than intelligence, in the case of Mary, is its fault, but is within the scope of this moral. (J, XI, 253-254)

February 15, 1867

Let no city allow white marble steps to houses: let every objector to this proposition be doomed to walk on the always wet, or always wettable, pavements of Philadelphia for one year, without being allowed to go out of a strait line.—This, then, is perhaps a stranger's cue to the motive of the incessant slop work on sidewalks here; that the least tread sullies a white doorstep. Not long ago, I stepped on the step of a house where an elderly female was laving the pavement in front; in order to avoid the torrent from her pail, heedless, I undid her labors in the rear; she hurled a torrent of curses after me, like a fish-monger, not in Hamlet but, in Billingsgate.—The cure seems worse than the malady; for a tread from a wet sidewalk sooner than from a dry one soils a doorstep. It rained yesterday & is not yet cleared off: yet a dash of water on the sidewalks, over the way, proclaims the servant & her pail. Perhaps another cause of this malady of slopping is: servants are glad of the chance to get from backyards into streets. (J, XII, 237-238)

February 16, 1867

It is a saying that, corporations have no souls: it is evident that they need housekeepers. I noticed to day that the interesting & valuable statue of Washington, in wood,[22] at Independence Hall, was standing within a few feet of a register, cracking in the hot stream of air. (J, XII, 251-252)

March 8, 1867

In the middle ages, society was farmed out to rapacious kings & barons; in this age, it is farmed out to rapacious speculators & middlemen. The centers of oppression & privation were once in baronial

[22] By William Rush, 1756-1833.

halls & ecclesiastical inquisitions; they are now in mercantile counting rooms & gambling bourses. There is progress as regards these centers in some, but not in all, respects. (J, XIII, 15)

March 13, 1867

. . . many women are not very particular in the management of their skirts—for I saw a man tripped up by becoming entangled in the flounces of one, whirled under his foot as he stepped over a gutter, on Bridge Avenue, by a woman who was stepping across in another direction. . . . (J, XIII, 48)

March 14, 1867

The improvidence of most people in domestic economy, as affecting health, cleanliness, & comfort, is evinced, once for all, in the, perhaps, universal habit of housekeepers & chamber maids to refil water pitchers daily, without discharging the unused water. In this way, a big pitcher in almost every chamber in the country holds water which has, in part, been standing in it since the pitcher came into service.—As to the pitchers being washed, even when they have been emptied, few, if any, boarders & lodgers can testify affirmatively. (J, XIII, 52)

June 11, 1867

In order to save the percentage of extravagant shop-rents, perhaps goods might be carried from house to house, or cried along the streets, like fruit, charcoal, & tin-ware. The delivery of letters at houses is one step in this direction. (J, XIV, 12)

July 5, 1867

The subjugated rebels were, at first, appalled at the succession of Johnson to the presidency, because they expected to find in him a man who was true to his word; but they were, at last, more appalled by the consequences of finding in him a man who was untrue to his word. Johnson's untruth to his word & to his party—in this case the words of patriots, & the party of the country—operated more against their scopes as rebels & factionists, than his truth to his word & to his party would have operated. His low tact in tergiversation, in demagogism, & in dissimulation, was such, that he was more than an enemy to those whom he undertook to serve. As between Congress & the Rebels, he was like a vicious & cowardly rider, carried by the trained & eager horse, which he rides but cannot manage, into the very front of the field, from which he, in vain, endeavored to turn him.—A sneering wit might say of Johnson that he was a patriot in disguise: so well did he, in point of indirect legislation, subserve the national cause, which he apparently betrayed & contemned. (J, XIV, 92)

July 30, 1867

. . . While sitting in the Wharton parade, yesterday af$^{n.}$, a crowd of boys came along & played a game of ball beside me. Such profanity, such vulgarity, such licence of performance at their posts, such querulousness, such loquacity on the part of some, & such reticence on the part of others, such precocious stamp of physiognomy, were, as a whole, rare & remarkable. The catcher of one nine, from the first, talked incessantly & gave directions, smoking a cigar while he played; the pitcher, was sullen & irritable; the third base man lay on the ground & was lazy, but was, perhaps because tall, good natured &, though undemonstrative, plucky—a priviledged person, laughed at rather than growled at; the pitcher of the other set looked as if he had a stiff-neck, but I saw, at last, that a short neck gave him this semblance; his own nine jeered him for his manner of pitching, but he was imperturbably quiet; he went by the name of chicken, though he was a big young man; he ran & acted much like a wooden man. The first pitcher got mad, because the catcher did not return straight balls to him, whereat the catcher rejoined that the pitcher could not expect him to serve balls all the time to the pitcher's hole, & that he must get out of his hole to take them. At last, the pitcher, deliberately & violently threw the ball at the catcher, &, leaving his place, went up, in pugilistic attitude, to strike him. The loquacious catcher did not seem inclined to use his fists as he had used his tongue; & the reticent pitcher found that sullenness & pluck were not identical, for, when a noble youth stepped up between him & his victim, his arms relaxed; moreover, the third base man afterwards taunted, & pulled him about, without eliciting any bellicoseness, excepting the exclamation usual in use, here, as a protest, "You are playing smart."—I had remarked . . . to a man near me . . . that I should think things would end in a fight; but, after this émeute, all went on tolerably well, until I left; that is, evidently, there was present more, on the whole, of a conditional heaven, than of a downright hell; & this predominance gave these crude & undisciplined youth more of unity than of disunity, more of peace than of war, more of muscle than of maudlin, more of sanity than of madness, & more of pleasure than of pain. (J, XIV, 164-165)

August 28, 1867

Men must not forget that they may be arbitrary through the predisposition of habit, as well as through the impulse of mood.—I am reminded of this by the thought that in the act of argument in these pages against democrats & against Johnson, I have, occasionally, pondered, during a momentary discursiveness, or even chronic or other doubt as to the motives & principles of these men, whether I could sincerely express myself in such terms of invective & of censure, as I had been accustomed to use, or as then came into my head; & yet that if I consented to use them, I may have sometimes been influenced by sheer wont & bias, & by compromise with an intention of future attention to the mooted case. I do not know that I ever allowed myself to write, under any reserve or condition, what I did not, at the nonce, bring myself to approve, for some cause or in some aspect; but my abeyance of a close scrutiny of these pages, in this regard, leads me to propose this statement as a fair remembrance & warning to myself & to others if I do not make it. If I make any review, this page will be cancelled.—I also consent to let the MS. stand as it is, because the weight of responsibility of judgment for it is thrown upon readers, whatever degree of it also rests upon the writer. Every wise man . . . knows that all writings are to be liberally received, generally regarded, & qualifiedly construed. Not only, may a man write, to day, what he would not write tomorrow; but he may say things in one sense which precludes other senses: he may assert by way of hypothesis, of conjecture, of suggests, of study, or of memoranda; he has a right to be interpreted by his motive & even by his condition. . . . (J, XIV, 263)

October 4, 1867

A wit might say[23] that, the other day, President Johnson was fitly made an honorary member of a Base Ball Club, first, because the club hailed from New York City, a den of copperheads; second, because of his propensity & practice in playing "foul". (J, XV, 27)

October 15, 1867

A man's lungs are to his brain, somewhat as undersprings are to a fountain. I was not surprised at the fine & healthy thought in the sermon, last Sunday morning, of a Broad Churchman,[24] after I had seen him breast the air, on the way to his pulpit, with his big chest. A little head, thought I, will go far with that wind. (J, XV, 68-69)

October 19, 1867

The irrationality & impossibility of basing morality on miracles is illustrated in the rumors which prevailed in many parts of the country in the matter of the death of the assassin Booth. Although the man was found, attacked, & slain, on his flight from the scene where he had murdered President Lincoln, it was for several months noised abroad that he was alive, & instances were given of his having been seen. Probably, hundreds of people believe him to be still in the flesh.—If such gross & wild gossip can find believers & can prevail, in an age of literature, of science, & of newspapers, what gossip would not prevail, & found sects, in ages of legends, of illiterary, & of superstition. (J, XV, 87)

November 21, 1867

Almost always, there is, more or less of flip-flap in the relation of thinkers & writers to the thinkers & writers from whom they learn, borrow, & plagiarise: in that, almost all of the former persons remain more indebted to the latter than they . . . acknowledge.—Flip-flap is the rogue's name for a sneaking game of thievery played here in Philadelphia, &, doubtless, elsewhere. A mean man in payment for a

---

[23] Newcomb has recorded a score of rather stiff "witticisms" in the course of his journal. It does not seem improbable that Newcomb was the "wit" and that he had perhaps made the remark in question in the course of the day's conversation.
[24] Phillips Brooks.

few cents worth of apples or nuts, offers to the huckster a two-dollar bill, &, after looking at the notes given in change, returns them with affected contempt, alledging that he does not want such trash; but, in the meanwhile, the huckster finds that he has abstracted, at least, a fifty-cent note. . . . (J, XV, 227)

November 23, 1867

Providence, R.I.[25] Coincidences occur in characteristics, as well as in circumstances. Curiously enough, after residing in Philadelphia, where streets are styled after botanies & numbers, the names of the first streets, which I read as I walked up from the boat today—were styled —as some would say, after the leading range of New Englanders, Dime, Dollar, Silver, Streets. That the coincidence is incidental, is proved by the occurrence of some such names in Philadelphia, & of some botanical names in Providence. (J, XV, 229)

December 26, 1867

The predisposition of many boys & men to maliciousness for the sake of combativeness, & the general proneness of people to pick quarrels for the sake of some sort or other of fighting, suggests & indicates, first, that warfare is an elementary, even though only mundane, condition of life, &, second, that a war of country[26] is a . . . scope for natural . . . bellicoseness of sentiment & energy.—I am reminded of this, almost every time I skate on the almshouse meadows, by the incessant fights going on there between the Schuyl-kill Rangers & the Eagles, sets of young men & boys, who live on opposite sides of the Schuylkil, & make, in winter, the frozen river a field of hostilities. I always stop to look on at them, with blended admiration, amusement, affright, & sorrow. Yesterday they mar-shalled with larger numbers than usual, & as, in default of home, I skated, for once, on Christmas day, I observed them with almost as much interest as armies of contending men or birds; & I recognised the mercy of a holy war where true men might do battle from true motives, where courage might be exercised without characterlessness. These crude & wayward boys played war with something of the

[25] Newcomb remained in New England for nearly two weeks.
[26] I think that by a "war of country" a defensive war is meant.

tactiveness & tactics of accomplished & veteran soldiers. They would at cause, or at what seemed to them cause, advance or retreat. The onset & the flight, the nerve & the nervelessness, were, in great part, determined by the mien & conduct of a few, perhaps of but one or two, in the crowd. Some were eager for personal collisions as for a duello between champions of each army. They watched & awaited each other like two armies: now encamped as in an entrenchement, now drawn out as in line of battle. Some had clubs, & wielded them demonstratively, like Indians; some had stones, &, hurled them stylishly, like ball-throwers. Yesterday, one young man had a gun, the effectiveness of which in emboldening him to advance alone against many reminded me of the advantage of a handful of arque-bussed Europeans against a rabble of unarmed savages, in the bygone days of voyages of discovery & of colonisation. This gun, & one which it procured on the other side, demoralised the fight as an engagement, by restricting it to the two who held them.—I could never see that either party beat, or was beaten; first one, & then the other, would make an onset, & the other a retreat. (J, XVI, 20-21)

March 19, 1868

The principle of sex, which requires males to give up softness, requires females to give up strength. Masculine women make effem-inate men, just as effeminate men make masculine women. . . . It is as much against a woman's nature & good as it is against a man's rights, & good, to vote in person. She who is so unfeminine as to go to the polls, should be so amazonian as to go to the wars, of a nation. Action in stead, & in behalf, of women was one of the significances of chivalry, & is one of the significances of soldiership itself. Knights refreshed & nursed their sinews in the smiles of ladies: warriors feel the special self-respect of doing the . . . mascu-line service of war. (J, XVII, 84)

March 20, 1868

The demoralisation of unmanly follies & of unwomanly fopperies are beginning to attract general attention & to tell graphically in themselves. The decadence of marriage & even, the prestige of women in society at large are become topics of discourse & discussion. Men are enervated & engrossed in tobacco, clubs, cards, stocks, equipages, dress, bar rooms, & sports; women are making milliner's blocks of themselves, & doing what they can to repel & disgust men by the shameless extravagance of their attire or by the abnormalness of their claims to civil independence;[27] as wives they tempt their husbands to an incessant & insane making, grasping at money for the support of their fashionable frivolities; as maids, they appal young men by the enormousness of income which will be necessary for their maintenance as wives. The madness of men, in respect of industry & of indulgence—making them either, gamblers or loafers in labor, &, indiscriminately, smokers & drinkers, conspires with the madness of women—making them either, dressy spendthrifts or strong viragos, &, indiscriminately, sensationalists & egotists—against love & life.— Indeed, selfishness & senselessness of all sorts, end in self. (J, XVII, 87-88)

March 26, 1868

That indeed must be, on its face, an abnormal & monstrous state & system of society when men, unless they emigrate into wildernesses, loaf & starve for want of employment not for want of energy; when stalwart & ambitious men are paupers, not because of idleness but of inability to find occupation. (J, XVII, 119)

March 27, 1868

The slight, twenty-five cent dinner of a young man who sat at a table with me at a restaurant at which I stopped for a dinner, yesterday, seemed as one explanation to me of the starved aspect of many young men. What between boarding houses & restaurants the chance of clerks at, either proper, or plenty, food is small. . . . A loaf of clammy bread which I bought at a grocers, the other night, smelt so disagreably when I broke it open, as to tempt me to throw it out of the window; but I thought it would kill the hens who got at it: yet

[27] Like his transcendental contemporaries Newcomb was somewhat interested in the temperance movement, in the abolition of slavery, and in reforms of working-conditions, as well as of dress, and of diet. He was, however, greatly opposed to the emancipation of women. For a fuller exposition of his views on the subject, see his entry in Section IV, for May 4, 1869, *281*.

such is the diet provided for people by this improvident system of society. (J, XVII, 122)

April 27, 1868

The beauty in the gorgeous spectacle of men & women—in part derived through flesh-colored tights, made such an impressive scene at the theater, night before last, that the incessant & inconsiderate abuse which, on account of attire, the piece, The Black Crook,[28]—has occurred for the year past, recurred to my thought as an act of impiety on the part of silly prudes, & of mongering conventionalists. The correlation of prudity with profanity is an inevitable conclusion from the correlation of every principle of divine, & of human, art with the mere person of god-erected & god-like man.—The entire indecency of the play consisted not in the dress, but in some double-entendre, unnecessary & untimely, in the speech of the fellow who played Steward: &, perhaps, in the gestures of one of the dancers, in one particular, Egyptian-like, dance.—Not only the morale, but the Maker, of man is maligned & insulted when the mere form of men & women is stigmatised as indecent. . . . (J, XVII, 259-260)

July 13, 1868

"After me, the deluge",[29] is the motto of every man who ruthlessly & wantonly sacrifices the health of his constitution, the order of his country, the fertility of the landscape, & the good of society—which are the patrimonies of men—to his own personal & paltry pleasure, at the present. The immethodicalness & mercenariness which strips the land of its natural & necessary covering of trees, for the sake of speculators in lumber, or of serving the wants of the present without regard to the wants of the future, is one of the sluices through

[28] *The Black Crook* was first presented in New York in 1866. It "created more talk than any piece of its kind before or since . . . the *corps de ballet* . . . caused the greatest sensation. There were a hundred girl dancers, most of them wearing the scantiest of attire. . . . 'The Black Crook' was the first show of its kind on the American stage to make a feature of the diaphanously draped or semi-nude feminine form." Arthur Hornblow, *A History of the Theatre in America,* Philadelphia, 1919, II, 101. In 1871 Newcomb saw *The Black Crook* four times between the first of May and the twentieth.

[29] A saying attributed to Mme. de Pompadour.

which desolation & deprivation shall stream like a flood. (J, XVIII, 209)

August 17, 1868

What with the noise, dirt in the streets, festering in summer rains, malaria around the stables, cruelty of drivers; danger to pedestrians & passengers, & the dust of incessant traverse [horse-cars] are nuisances, & should be, as they will be, superseded by some convenient application of steam to carriages. (J, XVIII, 316)

October 10, 1868

The democrats aptly & consistently complement their prostitution of party to an alliance with malignant sectionalists & secessionists, with its prostitution of the franchise to systematised & habitual frauds in naturalisation & in the stuffing of ballot-boxes. The city is filled with dismay at what would be judicial farce—if it were not an awful tragedy—which took place here, during the last month, of naturalising over 6,000 foreigners, 96 of whom in a hundred, perhaps, will vote the democratic ticket, & as many times at one election as they can. One of the professionals taken up, who was engaged in the service, confessed that he had voted, in one day, in New York, I think, twenty times over. Unfilled blanks have been found on persons, which had been signed by the Clerk, who cannot swear whether they are his signatures. Surely remedies should be found for these monstrous & disheartening evils.—The disregard of the democrats for principle & public good is attested in this notorious sin, which is done not only in the end of their party, but officially, & from head quarters; whilst if anything of fraud is committed in the republican party, it is, if committed at all, done by irresponsible persons & without the general connivance or cognisance of republicans, or, as is said of one Indiana Election, in self-defence, or locally. (J, XIX, 130-131)

November 4, 1868

On election days, the children of this city prepare bonfires for the evening, &, however the election goes, & although they are partisans —some of whom must be pained whilst they are pleased by the issue of the polls—light them & enjoy them. The brightness & benignancy of to-day's sunshine & air after the great nations great work of yesterday, which, in the main was glorious, but in part—as in democratical states . . . inglorious—reminded me of the part of the children in the bonfires, & suggested the innocence & childlikeness of Providence, & illustrated these traits in it. (J, XIX, 212)

November 20, 1868

Never, in the history of wars, of parties, of incidental retribution, or of judicial penalties, was such unexpected & admirable punishment inflicted upon a worsted & wrong side as was inflicted by the north upon the south in the great American rebellion. Revenge was taken without recourse to the means of revenge,[30] & without revengefulness of motive. (J, XIV, 279)

December 21, 1868

. . . In this fast age, presents, at holidays &, especially, at weddings, have been given in such excess & such indiscrimination, as, in at least the latter scope, to have disgusted the fashionable world, through, of course, their gross inconsistency with the original purport of gifts. I am not surprised to see that wedding presents are, at last, refused, in New York—excepting from the family—& that notice to that effect is printed on the cards of invitation.—Holidays & weddings, of all occasions, should be kept sacred from the defilements, allurements, & temptations of greed. (J, XX, 35)

December 30, 1868

Neither, virtue or vice ever lack witnesses in their own behoof— I had scarcely thought & written, yesterday, about the imaginary investments of ancient times by modern sentimentalists & visionaries, than I came across, in a newspaper, the result of the recent researches of some student of history in the Spanish archives, which,

[30] Newcomb was uncompromisingly opposed to any lightening of the hardships which the defeated southern rebels had to suffer after the Civil War. In 1865 when the Triennial Convention of Episcopalians invited the southern branch of the church to rejoin them, he was indignant. The Convention, he said, "went to ask an unrepentant prodigal to meet it, & to join in its feasts." (J, VII, 283) For a further example of his radical views, see March 1, 1865, and October 9, 1869, *200, 225.*

on their own showing, prove that Ferdinand, of the Romantic firm of Ferdinand & Isabella, in Young Ladies' Academies, declared his daughter Juana insane & an heretic, in the ends of putting her out of the way as the successor of Isabella, her mother, to the crown of Castile. . . . Of course I read Prescott[31] as I would have read an historical poem, or a fabulous legend; but I welcomed this attest of the absurd & crude tenure of most history. . . . (J, XX, 77)

January 22, 1869

The attitude, even if it is somewhat exaggerated, of Houdon's statue of Washington has a remarkable moral verisimilitude, which may be, in part, accounted for by the alledged fact that the sculptor, after difficulty in selecting a posture, depicted him in the position which the General assumed under surprise at the exorbitant price of a pair of horses offered to him at sale. Anger at imposition affords a meet motive for the mien of the founder of a republic as against a monarchy. (J, XX, 185)

March 3, 1869

Andrew Johnson appears to be a political pharisee. He is plucky with pretentious self-conceit. His thanking heaven he was a civilian & not a soldier, is in sequence with his plumings of himself on the offices he has held.—Whatever good there may be in Acting President Johnson, he is so chronically & systematically inferior in grade that he is overshadowed by Grant, somewhat as a wretched, but officious, stage actor, a mere supernumerary but a jack at a pinch, by a first rate actor.—The bitterest mortification & greatest humiliation cast upon the present administration, now in its last day, is the pure & active change of current which has already begun to set in upon the public condition. The matter-of-course-confusion & dispersion of lobbyists, rings, wire-pullers, & office-seekers, at the prospect of the accession of a true & efficient administration, is the most cutting of all commentaries upon the plane & prestige of the retiring administration. . . . (J, XX, 305)

---

[31] W. H. Prescott, *The History of Ferdinand and Isabella,* 1838.

May 17, 1869

. . . the unexpected sight, in the procession & chancel, of a Benedictine Abbot, as I took him to be, yesterday, interested me in a way
which, mainly sober as it was, showed me the poetical & romantic
influence which my youthful readings had probably infused into me.
This fellow was no more in his dress, if he had been the creature of
the time, than a Shaker,[32] or a Millerite,[33] would be, if similarly
attired; but legends, poems, & pictures had come between the Benedictine of old, & the Benedictine of today, which tended to intoxicate
the mind. . . . (J, XXI, 154)

May 29, 1869

I was glad to learn from the keeper of Independence Hall, today,
that the wooden statue of Washington, by Rush, which has pleased
& interested me so much, was said by Lafayette to be the best of his
likenesses. (J, XXI, 197)

May 31, 1869

Decoration Day, which came yesterday . . . was observed on Saturday by some—President Grant making the admirable precedence of
giving leave of absence to office-holders for the occasion—&, I hope,
will become one of our national holy-days.—One of the posts advertised in their programme that they intended to decorate the graves
of the confederate, as well as of the union, soldiers. The democrats
strain a mite of truth & swallow a mountain of falsity. They do not,
under any circumstances, see generals, in an issue between country
& party. The pretext of the post—probably a copperhead affair—was
the honoring, alike, of brave men; ignoring the meaning of the day,
which is the honoring of men because they were brave martyrs of
their country, not because they were brave men. . . . (J, XXI, 198)

June 17, 1869

I maintained to an aristocratical friend, last night, who said in
effect, that laborers could not expect to get adequate support, that

---

[32] A religious celibate sect which flourished in America in the nineteenth century.
[33] A follower of William Miller, an American preacher who believed that the
second coming of Christ was at hand.

every working man was entitled to the living of a man.—He objected to Grant's proclamation on the eight-hour law, as extra-official & unauthorized; I defended it on the score of a commendable desire & determination in Grant to administer the laws according to their spirit as well as letter. When Grant found that the law, which Congress had passed making eight hours a day's work, was understood, at the time of its passage, by its proposers, to involve no reduction of wages, he, despite the previous &, I think, crude, opinion of his Attorney General, on the literal executiveness of the law, decided to enforce it as it was meant. Such statesmanship will soon supersede, on its part, the epoch of technical quibbles & legal circumlocution. (J, XXI, 247-248)

July 19, 1869

Young men force cigars into their mouths, as young women force corsets on their waistes, for the sake of false & injurious show. I passed a boy the other day, who was leaning against a wall, reeling with the fumes of a first smoke; he was, in part, too sick &, in part, too good natured & wise, to resent my kindly rebuff as I went by him, of "O, you little fool!" A young girl slept in corsets, recently, & killed herself by her insane & unnatural ambition for an insignificant waiste; her ribs were found overlapping each other. How senseless a thing is sin; & how sinful a thing is senselessness. (J, XXI, 327)

August 3, 1869

. . . In the park,[34] fashion is obliged to pass in review before the mass of the people. Wayfarers sit on the benches & watch the equippages as they roll along. It is a treat to see the horses: the carriages are artificial things, of no account in themselves, however costly, like boots & bonnets; the occupants of them are the creatures who demean themselves to commercial gamblings & extortion.—The houses on Fifth & Madison Avenues are voluntary, pretentious, & tasteless prisons. I thought, as I passed by "the brown-stone fronts" of a cross street, on Sunday, that a man would, probably, be considered as

[34] Newcomb was spending a few weeks in New York. While there he visited Central Park.

eccentric who should keep his blinds open & have no window curtains, in these palaces of tradesmen, as he would be if he wore no
coat in the streets & went barefoot. Yet light is healthier, needfuller,
& cheaper than Saratoga-water & sea-side baths: but it is not the
fashion, & never will be, amongst people who delight in cosmetics,
carpets, upholstery, & false lights. (J, XXII, 11)

September 6, 1869

The gutters of Philadelphia are stinking sinks of malaria. They
are now in their glory after the long drouth. There should be a police
of health in every city.—The bad drainage of Philadelphia will drive
a man out of the place, or his health out of him.—New York is
noisiest, but Philadelphia is foulest. (J, XXII, 96)

October 9, 1869

I grieved to see the slaughter of birds on the neck,[35] yesterday,
by the sportsmen. I like the birds—not only because I dislike worms,
but also—because I like life, completeness, vivacity & song. Man takes
away a part of his own life when he takes away the life of birds. The
very landscape is divested of some of its beauty by the loss of birds,
for the reeds are enhancedly & especially beautiful when their ripe
& tall tops are reaped like harvest-sheafs, by the birds. There is other
food for the body of men than birds; there is no food . . . for his
soul but birds. Men had rather, if only on the score of general beauty
& economy, eat grains, like the birds, than eat the birds.—I wondered
at the skill of a huntsman whom I stood by, while on the narrow
road—the only land in the deluged district above League Island—in
hitting flying birds, as they flew over our heads. When I told him he
should have been a sharp shooter in the war, he said he had been
one for three years; & when I asked him if he saw any rebels fall
under his aim, he replied that had killed a hundred.—These birds
could have been better spared than those rebels; for they were
innocuous, useful, & not unnatural; they lived, & let men live, while
the rebels were slayers of men as well as stealers of men, & were
intolerant, venomous, fanatical & insane. (J, XXII, 212-213)

[35] A strip of land between the Delaware and the Schuylkill.

November 13, 1869

Philadelphia newspapers have been agog for several days over the unmanly, & therein ungentlemanly, behavior of some medical students towards a class of female students, because of co-attendance at the clinics of the hospital. The rude young men plead that they are deprived of their full share of instruction, because of the presence of women, & that the modesty of both sexes is shocked by such necessary exposures as are inevitably made on these occasions. Young manhood is right & manlike in its instinct against the unnatural intrusion of women in intellectual professions; but they show their displeasure & disgust in foolish, childish, & really effeminate ways. Nobody seems to put the main blame of what educational loss may ensue to the students, upon the demonstrators. It is the duty of these teachers to inform their pupils to the very utmost; they have no right to be reserved or prudish because women choose to be present; they should do their full duty, & if the women can stand it, it is weak indeed for men to succumb on the mere question of delicacy—saving, indeed, what natural & proper aversion there may be on the part of men to having women scientifically posted in such matters. . . . (J, XXIII, 4)

November 18, 1869

Thanksgiving-day.—Holidays are other days marked with red ink, mainly in the end of illustrating all days. They are emphasisers of particular lines in the general reading. They are specified notes of the daily music of life underscored for occasional fugues. They are the organisations of over-flow. They are the moral stimulants of moral feasts. They are the licenses of greater abandonment to overflowing thoughts & feelings. They are the merry-makings of culled harvests.— President Grant did right to appoint this old American festival earlier than hitherto, in the season; & the sweet weather seems to seal his judgment. (J, XXIII, 23)

December 7, 1869

Grant is one of those men, whose common sense is a brooding resource to them, in such kind, that they hesitate long before they speak, & speak crudely if they are forced to speak. His first message as President, yesterday, partly illustrates this. Its bias is true & able. He makes the blunder, & bull of saying the reconstruction measures turned out more successful than could have been *"reasonably* anticipated." (J, XXIII, 116-117)

January 20, 1870

I grieve to see that Grant does not carry his personal simplicity & prudent economy into the White house. If accounts be true, the state of a court, certainly that of, so called, fashion, is there emulated & practised. The servants are in livery; the furniture is extravagant & luxurious; & it is even said that, Grant is always addressed as, Mr President, or spoken of as the President. This is, neither first rate manhood or first rate republicanism. Washington practised a little state; but his times were not our times; & he might have pleaded, however speciously, only, that conventional gentility served to make a democratic ruler respectable in the eyes of the world, at a time when democracy was thought to mean ill-manners. I dare say the fault, at first hand, is Grant's wife; but Grant is, at first hand, responsible for it. (J, XXIII, 254)

February 21, 1870

The Irish are such a gregarious, unindividual, & unpositive people, that they may, almost, be said to have left Ireland for the same reason that, when one sheep jumps over a wall & runs away, the whole flock follows. It is a race at the mercy of leaders. (J, XXIV, 14)

February 22, 1870

Bonaparte meant himself, & the state under himself; not, like Washington, the state, & himself under the state. (J, XXIV, 18)

June 6, 1870

The air of the theater, the other night, smelt, as I entered it, as if a concocted mass of tobacco-juice, peanut-shells, old clothes, blacked shoes, & stale perspirations & respirations had been simmered & stewed down by the heat of the room into steaming dregs. All of our public and private edifices are badly ventillated; but theaters are scarcely ventillated at all. . . . (J, XXV, 68)

June 18, 1870

A young man told me, yesterday, that he once went into Wanne-maker's clothing store & when shown a coat for which $18 was asked, offered $12, & got it. This notable instance of the trickery & untrustworthiness of trade, Wannemaker is now the Prince of slop-shop-keepers, & is Vice President of the Young Men's Christian As[n]. It is said that it was the rule at his shop to let no customer off without a purchase, at whatever reduction of price. (J, XXV, 125)

July 25, 1870

The American young men bid fair to be lean, because of their blended fastness in eating & fastness in action. They are determined to work in their ways, whether they eat or not, & even if they have money to buy food with, they do not know what to eat, nor the importance of eating. It is a marvel, if, between insufficient food, & sleep, they live long. (J, XXV, 225)

August 12, 1870

The French system of pronunciation makes a sentimentalist & a rhetorician[36] of every speaker of the French language. (J, XXV, 262)

August 25, 1870

. . . Not imitative art—so to speak—in the person of some Shaks-pear, but original art, in his own person, makes Louis Buonaparte's pompous & crude affair at Saarbruck, the other day, in subtle keep-ing with his melo-dramatical entrance of France, years ago, with a tame eagle on his shoulders.—The French are the sharpest & the sorest of persons in detection of the theatrical & the affected in each other, on the terms that they are, in common, the most theatrical & affected of races. . . . A Frenchman, in some states, is, as ridiculous to a Frenchman as to an Englishman. It is a nation of glass-legs. . . . (J, XXV, 289)

August 30, 1870

. . . I was told, I know not how accurately, that the Red Stockings

[36] Newcomb went abroad to live in 1871 or 1872. It is possible that he was already studying French and planning his trip to Europe.

of Cincinnati, as yet the Champion of all American clubs—which has however been, this year, defeated by the Athletics & by the Atlantics, whom it beat last year—are compelled, by the rules of the club, the conditions of their professional hire, to go to bed at ten; & that they practise throwing, in winter, in rinks. . . . (J, XXV, 298)

September 23, 1870

Both the north & the south were more or less surprised by the great war of the rebellion, because the north did not know the full vice of the slavemongers, & the south did not know the full virtue of the republicans. The north did not think that the south would fight for such a cause, especially under the circumstances; the south did not think that the north would fight for any cause. (J, XXVI, 6)

October 16, 1870

. . . I always think that there was something of this intellectualism & thence, imaginativeness, in much of Napoleon Bonaparte's putative heroism. Like Frenchmen, to whom he, so far, & farther, but not totally, took as to moral kin, he was romantically impressed by his reading of Plutarch's Lives, & of other biographised heroes, &, forthwith,—somewhat as a young pietist takes, for a while, to be medieval ritualism, with which he has become preposessed—he hastened, at the first opportunity,—in part congenially &, in part, French-wise—to play the part, in his way, of a hero. This Bonaparte was a Frenchman in action of a sort. What most Frenchmen are in a war of words, he was in a war of men. Consistently enough, he talked, on much of French terms, of his previous history, as almost all Frenchmen talk before they have acted, & without much acting. . . . He indulged in talk, however summary in kind, as no genuine & wholesale hero ever indulged in it, or condescended to it, or cared for it. He incessantly endeavored to inflict blows on others by means of words. He had so little learned the true power of words as to be afraid of them in the feeblest of his enemies, & in women. His French predilection for rhetoric is shown in his epigrammatism, & in his affected brevity, general mannerism of style. . . . He had not the faith, the generosity, the candor, the quiet self-respect, the general primariness, of a first-rate hero. . . . The tenure of genius has been more, as well as more constantly, suborned to improper pride, envy, personality, & pettiness in France than in any other country. . . . (J, XXVI, 58-59)

February 19, 1871

Noticing two or three young women, apparently courtesans, in the gallery of the theater, last night, I thought, in answer to the sectarian objection that the presence of their class made the theater immoral, & unsafe to young men,—that it were, indeed, pity & outrage to debar these creatures from such a privilege of culture & morality; for, as most young men who sit in the galleries, & many of those who sit elsewhere, have, in effect, little or no intellectual opportunity than what they get at the theater, so courtesans have, in effect, little or, rather no, moral opportunity, in way of thought & culture, than what they get there . . . they serve as academies as well as drawing-rooms to those who get little tuition, & see little of elegances & manners, elsewhere. (J, XXVII, 42)

March 19, 1871

I was glad to have the President hear A New Way to Pay Old Debts,[37] at the Chestnut St. last night. . . . Many things in it must have mentally conspired with what he has seen of the world, especially since he became president. It was a pleasure to me to see him. I sat, fortunately, opposite to him, & did my part in greeting him, not with shaking, but clapping, hands.—A man's presence always excites something of enthusiasm in his observers, in the kind & degree that he is truly heroical, that is, manly; and Grant's face had renewed my liking for him, even if it had, at all, been shaken or worn. I noted, at once, in him a predominant energy which waited on his mind for counsel & cause & which, thus conditioned, makes him active & efficient, & at the same time, thoughtful & deliberate &, possibly, in case of default of thought, slow. His forced & unnatural position as president, & as, ex officio, a chief in politics, seems to have developed something of active thought in him,—somewhat as in other men of less energy, & executiveness,—more at large than is natural & convenient to him: still he has the ruling will for deter-

---

[37] By Philip Massinger, published in 1633.

mination & conduct, &, especially, for resisting what is not cognate & congenial to his proper individuality.—He did not applaud, but paid, mostly, close attention. I was sorry to see him in kid gloves.— What Grant does as President is not, under the circumstances, so pertinent & popular, as what he is as man. . . . Grant perseveres, apparently, against popularity as well as party, as in the San Domingo affair.[38] . . . He does not seem broad & developed enough for a model & complete president; but he is admirable in kind. . . . (J, XXVII, 140-141)

SECTION IV. MAN AND MORALS

May 24, 1852

Literary abstraction is dangerous,[1] because the mind wanders from the body, loses its centre, & is detached from will. The phenomena & results of magnetism show the mind has powers of unknown reach— but while the man is in an unnatural & unhealthy condition, repugnant to order. Literature is of use in forming a man, though it is not such as it should be yet; but the man is for a life which is overlooked in literary exclusiveness. (J, I, 16)

June 12, 1853

There is a way of reading which calls out imagination, & suggests associations, that make the text agreable & serviceable whatever its literal value may be. Poetry thus read is like clouds whose rich & full texture outline general shapes to the eye. But I doubt if this will not induce a habit of reverie & musing, & of unexact observation & consciousness, which would be evil. Will not a simple, open, timely, exact relation to nature & art, give opportunity for the true relation to ensue, for the mind to find out the sacred beauty whose entireness will meet the entire spirit? When I ask of the poetry I read what it has to give me, I find little, I think; but when I read it, abandoned to my own impressions, it is rich with fancies; but the quality of the

[38] Grant's imperialistic foreign policy led him to urge the United States to annex Santo Domingo.

[1] In Newcomb's eyes literary abstraction was responsible for eccentricity, inertia, isolation, intellectualism, celibacy, and the other evils, which reduced his life to a tragic, frustrated existence.

riches & the truth of the fancy are what I doubt. This suggestive or loose reading may have its use in developing the intellectual faculties, in young & old, evoking clouds which obscure for a while, but fall in rain. Its abandon may give room for instincts to arise & operate. The profound literature of life itself has not appeared. (J, I, 29-30)

March 25, 1854

Such is the sickliness of genius that, passive in will & conscious with thought, it seeks to find basis for its incorporeality in a living form of another than itself, a form of promise & hope, redolent of natural life, which it thinks it finds in youth. . . . (J, I, 32)

September 15, 1856

The habit of hastily, or habitually, *recording thoughts* is injurious because it prevents the truths from assimilating with the will. It tends to externalise the thoughts expressed, tearing them from fostering relations, altering their associations, giving them a place without the affections or the causes which disclosed them. . . . A thought should ripen in the man. Then it is fostered & cherished by every due occasion of its own application or suggestion. It becomes apropos to the time; the time calls it out or gives to it. Life is with it, & helps the understanding to see it & its relations. But when the mind quickly seizes it & plucks it, it plucks it from the tree which should ripen & keep it ripe & fresh. . . . Thoughts, when expressed unduly, are apt to become estranged & foreign. The excitement of thinking or of writing or of speaking gives it[2] a momentary prominence, emphasis, & luster which change after the heat of expression. The will then is obliged to recal it, instead of possessing it already, & cannot always recognise it when the will is in its normal state. What was in us becomes without us. Thought was ahead of the will, & presents to the will, such as it is after its violation, a truth which is no longer part of the will because it was torn out of it. . . . (J, I, 74-75)

January 7, 1859

Any one can see how obviously marriage is a normal condition &

[2] "It" evidently refers back to "thoughts."

necessity of man, from the fact that it is the exact reverse of isolation. That isolation makes man a monster, & unmans him, is well known. Marriage is the counterpart of isolation. That principle which makes man, from infancy, a dependent on society, makes him, from youth, dependent on woman in marriage. Any argument for society is an argument for marriage, & the argument for marriage is the height of the argument for society, because woman is the special partner of man, & the home of the married is the innermost sanctuary of society. As isolation is death, marriage is life.[3] . . . (J, I, 136)

June 29, 1859

All oddity & eccentricity of dress & manner are violations of the social order of relationship, of the law of mutuality. They separate a man from his fellows. (J, I, 159)

August 4, 1859

It is a remarkable, & inexpressibly sweet, fact, that in all the Bible there is so little morbid sense of sin. Sin is seen, acknowledged, put away; & the reformed goes on his way rejoicing, delivered from his enemy. . . . (J, I, 170)

September 10, 1859

My nephew[4] returned home lately. One furnace of life's heat went with him. He reminded me anew how affection is the life of man; for whilst he was much to me in constant companionship, he reminded me of the different & far superior & only adequate delights of that other relation in which man meets, not his own sex, but his counterpart. (J, I, 182)

October 16, 1860

The absence of the bosom in man well indicates that the woman was taken out of him. His breast is ribbed with strength like a battlement. (J, I, 257)

---

[3] Compare "Marriage is necessary for man to be like God, to be joined to God, to be a whole man." (J, I, 98)
[4] One of the children of his sister, Sarah Gallagher.

October 18, 1860; N. Y.

Church service cannot be adequately sung by a choir of boys alone, or even where they predominate. The celebration of the Lord's praise should not be confined to the class least able to praise. . . . (J, I, 257)

February 15, 1861

Levity of manner & undue familiarity break or impair the bond of earnest relation. They proceed from lightness & whim, & partake of hysteria. They establish impulsive & loose associations & connections. Love is earnest & wisdom is dignified. Enthusiasm must minister to action. Nerve & muscle must intertwine. Happiness proceeds from health, not from excitement. Action conveys joy into lasting garners. An idle tongue & all aimless relation dissipates that which earnestness would reduce to order. . . . Earnestness has a sure & constant link with life. Levity, like deeper folly & insanity, trifles with this bond, & plays over it. Levity is the enthusiasm of folly. (J, I, 291)

. . . One cannot see a man smoking or using tobacco, without feeling that a corroding worm is in him that will gnaw out what strength he has. . . . (J, I, 291-292)

March 21, 1861

The waves as they rise bear up both light & darkness, & thus man, while in the regenerating state, carries both states with him. In some, evil is behind, as, in the sails of ships at sea, the sail is dark when seen behind, while in front it is illuminated by the sun that shines on it. In front, the sail is a reflection; in the back, a shadow. (J, I, 303)

April 13, 1861

What spiritual culture the husbandman wants to understand & enjoy the music of the birds & the beauty of the blossoms around him. And so with all men to all life. The spiritual gives the real sense of things. It, only, defines. All real significance is taught by it. The spiritual demands a loving heart. Otherwise the man is not spiritual whatever his abstract intelligence may be. A man is as his heart is. Life answers to life, as joy to joy, heart to heart. Life adjusts relations to all things, & thus to the birds & the blossoms. Wisdom requires a wise life. The spiritual addresses the whole mind, as well as the heart: it joins imagination to reason, & makes all the faculties part of understanding. It is the highest generalisation. . . . (J, I, 311)

November 1, 1861

Industry is incarnation. It brings forth the spirit into forms. It organises & manifests the invisible. It is the guage of ability & vigor. (J, II, 25)

November 9, 1861

There is a most womanly beauty in married women. There is a softness, brightness, fulness about them. There is a store in them of that which they give. Their tempered brightness reflects the light of their husband's judgment. They have the ease of place. In marriage is the axis of life. In married people there is the rounding facile presence of orbit. Their natures are brought into the play of unselfish relation. They have the development, the swell, & the glow of movement. Their wills are in circulation. The men are active as men, & the women as women. Celibacy has its pivot in self; or, if unwilling its condition, it only emulates the true pivot like a would be volunteer running after soldiers.—Marriage is very ground of illustration that He has not found his life who has not given it to another. (J, II, 28)

November 29, 1861

In a free country every man should be a soldier. He should belong to an order able & ready to protect his country & his home. Every man should have a man's arm & be in the place of a man. No freeman should be in needs to fight by substitute or hire. The military drill should be part of the common education, & the regiment should be part of the civil organisation. (J, II, 31)

January 15, 1862

There is a great deal of freshness & sweetness in the middle classes. I saw this long ago in my skating & pedestrian companions, most of whom are young mechanics. Perhaps there is the want in the middle class as a whole, as in youth of all classes, of a precise bond of relation & place, so that you can depend upon them only for the time. They are somewhat, in their place, as youth is under manhood. The men of the higher class have perhaps a more manly reserve & attentivity, & are more sharply cut. The middle class do not commit themselves to the exactions of high bred life in loyalty to companions, but are simply good natured & lazy for the time. . . . They do not mature, perhaps, in executiveness of manly will so much as the upper classes, having less complicated & generic care. . . . (J, II, 43-44)

January 29, 1862

Old age attests the spiritual reality of life. Its character, ripening in the midst of physical attenuation & decay, shows that the body is the servant of the spiritual & that time is secondary to eternity. It shows that the man is inside of the body, & that he is formed by life in time. The physical weakness of age is its spiritual strength. (J, II, 54)

February 10, 1862

. . . The heart is the stomach of the brain. . . .[5] (J, II, 58)

November 17, 1862

The spirit is the fruit of life. Old age is the autumn of man. The spirit of the good shows through the attenuated body, whose energies it has absorbed into its own, like golden fruit hanging on leafless trees. (J, II, 102)

February 14, 1863

The greatness of God is the greatness of man, not comparatively & inherently, but relatively & subordinately. Man has not the power of God, but he has the results of that power. The Created is nothing

[5] Compare January 8, 1867, *260*.

compared to the Creator. . . . I remember sitting on the porch at the Glen House, at the foot of the White Mountains, beside a man who moralised in the not unusual strain that the grandeur of the mountain scenery & the immensity of creation made him feel the littleness of man. I expressed the feeling that the greatness of nature was the greatness of man, because nature was made for man, is subordinate, under God, to man, & is the work of the Father of Man. . . . (J, II, 190-191)

. . .

The Greek mythology is rather an acknowledgment of supernatural powers than of Divinity. It shows a sense of organism in the spiritual world. It distributes & locates spiritual principalities in different departments of nature. It is rather polyangelism, than polytheism. The Greek mind was not spiritual enough to recognize unity. . . . They thus regarded their deities as sovereign rather than as parental, as judicial rather than as reformative. Thus, also, they did not know the unities of men & women in marriage, nor of divine & human principles in regeneration. . . . Accordingly, among all savage nations & among merely intellectual nations & classes, the sturdy, combative, defensive, executive form & character of men is better appreciated than the softer & finer form & character of women. Thus the Greeks idolised men & boys, & underestimated women. The intellect of the unregenerate world is disproportionately developed to its affections. It has more mind than heart. . . . (J, II, 192-193)

March 2, 1863

The difference between men who live in the present, & men who live in the past, illustrates the difference between sentiment & sentimentalism. To form associations around a fact or a principle, exercises sentiment. To form associations around what men so like that they wish it to be fact or principle exercises sentimentalism. Sentiment regards truth in the first place: sentimentalism regards fancy in the first place. Men of sentiment square the present to what should be: men of sentimentalism mould the present to what was. . . . (J, II, 213-214)

March 7, 1863

He who only thinks & thus does not live, is as unpractical a starveling in life as he who studies corn & water & does not partake of them. . . . (J, II, 224)

April 28, 1863

. . . To detach a thought from life is to pluck it out of its soil. Many men have thoughts which they would not have had if they had lived aright. Their record bestrays their illicit experience. They are like soldiers, whose extra supplies & knowledge of the country attest their unsoldierly straggling. . . . (J, II, 289)

May 28, 1863

Abstract beauty is like a flower that fills the pasture with weeds. The daisy with its bed of golden pollen & its lily rays of leaves is morally hideous to the husbandman wanting grass for his cattle & corn for his household. All abstractions are eyesores & impediments to a man desirous, as all men should be, of the bread of life. Beauty is not an abstraction, but men make it so by their relations to it. (J, II, 318)

June 8, 1863

There are three classes of men in society. First, those who are manly in standpoint & desire to be reciprocally met & to meet others reciprocally in the normal relations of life. Second, those who are more passive in their own position, but will respond if manfully met. Third, those who are headstrong in moral waywardness, & surlily or coldly repel moral advance & fellowship. The second class are the most numerous, at least relatively so to those in the more respectable degrees of society. The first class should never despair of the second, but they will find that they can depend, more or less, on their co-operation & good will if they address them with tact & otherwise rightly. . . . (J, II, 326)

August 18, 1863

Due reserve amongst fellow-lodgers at public places is necessary. This is right in itself, because pleasant & reliable companionship must be based upon character. It is shown to be right also by the consequences of imprudent & hasty acquaintance. A wellbred person is exposed by premature association to constant contact with disagreable, illbred & uncongenial persons. This is especially obvious during a long stay at a hotel. Illbred people put themselves forward, & make themselves hindrances & annoyances if they are not prudently & steadily met. It is not a slight to any one to postpone familiar intercourse with them until they are known. It is, on the contrary, a conformity to the rules of society in maintenance & observance of which all are interested; & will both, command respect, & be, as far as it goes, a guarantee of social qualification on the part of those who rightly conform to it. Reserve differs from exclusiveness by being based on principle. Exclusiveness is selfish, personal & inconsiderate; is a painted, showy, & empty bubble, & is soon seen to burst. (J, III, 50)

September 16, 1863

Intellectualism exaggerates truth, as reflection in the water elongates the object which it reflects. It magnifies through its superficiality. As the star is brighter & greater in its place in the sky, than its pendent & dripping shadow can reproduce or imitate, so truth in its place in life is brighter & greater than its detatched picture in the thought or memory can express. . . . (J, III, 79)

October 21, 1863

The fruits leave the trees on which they grow, & fall to the earth but not to remain there either. So man leaves the body in which he grows, & the world in which his body abides. The spirit is heir to the flesh: heaven is heir to the world. The falling fruit bruises the ground: the falling spirit bruises the body. (J, III, 125)

November 10, 1863

Sometimes, sham is to be taken for the reality which it counterfeits. Affectation often expresses the secret & earnest bias of a man. Many men should be taken for what they would be taken, because they will soon be that which they heartily assume to be. (J, III, 149)

December 22, 1863

It is often of more importance, relatively, how a man speaks the truth than what truth he speaks. Declamation against evil from an evil spirit detracts from the force & eloquence of the argument. The difference of truth spoken in manly indignation & sorrow, & of truth spoken in unmanly rage & disappointment, is exemplified, to a degree, in the difference in the invective in the 23d of Matthew compared with the invective of Timon in Shakspear. It is the difference of the voice of regret & despair, of steadiness & unsteadiness, of wise circumspection & of headstrong indiscriminateness, of love & misanthropy, of calm justice & of morbid recrimination. (J, III, 231-232)

March 12, 1864

The world is the common, normal field of men. The privilege & duty of life in the world, involves the sequence that, on the one hand, all who live in it, as they are bounden to, must expect to be exposed to the evils prevalent in it, & to all evils incidental to human nature: &, on the other hand, that all who are conscious of particular or general evils in themselves have not only the right, but also are bounden, to live in it, notwithstanding the injury which their evils may inflict on others. (J, IV, 24)

March 29, 1864

Fine life, as well as rough life, is a condition of full manly quality. Delicacy is also a part of even strength. The tree that stand exposed to the unimpeded force of the winds is somewhat deformed & dwarfed. The tree that stands on the sea cliff is coarse & brawny as a professional wrestler, but it is shaggy & crude. On the other hand, the tree that stands amid the genial homestead, fostered in strength by the tempered winds & fostered in fineness by the sun-warmed earth, is the model tree. Man is to be moulded on all sides. As a citizen, he is to be ready in both war & peace. He is to be trained in both muscle & nerve, in both energy & sentiment, in both mind & feeling, & in general effectiveness. (J, IV, 60)

April 16, 1864

In some sense, ideas are the inward shadows, as reflections in water are the outward shadows, of facts. (J, IV, 100)

May 2, 1864

As I walked down the bayside, day before yesterday, saw a naked boy standing erect, like a statue, with his back to me, at the edge of a pond; & the majestic beauty of the form of man, the culmination of art in form & outline, the peerless crown of natural forms, was expressed in the candid, undisguised, revealed, significance, amid the glory of a vernal sky and earth, of a boy. The dark clothed figures of the fisherman in the boats, whom I afterwards passed, seemed, in contrast to the nudity of this boy, to be in mourning. How subtle & comprehensive a thing is human life that it expresses the beauty of the human form in its results, although so much of this form is hidden, like a tapestried horse, from view. . . . (J, IV, 143)

May 19, 1864

How few men think, speak, or write, earnestly enough, with sufficient interest in the end of thought, to find not only reward, but pleasure, for their labor in its attainment. (J, IV, 182)

.   .   .

Religion is so identical with the spirit of a man, as it should be, that a man cannot be a man without being religious. The spirit, that is adequate in its order, is essentially religious. As it thinks of Providence, it is reverent, grateful, prayerful, dutiful. As it thinks of life, it is apprehensive, resolved, & energetic. As it thinks of man, it is friendly. As it thinks of woman, it is altogether manly. Sentimental worship & abstract ritualism are no more identified with manly religion, than is sentimental vagueness for the Fathers of a country identified with manly regard & esteem for them, & with following their example. . . . Action is worship in the concrete, because it is full respect to the will & character of God; full appreciation & acknowledgment of its very end & plans; full compliance; energy as well as sentiment; taking & giving, as well as asking; obeying as well as acknowledging; realizing as well as aspiring. . . . He who does not feel deeply & broadly the sublimity & significance of the Ineffable, cannot feel deeply & broadly the sublimity & significance of the principle of humanity. He who does not worship in due degree, does not live otherwise in due degree: but he who worships in due degree, will be the very man, who, co-relatively with his due worship, lives, in all its degree, the life of a man. . . . (J, IV, 184-185)

June 21, 1864

Reproduction is a primary law of all life. It is as obvious in nature as in man. The summer, from the rosy clover in June, to the golden pumpkin in August, is a field of sexuality. The grasses are arborescent stalks of seeds. The growing fruits are green pods of seeds. In autumn, vegetation, like life, perishes unless taken at its ripeness, & nothing of it, as an organisation survives but the seeds which it exudes. Life could be named sexuality. The world is better designated as fruit than as beauty.—Generation is typified in all the seasons. The spring is salient; the summer is pregnant; the autumn brings forth; the winter is negative because it is barren.—The moral is patent, that the primary & full joy of life is in love. The very consciousness of so central & engrossing an existence would be the sentiment of love. The very condition of such an existence would be the relation of marriage. Men of Genius show their subtle appreciation of human nature, by making love the pivot of the plots of their dramas, novels, & philosophies. (J, IV, 239)

July 14, 1864

Drapery has the significance of merging the human form in the form of life at large. A man may be considered dressed, in this regard, not when he is a nude form, but when he takes a part in common life which vests him. It is well, perhaps, that, at least for a while, the exquisite beauty of the human figure should be veiled in the overshadowing symbol of the more exquisite beauty of its moral sphere. . . . (J, IV, 279)

July 23, 1864

Morality is positive & absolute. It is not relative or conditional, but intrinsic & requisite. Men are adjudged & measured by its standards, whether they recognize it or not. Unbelief is a sin & monstrosity; doubt is incipient unbelief. Both are abnormal. . . .

The superficial & vain assertion that men can not help their condition & therefore are not responsible for it, & therefore do not deserve to have inflicted upon them the penalties of their conduct, so far from palliating restraint, adds, if it were true, an additional force to their danger & to the propriety of their correction. If men are evil, & do evil, & do evil from constraint, then they are not only as mischievous & perilous to society, insofar as they do evil, as if they were free, but are more so, inasmuch as they are bound to evil until they are become free. The immoral influence which constrains them requires, if possible, that they should be restrained the more. If evil is necessary in them, it is necessary to correct & subjugate it.[6] . . . (J, IV, 282)

October 24, 1864

It is sometimes the case, that a man is most superficial on the subjects about which he has thought the most. The very fact that he thinks so much, if it be too much, about it, is proof that there is something wrong about him & that he has not got at the point of the subject. He gropes a long time because he does not see clearly. He is fussy because he is not energetic; he is overconscious because he is not duly active. Right thought is, more or less, a matter of course in right life. . . . (J, V, 102)

October 27, 1864

Though a beast can never be compared to a man, yet a beastly beast is a foil to an unmanly man. . . . A rider is pleasing in proportion to his full personication of the manly & superior traits which both characterise him as a man & give & ensure him the mastery of the animal; & a spirited animal is exalted by its free & sympathetic subjection to his natural superior & master. Big & powerful as a horse is, a manly man on horseback, not only appears, morally, the biggest & powerfullest, but his broad chest rivals & crowns the chest of the horse, & his expressive figure far excels the figure of the horse in real athletism. The form of man is, in itself, a compact & powerful equivalent for mere size in animals. . . . What he has of the animal in him is the quintessence of animals. (J, V, 111)

[6] A modern version of the doctrine of man's responsibility.

December 1, 1864

Undue naturalism is better & safer than either undue intellectualism or undue spiritualism, because it is the only ground on which, & through which, due intellectualism & due spiritualism operate. Naturalism is the very matter of the case of life at issue. It is the thing that was created & the thing that is to be recreated. It is the germ of what men are to develop, & of what they are to be through the intellectual & the spiritual. The latter without the former would be like rain without a soil to rain upon, or like light without an object to fructify, or like a graft without a tree to insert it on. Humanity is the very thing that God makes, needs, demands, & loves, in men. Abstractions not only demoralise humanity, but thwart the will of God in humanity. They destroy man because man is nothing but as he is human. Humanity is always, at first, natural; through moral culture it becomes normal.[7] . . . Abstractions not only thwart the will of God, but violate the divine nature of God in whose image & likeness he created man. . . . Man was born to live under God, not to be absorbed in God; to be found in humanity, not to be lost in divinity. Abstractions are as unnatural in man, as they would be in nature, if waters ran to, instead of from, their fountains; if rays of light streamed inwards, & not outwards, from the sun; if the earth resolved itself into its constituent gasses. . . . Inward things of truth if unhindered & cooperated with by men, by their very quality tend to turn themselves into the outward things of humanity, as sunlight, if unhindered & cooperated with by husbandmen, turns itself into the kernel of the corn, & into the juice of the grape. (J, V, 211-212)

December 5, 1864

. . . Writing, if it be practiced, must be of the nature of record, memoranda, data, solution of problems, hints for others, laws for organisation & guidance; & as landmarks in the practical survey of life; or, if it be more scholastic, & thus more technical, elaborate, & rhetorical, it must be of the nature of more special & detailed culture, & as school tasks for school hours. A man may take themes for study

---

[7] Elsewhere Newcomb has defined naturalism and normalism as, respectively, nature and grace.

& thought, & assign so much time in a week or month to them: but he must be true to life as a whole. . . . (J, V, 222)

December 22, 1864

. . . Hypocrisy convicts itself of dereliction, in the fact that it does not intelligently follow what it cunningly simulates. . . . (J, V, 283)

December 29, 1864

The fact that marriage is moral as well as physical indicates the immortality of the soul. That love increases, though the body decreases, suggests that the soul increases though the body decreases. The physical is a necessary & normal but an intermediate & temporary condition of the moral. The building cannot be built without a scaffolding, but the scaffolding is rejected when the building is completed: the seed must be formed in the fruit, but the fruit rots when the seed is ripe. . . . (J, V, 309)

January 7, 1865

A man must remember, amongst other principles, these four things: that he will have only what he gets & takes; that he must be masculine; that he must show, & serve, masculinity by the effective helping of himself to masculine relations through masculine strength; that he must seek to serve, & to be served, in human good & pleasure; but, last, first, & throughout, that he will have only what he gets & takes. . . . (J, V, 330)

January 12, 1865

. . . The divine economy of Providence reveals the significance of active, prompt & energetic conduct. It accords to men what they take from it. The earth is as a stone unless the husbandman breaks & sucks it. Fire will burn & consume unless men graduate it; cold will wither & blast unless it is tempered. Ores are hid in mines, & must be both sought & worked. Gems are sheathed in films like corn in shocks. Man is naked unless he clothes himself, & foodless unless he feeds himself. Men suffer much more in not attempting to do, than in crudely attempting. . . . (J, V, 340)

February 17, 1865

Life is the nut, which he who lives, both scents & eats: thought is the scent, which he who merely thinks, gets instead of the meat. Even the true flavor, however, can be had only in the eating. The pleasure of using is part of the pleasure of tasting. He who eats thinks less of the scent, not because he does not perceive & enjoy it, but because his eating gives him far more than a scent. . . . (J, VI, 81)

February 23, 1865

The artificial strength of masculine women is as brittle as ice, though it cuts like ice. It may be chronic, like ice in cold climates, but it cannot endure the heat of anything like summer. Its abnormalness & coldness repel in greater degree than its serenity & force avail. . . . (J, VI, 98)

March 3, 1865

There are few men of fine traits, who are so resolutely & normally balanced but that some irrelevant & superficial, but mischievous & abnormal, quality can be detected within them, which inwardly undermines & may forcibly overthrow them. As men, by foolish doubts, will obtrude dark & cold error on plain & cheerful good sense, so men, by other foolish foibles, obtrude perversive & deforming whims on otherwise upright & symmetrical dispositions. One occasionally meets men whose virtues are fragrant & effective in their range, but who bear within them, like an almost imperceptible canker, in an apparently splendid fruit, the wilful germ of a rotten core. (J, VI, 120)

April 10, 1865

Thanksgiving does not forclose supplication: joy does not forclose hope. . . . A man cannot bless Providence for a gift of Providence, without adding a prayer that it may be blessed to him. Thought of this during the ringing of bells & booming of cannons which proclaimed, at midnight this morning, the surrender of Lee & his army. Joy has its vigils, its cares, & its penalties, as sorrow has. . . . The majestic tide of mighty success should not have rolled by unheeded

in the night though men must be awakened to meet it: & it was wise
to make the joyful noise that responded to it, & that summoned all
men to respond to it. . . . (J, VI, 242-243)

May 18, 1865

Happiness is an attest of wisdom, for it is the success of wisdom.
An unhappy man is unwise in the fact of his unhappiness. He does
not know what life is, nor how to live, unless he is happy, or has the
hopeful clue of happiness. (J, VII, 7)

July 5, 1865

The fact that the death of a loved, honored, & sacred person, with
whom intercourse has been dear & near, in no wise affects the substantial character of the past, & seems, in comparison with it, as a
transient & in some sense unreal event, indicates immortality. Not the
presence, the soul, & the relation in the past, but the comparative
evanescence at the death, were, in any sense, indefinite or mysterious.
Life is as positive as is good; death without immortality is as negative as is evil.[8] (J, VII, 84-85)

July 11, 1865

Death has under Providence, its own beauty. The breath ceases as
gently as the tide ebbs. The room where a loved mother died is holy
ground. The desolation of loss cannot impair the sweet & holy nor-
malness of the way of loss. The death was part of the experience of
a cherished being. It cannot henceforth, when thought of in their
history, be dissociated from the humanity & the condition of the
dead. . . . It is as soft & noiseless as an afternoon shadow that rolls
over a rich field & leaves whole in its track the light which it seemed
to break. . . . It is the consummation of condition. . . . (J, VII, 91)

July 12, 1865

. . . Every man in whom principle is not domesticated is a stranger
to himself. He can neither be sure of, or know, what he is or what
he will do. (J, VII, 93)

[8] This passage was written a few days after his mother's death.

July 26, 1865

The relation of a son to a mother is a subtle & suggestive attest of the normal & indispensable law of marriage in the economy of life. . . . Her death would be, under all circumstances, a loss to him; but if he was unmarried, her death would be to him & to her other unmarried children a peculiar & unnatural desolation. The relation of an unmarried child of mature years, to a living mother, is eccentric & abnormal in many essential respects. . . . However much parents are, while they live, to their unmarried children—their children are deprived even of that much when they are bereaved by their death, as in the order of nature they probably will be bereaved. . . . (J, VII, 107)

August 2, 1865

New York. Virtue is an essential of manly beauty & strength. Was reminded of this as I walked through a market on the side walk on my way from the boat yesterday. The butchers were an extraordinary sight. They were a sort of athletic monsters: bullies whom indiscriminate violence & vehemence had partly tamed, & whose demonstrative ardor the nothingness of vice had partly sobered. They were so peculiar, strongly marked, & repulsive, & illustrative, that they would have been deemed studied & farfetched in a picture of hell. Gymnasty without morality turns muscle into stone. . . . (J, VII, 115)

August 16, 1865

Cheerfulness is not an inconsistent accompaniment of mourning. A bereaved man may answer buoyantly & promptly to some relations, as he ever did, & yet be sore stricken at heart in the sundered relation. He cannot have truly loved, who morbidly mourns. . . . (J, VII, 133)

September 5, 1865

Many thoughts are less interesting in print than they would be in conversation, because they are less opportune to the occasion of the readers than to that of the conversers. (J, VII, 188)

September 16, 1865

Undue thought not only compresses, distorts, & angularises the mind through a onesided & forced focus, but it precludes the thinker from other relations. It is like a telescope which, at the same time, strains the eyes & shuts out collateral objects. It aims at perspectives & neglects forgrounds: it forces the sight & neglects the arms: it keeps a man on tip-toes.—Mere thinkers always forget that man has other functions than to think, & other organs than the brain. They take miserable pleasure & pride in what seems to them mental accomplishment, but take no shame & disgust in their general moral perversion. A man should cultivate all his nature for the same reason that he cultivates his thought. He should joy as a man. He should peristently remember that action includes all the qualities of a man, in its broad, profound & full scope. (J, VII, 217)

September 19, 1865

Undue thinkers lose their manly condition, as overused & untimely-used horses lose their mettle & shape. They become hacknied, sparse, dry, bony, spiritless, abject with thought. They are always on a race, & are nothing but[9] racers. (J, VII, 227)

October 7, 1865

Some thoughts may seem very commonplace in a book, which are very effective in a life. There are inky scrawls which are the trails of a living man who has passed on, whilst the track behind him may be uninteresting to some because he is not present. A fire may be burning elsewhere, though it has left only a charred ground behind it. (J, VII, 266)

November 30, 1865

They who seek substance, find substance & beauty: they who seek beauty find neither beauty or substance. Conduct comes from principle, not principle from conduct: complection comes from health, not health from complection. The aroma does not make the flower, nor does color make the gem. (J, VIII, 39)

[9] A racing horse, not a horse, as Emerson might say.

December 1, 1865

Men do not know nature, who do not know human nature. Timon did not discriminate between good & evil in man, & he fell; when he found out some of the evil that was in man, he did not even then rightly comprehend it: & he envied his crude apprehension when like many men who praise nature as a wholesale foil to man, he hugged nature as indiscriminately to his breast as he had hugged men. There is miasma, rottenness, sterility, foulness, in nature as there is in humanity. There is selfishness, cruelty, & savageness in beasts as there is in men. (J, VIII, 40-41)

January 19, 1866

Character is generic. Morality is the general peerage. There will be more essential unison & affinity between two persons, one of whom is more cultivated & refined than the other, but each of whom are moral in principle, than between two persons, both of whom belong to the same social caste, but whose characters do not rest on the same basis of principle. Morality is in itself a refining element. Culture & habit are necessary to its development & pervasiveness, but it is the source of all humane accomplishment & refinement. Many a so called low-born man is more the peer of a true gentleman, by virtue of his honesty, industry, & general moral traits, than is a merely conventional gentleman. (J, VIII, 133-134)

January 22, 1866

As the significance of architecture is directly moral in that it subserves the good of men, so it is indirectly moral in that the scope of its resources & suggestions as an art are moral. It provides a shelter for men: but whilst men are building for shelter they are also reproducing, in their range as men, the organising or formative principles of Providence. Pillars uphold the vaults; but they indicate, also, both that men under Providence must maintain their method of life, & that human art is secondary inasmuch as it must use pillars whilst the primary art of Providence suspends vaults & worlds in the air by mere strength of will. The mechanical & the symbolical are correlative. (J, VIII, 137)

February 3, 1866

Thoughts invest themselves with words according to their range. Rhetoric, like a wardrobe, shows the tastes, habits, & haunts of men. . . . (J, VIII, 181)

February 6, 1866

The dress of men is badly arranged: it is left to the wisdom of heedless fashion-mongers & selfish tradesmen. It seems as if something might be provided to take the place of suspenders; but these, inconvenient as they are as trammels to the chest, are much preferable to the device which many have for getting rid of them by wearing belts, or tight breeches over the loins. The shoulders can bear more than the stomach. I left off suspenders this last summer & relished the free play of the chest, but found that serious affections of the stomach & kidneys would probably ensue if the weight of the breeches were not restored to the shoulders. (J, VIII, 196)

March 14, 1866

The bleaching of the hair indicates the process by which the soul absorbs the bodily forces, & vacates the body. White hair shows grossly that the soul has sucked its juices, so far. The premature turning of the hair attests that the mind has fed on the body quicker than the body could feed & renew itself. . . . (J, VIII, 336)

March 23, 1866

Heaven is ever true, whatever man is. Truth is bright & fair, however men receive it. Lakelets of pure rain bestrew the barren landscape, their fresh azure blue sparkling amongst the stale grasses like a gem on a faded garment. But the beauty of the lakelets is not in vain; for, the turning earth will joyfully respond to it: as the water now glows like a turquoise, the ground will soon glow like an emerald. Humanity must be likewise responsive to heaven. (J, IX, 12)

April 9, 1866

Far more men think & scheme how to divert time than how to

use it; how to pass it, than how to meet it; how it kill it, than how to vitalise it. (J, IX, 74)

April 10, 1866

Sentimentalism prates from superficial thought. It whines that the pretty bird should eat the hideous worm:[10] it does not consider that the hideous worm, is by this eating, transformed into the pretty bird. It mourns at the desolation of war: it does not consider that war is the ploughshare of peace. (J, IX, 80)

April 12, 1866

It is an essential part of all moral culture to prepare men for the good & evil things of the world. Not only the order of action, but of balance & health, require premonition. The general art of Providence abhors suddeness & surprise. The sunlight streams in & flows out as gradually as a tide; the clouds deploy for rain, as armies form into line of battle; the seasons interblend, like colors in the sunset-sky; fruits ripen slowly before the expectant husbandman: & the very lightenings flash from black thunderclouds as systematically as cannonballs follow the fires of artilleries. The mind & feelings tend to be injured by unexpected & unprepared-for thoughts & emotions, joys & sorrows, as the muscles & nerves are injured by unexpected & unprepared-for mis-steps. Men must be taught, from childhood up, to be on their guard, like soldiers marching through the country of an enemy. They must know what to expect, & to be prepared for what they do not expect. . . . (J, IX, 89-90)

April 13, 1866

The great prestige of woman in society & in the household, might suggest, to a superficial observer, the thought that the feminine element ruled. But it is man who accords this prestige to woman, & fosters it in her. It is he who upholds her, knows her, develops her, & gives her place. The masculine element is the backbone of society & of home. The greater power of man joyfully gives prominence to the greater beauty of woman: but it is none the less the strength of that beauty, as that beauty is none the less the motive of that strength.

[10] Newcomb did not like worms. See entry for October 9, 1869, *225.*

An army is not led by musicians though musicians take the lead in all parades, pomps, & festivals; trumpets & drums are not the weapons of an army, though they resound whilst the artillery & muskets are silent; soldiers are none the less sober & grim in the line of battle, because they are smiling & gentle in the procession of triumph. Woman is the mate of man, & as such is, relatively, his equal: but, in some respects, it is the very preeminence & power of man, in his scope, which induces & delights him to put her forward & to make her the leader of some of his relations, as it is the preeminence & power of parents which induce & delight them to put children forward & to make them center of some household sports. (J, IX, 96)

April 18, 1866

It is an unmasculine error to allow fastidiousness to supersede pluck. Many a man hates to make a fuss when he is imposed upon, & had rather endure a petty, however inconvenient, wrong, than make demonstration against it: but the duty of a man is to maintain right as right, & to be as steady in little, as in great, things for the sake of the principle. To passively endure imposition, is to make a wedge for demoralisation in society & in manhood. . . . (J, IX, 109)

April 20, 1866

People frequently ascribe their excitement from morbid anxieties to the nature of the themes about which they worry; whereas the secret of their excitement is not in the subject, but in the nervous agitation which any unduly regarded subject would, in their condition,[11] produce in them. (J, IX, 123)

May 5, 1866

Drowning men, the adage is, catch at straws; hungry men catch at prey: & this is the nature of the hold of most lawyers & physicians on the hapless victims of their traffic. Professions that invest capital in the vices & infirmities of men must, as most men are, be expected to be, in great measure, what all tradition represents them as having ever been, in great measure, obnoxious & tenacious harpies, imposters,

[11] Sigmund Freud upholds this theory of anxiety in his *Introduction to Psychoanalysis*.

& usurers. . . . Society should discourage the evils of mischievous &, virtually, idle, but really worse than idle, middlemen in law & trade, by making the access of all citizens to courts, to a knowledge of the Statute law, & to markets as direct as possible. (J, IX, 200-201)

May 15, 1866

The merely intellectual man sees the fatuity & abstraction of the merely spiritual man, but he will not see his own. . . . (J, IX, 230)

June 6, 1866

One of the evils, fostered by a diary of emotions & general conduct, is unduly concentrated & abnormally isolated consciousness. Part of the evil fostered by a diary of thoughts is less in that kind & degree, but, more or less, is otherwise the same. Both tend to make men think too much of, & by themselves. They disintegrate life by forcing an analysis of it. They demoralise power by confining it in the scope of portraiture. . . . (J, IX, 273)

June 15, 1866

Noticed in a small camp of Gipsies, today, that camping out & pure air were not necessarily correlatives. The place stunk like a menagerie, whether because of dogs lounging around or of blankets hanging about, or because of both, I could not tell. The little children had a look of full blood about them like animals; & the elders were ruddy, though tawny. (J, IX, 291)

July 3, 1866

The effect of liquors seems to corroborate the general verdict that they are, almost without exception, adulterated. A glass of lager beer, which I took last evening, rolled through my veins like a turgid & poisonous current. My long walk gave to my blood, perhaps, unusual sensibility to the foul intrusion. (J, IX, 305)

July 5, 1866

Men must not form opinions where they see only enough to form hopes. They have more opportunity for generalizing on what may be, than on what is, or has been. It requires a wider scope than they can get in the streets or in parlors to acquire a knowledge in full of the average career of men whom they note.—Yesterday, I was pleased to the heart by the family groups walking together in the thronged streets or sitting together on the grass of the park. One scene brought the subtlest relations of life into the national public holiday. Near the corner of the station, a young fireman, or tender, of the cars, in his working dress, & with uprolled sleeves, stooped down & kissed his child, & then kissed his wife, & went to the waiting train. As he kissed his wife, I saw into the eyes which saw only a wife & a mother; & the depths of all nature were unveiled before me. Later in the day, a father & mother sat by the trunk of a tree in the park, with four children before them . . . character gave a beauty to their faces. . . . Such domestic substance was worth ten million times the drudging labors that those parents doubtless underwent to maintain it. Another family scene, the one which suggested the moral of prudent generalisation, was at my side. A young father sat with a fair little boy between himself & wife. He seemed devoted to it, & kissed it. There, I should have thought, if I had seen no more, was another happy household. Presently he swore at his wife; she told him not to swear for she would not bear it; he ordered her to go home then. This latter scene taught me that I had, all day, seen only so much as I had seen. . . . (J, IX, 307-308)

July 26, 1866

The palm of the hand, with exquisite effect, prepares for the breaking of the arm into fingers. It is a sort of lake into which the arm flows, & from which it issues in streamlike points. (J, X, 6)

July 31, 1866

The likeness between animals & animals, between animals & men, between minerals & vegetation, indicates so much as this, oneness & unity in Providence. The juxtaposition of specimens of creation, as at the Academy of Natural Science in Broad Street,[12] reminds one of the collection of the works of one artist.—That a monkey somewhat

[12] In Philadelphia.

looks like a man argues the common hand of the Creator, not the common tie of blood in man & monkey."[13] . . . (J, X, 27)

August 13, 1866

The female partner of vice is, in some respects, more criminal than the male, because her relation implies more deliberateness & organisation. The vicious man accosts, or is accosted, he enters the den of vice, revels there for an hour, & goes away, perhaps never to enter it again, &, at any rate, he passes to planes where his thoughts & feeling are, more or less, alternated, & perhaps mitigated & changed. The vicious woman makes a trade of what a vicious man makes a diversion. She lives for the commission of one particular sin. She maintains a household, eats, dresses, sleeps, & goes in & out with the exclusive consciousness of her foul avocation. . . . Successive groups of men maintain the haunts of vice; but the same groups of women are maintained. . . . (J, X, 70-71)

August 23, 1866

Physiologists, who have experience in gymnasty, now begin to concede, if I remember rightly, that gymnastic exercise will develop muscle & strength even in elderly men: now, let elderly men, who have wasted soul as well as body, or either, straightway begin, & attempt what moral, as well as physical, gymnasty will do to develop & establish a manly will in them, however much they have previously neglected it in either respects. Let the celibate, even if he is older than Benedict & Valentine, study & foster in his heart manly love of woman which includes manly longing for her counterpartship. Let the overeager & onesided scholar, even if he is older than Biron & his fellows, pursue conduct more, & reading less. Let the sedentary tradesman seek strength & shape in pedestrianism & in games. (J, X, 111)

September 8, 1866

. . . A diffident man forgets that pluck is as much a manly duty as is modesty, & that he must walk the streets, & enter rooms, with as

---

[13] In several places Newcomb tries to show the absurdity of the theory of evolution.

much downrightness as unpretension, with self respect as well as with respect of others, with positiveness as well as with pliancy.[14] ... (J, X, 172)

September 13, 1866

The church of Rome is so comprehensively hostile to society, it may be called the organized enemy of mankind. It undermines, perverts, & continually menaces human good by denial of the fundamental law of marriage; by its honor & culture of celibacy, solitude, & idleness; by its honor & culture of euthanasy, ecstacy, & sentimentalism; by its denial of the right, duty, & responsibility of private judgment; by its incursion & aggression in the practice of confession on domestic sanctity & peace: by its maintenance of a standing army of men who have no bond in common with men in society, & no interests but those of their own dogmas & orders; by hostility to liberal education & literature; by its tendency to fierce bigotry as well as to morbid fanatacism; by its ignorance & denial of true piety & wisdom in general; & by its general, & intrinsic, addiction to abstraction at large. (J, X, 186-187)

September 17, 1866

The lives of men are becoming so peculiarly concentrated, intense, & onesided, in an age that especially addresses, mental & emotional faculties, that they are painfully & grossly affected [by] the physiognomy of men. The young men of the times are almost protesquely thin, acute, onesided, nervous, & generally jejune in face & mien. They appear in the streets like bold & extreme personations of their habits. (J, X, 208)

September 19, 1866

A newspaper that can be neutral in critical times has a bias to the wrong side, & will evince it in its general policy. ... (J, X, 213)

. . .

A surly & ill-bred man does not consider that he gives, on some plane, a warrant for neglect to himself, to the very men whose

[14] Such an observation must have had its source in extreme self-consciousness.

proffered presence & regard would be most valuable to him. Well-bred men prefer, on many accounts, the society of well-bred men: but when they extend the courtesies of their circle to those whom they meet at large, they are virtually bid by the rude manner in which they are met & answered, to keep away from people who, in respect of breeding, are already . . . disagreable & uncongenial to them.—Yet this is true only in some grounds. Patience is not only a reaper, but a sower. Good manners may so endure & treat bad manners as to over-come them in time, & implant better manners in their place.—More-over ill-bred men do not always mean by their manners what well-bred men would mean by them, if they resorted to such manners. Was reminded of this by noticing, the other day, at a base-ball match, that a man who sat beside me, seemed gruff & morose when I addressed him, but that he also seemed more or less, so, in his manners to his friends.—Well bred men are, generally, masters of ceremonies, if they manage rightly, in most of what companies they get in. (J, X, 216-217)

December 1, 1866

Purpose & erectness of mien are not only correlatives, but provoc-atives, of positiveness. A man, who indulges in a slouchy & crouch-ing attitude, whether in walking or sitting, is off the center of his power as well as of his balance. Determination to be physically upright favors the spirit of moral uprightness. Few men consider that it is as easy to be straight as crooked, so far as even corporal con-venience is concerned; & that it is far easier, so far as moral condition is concerned. The self-respect, which suggests dignity of mien, suggests dignity of scope. There is a manly position for men as men, in life as a whole, as there is for them in such special relations as soldiers, hunters, or dancers. The influences of life require a manly posture for their due reception & range. . . . The act of will, which throws forward the chest, backwards the shoulders, & upright the head, infuses the whole person with new blood as from opened sluices. Inert men evince that they need positiveness if only by their indifference to positive physiognomy. Slouchiness is an indication of negativeness. The motive, energy, & action, required in assuming

& keeping an erect posture, furnishes both, a base & battery of resistance to inward & outward evils. (J, XI, 186)

December 3, 1866

If a man needs a thing, he can have it: accordingly, what he needs, & can have, he should have.—Men are prone to dodge having, by dodging the discomfort of not having. They take up with evil, rather than mourn for good. They conform themselves to privation, rather than suffer a healthy craving for nutritive meat. They live in pinching cold, rather than kindle a generous fire. They furnish a petty & dreary house rather than build a spacious & handsome homestead. (J, XI, 192)

December 19, 1866

That superficial men should be colder than profounder men is a matter of course, just as shallow lakes freeze faster, thicker & harder than deep lakes. Because the intellect, in the form of logic, is more on the surface of character than is intellect, in the form of sentiment. Metyphysicians are, at once, in general, more superficial & coldhearted men than are dramatists. Shakspear is warmer, quicker, & livelier than Bacon, in that he is broader deeper, & fuller in his condition. The drama is nearer to the hearthstone than is science. (J, XI, 262)

December 26, 1866

. . . A man who rudely speaks or acts, from a right purpose, is, generally, more regarded as to his purpose than as to his manner. Hence, it may be seen that a secret of effectiveness in address is moral determination.—Was reminded of this, lately, at the Romish cathedral . . . when an old woman, over seventy, who had been long standing up beside me, in the heated & close room was so overcome by her fatigue as to be falling: I vigorously punched a man, who stood near the vergers, who guarded the empty pews from outsiders, & told him to ask the latter to give the woman a seat; I exclaimed that she must have a seat. The verger was taken aback at such unusual licence toward him by a person who stood before the powers which held the keys of a papal heaven & hell, & exclaimed,

"Must!" I said, without parley, "You wicked beast, the woman is fainting;" & way was accorded to her. I could but see that I, at least for once, spoke forcibly, & because forcibly, effectively, in that I spoke from manly sentiment. (J, XI, 298)

January 8, 1867

A man of thought may hear something of the music to which the march of life is set, but, unless he joins the procession, he hears it only as the accompaniment, incitement, & commemoration of other men. The music is as the echo of steps which proceed to triumph in service & to the collection of nobly won spoils.—It is a mean & unprincipled pleasure for a bystander, to enjoy the harmonies, beauty & pomp of a relation in which he refuses to join. He should blush to be seen on the sidewalks gazing idly at the parade of heroes. —Yet what pleasure he can take, is his if he can have it, & so long as he can have it: he may beat time with his feet, though he does not march with them: the occasion may bias him towards action thenceforth; he is drinking in through some sense, the melodies & sweetness of manly relations: he is piling up witnesses, in thoughts & sentiments, against his poltroonery & inaction. (J, XI, 354)

.   .   .

The lungs play the part of bellows between the fuel in the stomach & the flames in the brain. They are the draught-chambers between the furnace & the machine-room. (J, XII, 2)

January 9, 1867

Men utter truth more from intellect; women, more from character: that is, each, at first hand, tend to this difference of motive. Accordingly, the thoughts of men are more as prose; & those of women more as poetry. Men deliver truths, as wrestlers deliver blows, with knotty & rigid muscularity of action; women deliver truths, as dancers deliver steps, with rounded & soft rhythmaticalism of action. Men are as logicians & judges; women are as improvisatores & musicians. . . . (J, XII, 3)

January 10, 1867

A man blunders when he presumes on his caste as a so-styled gentleman, to be shabby & odd in his attire: he forgets that eccentricity can seize & injure a gentleman as well as a vagabond; that the law & order of society, not mere conventionalism of place in society confers & determines precedence, grade, & character. (J, XII, 16)

January 11, 1867

Skating makes a boy of a man, & a man of a boy. I looked with delight the other day, when skating on the Schuylkill,[15] at the hearty & simple pleasures of a father & son contending & sporting together in the game. The one played the most; the other labored the most. The one did what he could; the other endeavored to do what he would & each was happy & innocent in his way. The boy, grown up, was as earnest, unaffected, eager, & rapt as an infant, in his frolic & activity: the father, not only lived over again in his son, but became the fellow of his son in a common pleasure & exercise. . . . (J, XII, 19)

January 12, 1867

The scholar makes a wretched &, on its own ground, irrelevant mistake when he thinks that he must smoke, drink, & curse, to be admitted into the society of what rough & convivial men he encounters. Even such scope as he addicts, would lead to the reverse of such policy. Sometimes, on some occasions, rowdies may require coarseness & obscenities in a stranger as shiboleths of sheer self-defence, just as a band of robbers might make sure of a new comrad by witnessing his act of thievery; but a tactive man can better give an assurance of his liberal relation to rowdies & others, by sheer & simple unaffectedness of what terms he makes, than by wanton & artificial affectedness. . . . The very contempt which vicious men have for vicious women, should remind super-refined scholars, wandering amongst rough & coarse men, that partnership in crimes & abnormalisms is no test in the world for either esteem or tolerance. (J, XII, 26-27)

[15] Newcomb was always an enthusiastic skater.

January 14, 1867

Few lecturers & preachers think how much more interesting, persuasive, & effective it is to speak as childlike & sympathetic students at truth, than as pretentious & egotistic masters of truth. A man who ambitiously & selfseekingly manipulates his theme, shows no more intelligence in one scope, & shows much less intelligence in other scopes, than does a deferential, unselfish, & congenial handler of truth. (J, XII, 34)

January 17, 1867

The largeness of the relation of a son to his mother is next to that of his relation to his wife. That his wife is first in his regard, is not only a necessity of the order of all things, but in keeping with the fact that his father is first to his mother, &, thus, that the precedency of his own wife is due even to his mother's precedency as his father's wife.[16] The mother would have the son disposed of in marriage, as she herself is, & must have been. The largeness of the filial relation, especially during a mother's widowhood, is attested in the fact that there are occasions when a careful & wise son may serve a mother's need of counsel & even maintain her womanly character, by respectful, manly, & timely advice. What a son can do in that way, is illustrated by Shakspear in the expostulations of Hamlet with Gertrude. (J, XII, 57)

January 24, 1867

Hell is a generalisation of the ultimation, & of the tendencies of moral evil. Evil is, in itself, hell: evil men are, by virtue of their condition, in hell. Practive philosophy cannot, as visionary optimists pretend to go, go beyond the fact that evil & hell are, & always will be, correlative words. A gambling-saloon, & a brothel, are, in themselves, hells; they are regarded as such, & are entitled as such, even by their inmates & frequenters: accordingly gamblers & letcherers, are literally, denizens of hell. The Eternity of hell is but

---

[16] In a letter dated April 17, 1836, Newcomb's mother let him know that she always expected to be first in his attention even if he married.

another name for the chronicness of evil. Whether evil is intermediate & disciplinary, &, thus, finite, is one question on which some men speculate: but that hell will endure, while evil endures, is an incontrovertible maxim. Truth to science required Swedenborgh to assume the enternity of hell, just as it required him to assume the eternity of humanity as it is. Verisimilitude to the experience of life, requires Shakspear to leave his villains in the dusk of a dark night as on the brink of a fathomless pit, whose depth & duration he could not, & thus did not, sound, & record.—Hell is hell, whether men allow themselves to think that it is an eternal balance to heaven, or that the overlaying weight of heaven will finally assimilate hell to heaven. (J, XII, 95-96)

February 12, 1867

Fortunate young man, whom a fair young woman gladly greets & joins, the unfortunate young man, who looks at your felicity with eyes of sad fire, who envies not you, but your opportunity,[17] who is hostile not to you, but to his own impracticability, rejoice & make the best of your fortune: you are first now, & because you are now first, you may, if you are true to your place, be always first; but, whether you will continue first, because you are true, or whether you become last, because you are inadequate, one is behind you, who is perfecting himself in the art, not only which you have but, which you should have; you are a spectacle of instruction as well as of pleasure, of discipline as well as of mourning, of ambition as well as of aspiration, to a fellow youth, who will keep close to you if you progress, or who will surpass you if you lag. . . . (J, XII, 209)

February 26, 1867

Man has, on one side of him, the light of the orb of truth, in philosophy; &, on the other side of him, the verdure of the fertile & flowery earth, in woman. He stands between a glittering rain of sunbeams & a soft landscape of soils. The earth is not more for

---

[17] Newcomb was tragically unhappy about his bachelorhood. There is no hint in his writing, however, that he made any practical attempt to change his condition.

the sun, than the home is for man. Man interprets philosophy for woman; woman realises philosophy for man. (J, XII, 307)

March 25, 1867

Science will have demonstrated an old maxim, downright or implicative, of motion in morals, when it has exhibited that motion in physics is not only a sign of life, but is life itself.— What morality calls action, science calls motion. (J, XIII, 108)

April 6, 1867

Courtesy, punctilious, though not altogether formal, should be maintained even between familiar friends. It serves for practice, for assurance, for base, & for propriety. No man can always tell that he is welcome, even to his best friend: hence he requires demonstration in manner to, at least, assure him & set him at home. . . . (J, XIII, 152)

April 19, 1867

It does not appear to have occurred to anybody to try grass as a salad. Yesterday aft^n, as I reclined on the ground of Fairmont,[18] watching groups of boys at play, the sweet & juicy taste of some grass which I picked & put into my mouth, tempted me to eat more of it. I eat it, as people eat sorrel or lettuce. I eat in the mood of finding something in season for a man's blood in spring-time. I am not sure but that the effect was exhilarating. The thought that grass fed the brawny cattle enhanced my pleasure in the relish of it. Certainly, it is more harmless than tobacco, even if it is undesirable as a diet—but the latter may turn out not to be the case. (J, XIII, 193)

April 24, 1867

The allegation of invention & superstition made by less superstitious, against more superstitious, sects, as of protestant consubstantialists against popish transubstantialists, reminds one of the play at indignant remonstrance made by some villagers, against a

[18] A park in Philadelphia.

milkman's watering his milk at a spring instead of at a well, when they found that a lizzard had been introduced into a customer's porridge. . . . (J, XIII, 213)

May 30, 1867

Old age towers, amidst other ages, like an old & tall mountain in a range of lower hills, grey with snow, gullied with ancient water-courses, bold with denuded buttresses, mellow with the corrosions of time, & preeminent in ruin as well as size. . . . (J, XIII, 334)

May 31, 1867

Disappointment with oneself has, in most cases, probably much, or something, to do with disappointment with another. (J, XIII, 338)

June 29, 1867

Perhaps it may be said that—he is a man indeed who can be original without being odd; who can move in the circle of principles without falling into eccentricity; who can, at once, lead & be led; who can conform to both the ideal & the practive; who can be both individual & social; who can unify comfort & custom; & who can, by manly & simple conduct, commend to others what commends itself to him. When originality leads to isolation & abstraction, it is indeed oddity, for it is unmatched & unmated; & it is indeed eccentricity, for it is the range of wildness & remoteness not of order & co-ordination. (J, XIV, 77-78)

July 12, 1867

The steady & practive conduct of an urchin out in the street under my window, in persistently keeping with his fellows, despite rebuffs & even blows from them, &, in persistently keeping his temper, reminded me of the lesson which Timon, & all Timon-like men —who are the next most numerous class to Hamlet-like men—might have learnt from children, in regard of patience, endurance, & magnanimity. If every boy should run to the woods in revenge for hard temper, hard words, & hard knocks . . . society would soon be a solitude. (J, XIV, 117)

July 16, 1867

The lives of fashionable women is frivolity itself. Inanity conspires with luxury, inertness with excitement, to invalidise & pervert them. The lives of women who are shut up in eastern harems is notoriously imbecile & trifling: but nobody seems to consider how essentially indentical with these, on other planes, is the lives of women who are shut up in western society. What between fathers who pore over gambling-like business in close counting-rooms all day, & mothers who are never on their feet excepting in heated & midnight assemblies, children born in fashionable circles have indeed poor prospects.—I am reminded of this by the contrast of the row of shop-keeping women, along the street opposite my present residence, to the self-pampering women in other streets, who do nothing at all.—Of course, these are extremes; women being as unfit for merchandise as for mode: yet, the contrast is suggestive. (J, XIV, 125)

August 13, 1867

Not to be everything, is a condition of being something. This rule holds good, as in effeminacy on the part of men, & in masculineness on the part of women, so in matters of mind, feeling, society, & action. (J, XIV, 213)

August 14, 1867

One good from the gibbeted carcasses of traitors, as they hang in public memory, is the genuine unmistakable odor from them which pervades the sentient mind of their country. Such men, like crushed vermin, stink more after their death than they stank in their lives. (J, XIV, 219)

August 26, 1867

A red-shirted fellow, with a cigar in his mouth, whom I encountered as I came along the street in the translucent & cleanly air of early morning, seemed to me an invalid who was pampering in himself a nervous fever, with which he was afflicted.—Beyond cavil or question, there is something hyppochondriacal in the use of tobacco.—This reminds me of the pure & positive tone of color, which art in providence has given to normal articles of food. Corn is white, tinted with gold: apples are white, red, & golden; grapes are purple as if they fed on a soil of crushed amethysts;[19] water is transparent as if it was distilled crystal; milk is white as if it was distilled pearl; & so on. Tobacco has a dirty hue. But this is only a suggestion, & as by the way. (J, XIV, 251)

September 12, 1867

. . . . Recrimination, constant amongst evil men, because every man desires something of good to be done to him, whatever evil he desires to do to other men, is incessantly replete with references to the moral code of life. . . . (J, XIV, 309)

September 16, 1867

The Romish church makes a trefoil appeal to foibles in females through its ceremonialism, its millinery, & its poetasting. I was reminded of this, yesterday, at the Cathedral, in thinking of the impression which the curtsies of popish women at the doors of their pews & the prostration of the devotees upon the pavement at prayer would make upon the manner-loving & dress-bewitched Protestant women, about me, who looked on. Then there were the altars bedizzened with lace, lights, & flowers; the priests bedizzened with yellow, white, & gilt; & . . . the perfume of the incense; the soul-touching music of the psalter, thrown in as the more substantial bread amidst so much intoxicating suck, to wind up the charm, as the Witches in Macbeth would say. (J, XIV, 318)

September 27, 1867

No one man is the same as another man, yet who gets hold of one man, gets hold of the race; so, no one truth is the same as another truth, yet who gets hold of one truth, gets hold of all truth. (J, XV, 2)

[19] Compare Sylvester Judd, *Margaret,* Boston, 1845, p. 285.

October 22, 1867

The degree to which imagination can insensibly go in ecstasy is suggested by the degree to which it patently goes in outward affairs. On the Wharton parade ground, yesterday, after I caught sight of a dead horse in the distance, I thought, or feared, I smelt it; yet, this may have been the work of fancy, for the wind was against it, a bystander did not smell it, & it may have just died, for all I know. (J, XV, 97)

October 25, 1867

Remorse is the phariseeism of melancholy pride. It is cold conceit ironsided in its heart.—I was reminded of this, yesterday, whilst thinking, during a short scrutiny of my pleasure in finding that I had not been quite so froward in some matter as I feared I had been, that phariseeism is as truly predicable of the comparison of our better selves with our worst selves, as it is of our more immaculate selves with our more maculate neighbors. Thanksgiving that we have not done in full what we did in part & what we might have done in full, may be so made as to be as vicious as the thanksgiving that we have not done what other men have done. (J, XV, 110)

November 4, 1867

Character should be in ratio, not in reverse, of culture. The mere worldling regards character as inconsistent with culture: the mere intellectualist regards culture as inconsistent with character. (J, XV, 145)

November 20, 1867

To make sure of gold, make sure of good. What money gives, is given absolutely & forever; what money may give, is, as yet &, perhaps, for ever withheld. A man may, through outward loss, lose his money, but he cannot, through outward loss, lose the training & life which it was the means of giving him. Used riches can no more be taken away from a man than used blood or food. (J, XV, 221)

January 4, 1868

A man, who is confined in a city is forclosed from nature, like a tree planted in a hothouse.[20] He is, essentially as well as virtually, a stranger to the sun & to the soil. He is deprived of the landscape, as is the sun itself, when as an active or a passive, a giving, or a receiving, power. The air breathes into his face redolent with bricks, smokes, & gutters; the sea of light is diked before his eyes like a ditched water-course in a drained peat-meadow. The same genial weather enriched this afternoon, which had made yesterday, & a week ago today, so exquisite & enticing: yet, because I walked up & down Broad Street, within the city, I was deprived of so much good of it as it might then, as before, have yielded, if I had walked along the rural suburbs. The summery atmosphere, without the show of broad fields, is like a splendidly illuminated theater in which a green curtain hides the stage.—A man should be neither a cockney, or a rustic: he should be deprived of neither men or nature. A mere garden enclosed with houses, in a city, is better as a residence than a houseless campagna in the country; excursions to the country are necessitated by a residence in the city. (J, XVI, 72)

January 28, 1868

To make all weathers welcome, make work for them. The snow which disfavors my skating, today, favors my inn-door exercises & visitation to my friend. The cloud, which forshadows idleness to a onesided man discloses a change of industry to a many sided man. The vane shifts at the wand of Thrift. Change of weather is a change of pleasure to a practicable person. (J, XVI, 174)

February 1, 1868

The light of heaven fills hell with horror, because it discloses to them through contrast, as well as through character, the evils of their condition; so, somewhat, a winter's day is sometimes more cheerless than a winters night, because the sun reveals the cold

---

[20] Compare with Newcomb's sketch, *Dolon.*

color of a snow-covered landscape; & so somewhat, broad daylight is dreaded by painted & passé fashionables. (J, XVI, 199)

February 3, 1868

Manhood, like metal, is tested by its ring. As is the morale, so is the melody. The more vigorous the strike, the more telling the sound. (J, XVI, 207)

February 14, 1868

Love me, love my horse, says the jockey: love me, love my head, says the logician. (J, XVI, 269)

.   .   .

Wrinkles are, perhaps, sometimes, marks of strength in conduct as well as, sometimes, of weakness in care. They may, in some cases, be called the muscles of mourning; the bold under-lines of as yet unformed flesh. (J, XVI, 269)

March 4, 1868

Humor is happiness in some of the senses of the sentiment. It is a glee of genius; it is a frolic of faith; it is a fun of feeling; it is a catholicity of character; it is a playfulness of principle; it is a vivacity of virtue. . . . (J, XVII, 15)

April 27, 1868

Hell has its heroes, its saints, & its martyrs. Despotism, Jesuitism, & dissipation, are the fields of its elect. (J, XVII, 261)

May 2, 1868

Many vicious men may be called misers of morality, in that they hoard, in secret, intentions, for future use, unused & under-developed motives & methods of life. Although, at the present, they starve themselves in respect of good, they have something of the same vague sentiment & scope of future reform that misers have of future resource. They fancy that they save their good, while they spend their evil. (J, XVII, 285)

May 11, 1868

Part of the tragedy in drinking is—that wine makes a promise to the sense which it breaks to the soul. The abandon, the humor, the vivacity, & the artlessness of sots seem for the time, to others as well as to themselves almost compensations for the penalties & pains of drunkenness & spendthriftness; but the upshot is imminent & palpable, & condemnation of drink, not compensation for drink, is the painful & gross conclusion. The virtue of wine is not the virtue of blood: a man flares up, for a while, with some special semblance of merriment & geniality, but the inevitable flickering out reveals a consumed, not a constructed, man. I was reminded of this at the ball-grounds this af^n. An athletic young carter made the vicinity . . . light with his jovial farce & merry with his exuberant form; I felt manlike love for him; but I saw that he was putting the elixir of—worse than stupidity—madness, into his blood, & that idiocy or insanity would be the result of his diet of hellish nectars. . . . (J, XVII, 323)

July 4, 1868

Holidays set in like swelling tides in which people sport like bathers in a fresh, full, & flashing sea. Noise is part of the scene & occasion. The bells resound like the billows; the cannon crack like the breakers; the fireworks sparkle like the sunlit waves; processions heralded with peans of music, play at pilgrimages in the track of the glorious past; the subtle presence of the fathers is symbolically assumed in outbursts of sounds.—Holidays are double plays of happiness: they commemorate, in one, the successes of progenitorship & of posterity. Labor is suspended in honorable tribute to what rest has come through the works of the one, & in tentational enjoyment of what rest has come through the conjoint & complementary works of the other. . . . (J, XVIII, 174)

July 6, 1868

Men doubt, despair, & die through imaginary dreads.—To find means, find morality & manhood. Duty precludes all denial but of selfishness & sin. Will & way are as virtue. Scope is as strength.

He must be a mean man who has no means. Happiness is as cheap as health & honor. Substance is as sure as soul. (J, XVIII, 179)

July 7, 1868

The sun-&-shadow-like contrast of a fair little white child attended by a swarthy negress in the back ground of the door, on the marble steps of a house, which I passed yesterday, suggested the correspondence of the difference between races with that between day & night. It was as if the zenith & the nadir each had its children as well as its complection. (J, XVIII, 188)

July 11, 1868

The misery of idleness is a proof of the morality of industry.— Unhappiness is one symptom of the unhealthiness of inertia. (J, XVIII, 207)

July 17, 1868

So much dress is so much loss of lung: so much exclusion of air is so much exclusion of breath. So soon as I opened a window by my bedside, today, & a hall-door in the next chamber, & returned to bed, in the close morning of a series of days in which the thermometer has been near 100° in the shade, my lungs heaved like a life-boat on a surging sea. . . . (J, XVIII, 223)

August 3, 1868

Mourning imparts to a man the physiognomy of vivacious & vigorous hope: melancholy, of vacant & dreary despair. (J, XVIII, 271)

August 4, 1868

There are pharisees of morality, as priests, professors, & prudes; of mind, as writers, critics, & pedants; of fashion, as fops, exclusives, & belles; of vice, as rakes, rowdies, & scoffers; of trade, as wholesale merchants, titled-physicians, & office-holders; of custom, as tobacco-smokers, profane-swearers, & wine-bibblers; of routine, as mannerists, imitators, & gossips . . . of muscle, as prize-fighters, champion-rowers, & expert gymnasts.—Phariseeism is predicable of all persons who prostitute principle to pride & who put self between others & the general scope. A pharisee thanks providence—not for making all men but—for making himself peerless. (J, XVIII, 275-276)

.　　.　　.

A man will not wonder at the slow recognition of him by strangers, when he reflects that they are possibly wondering whether he is not a pickpocket. (J, XVIII, 279)

August 13, 1868

A man should be as much ashamed to give to beggars,[21] as he should be ashamed to beg. It should be harder to compromise with principle, than with pride. (J, XVIII, 303)

August 18, 1868

As I stood, yesterday afternoon, amongst boys & young men, at a game of ball, & thought of the offshoots of vices from virtues, I thought that the doctrine of the unpardonableness of sin, & of arbitrary punishment, on the part of providence, for sin, was, indeed, the sin against the Holy Ghost. Vices may be called one-sided virtues. One man sees a warm coat, & he steals it with the same end in view that the owner bought it. He is a thief. He recognises the rights of persons to clothing, not, in another's case, of persons to property. Another hears that there is money in the pockets of a traveler, & he kills the traveler for the sake of the treasure, with the same end in view that the traveler was conveying it & had collected it. He is a murderer. He sees the connection between money & life, not, in another's case, between life & property; he takes care, as he thinks, of his own life, but ignores the life of his victim. Sensualism is a vice founded in the virtue of sexuality. And so on, through all the sins. . . . Not to be a fair man, is to be a fiendish man. No offender against other men is so obtuse as not to see the unrighteousness of offence against himself. Onesidedness is monstrosity in soul as it is in body. Negation in virtue implied positiveness in vice. And so on through all the enormity & culpability of sin. (J, XVIII, 320-321)

[21] Both Emerson and Thoreau expressed similar principles.

September 19, 1868

Miserlike people have not learned the cunning of measuring their gains by good.—I, who am prudent in my expenditure, living upon my income, & looking to a home, have begun to reckon generous & beneficial pittances as investments, not as expenditures. This is the miracle of miracles to turn gold into good. The transmutation of metals is nothing to that of morals. Iron is, in itself, a metal as is gold; but gold, in itself, is not good. Lucer is a fiction; life is a reality. (J, XIX, 66)

September 28, 1868

Mourning keeps the heart free & open as a load-stone for the reciprocal attractions of life. It enables it to feel for what it has not got; & it enables it to feel for what is near it, or comes within its range, but might, if the heart was not in a vigilant & attractional condition, stay, or pass by, unnoticed & unmet. (J, XIX, 87)

November 7, 1868

The streets of cities should be broad for the sake of sunshine as well as of ventilation, convenience, & beauty.—I gladly left Arch, today, which is a broader street than Chestnut, for broader Market, in order to get the sun in the chilly afternoon, on the northern sidewalk. But even Market is not broad enough. The angles of streets should, if possible, be compassed with reference to the winter's sun. Winter is four or five months long; & the comfort & cheerfulness of cities wants the warmth of the sun in winter, as it wants the general vitalism of the sun all the year round. (J, XIX, 228-229)

November 9, 1868

Vice makes speech obscene on the terms that it makes scope obscene. What is virtuous in action is, other things being equal, virtuous in mention. If it is, under all circumstances, obscene to speak of certain things it is, under all circumstances, obscene to do certain things. Inasmuch as the counterpartship of the sexes is a supernally appointed condition of the human constitution it cannot be vulgarity to discreetly & fondly speak of it, but it must be profanity to call manly sentiment & speech concerning it vulgar & filthy. Obscenity applies to lust, or lewdness, not to love, or counter-partship. Bawdy speech is that speech which deals in perversion & in prostitution, not in candor & in play. It is based on the manners & morals of a brothel. I passed a man, on Chestnut St. the other night who was singing, in a crowd, a song, which I held to be obscene, because it commemorated vicious conduct, not because, it was expressed in what is called vulgar language[22]. . . . (J, XIX, 233-234)

November 16, 1868

. . . I saw a scene which became an asylum of lunatics & of idiots. Young men, wan, depleted, frenzied, vacant in face, stary in look, brain-shattered, through drink, were singing & capering together. The sight would have been sickening to them as it was to me[23] if they had not submerged the best part of their senses in whiskey. . . . (J, XIX, 260)

November 30, 1868

The beauty of a pugilist, trained for mere & avoidable fight with pitiless rivals, is like the beauty of a tree, formed in fierce combats, at exposed situations, with the blasts of inclement & inhospitable winds. As all the expressiveness of a gnarled tree, stripped for the encounters of winter, cannot make up for its deprivation of graceful symmetry & of genial verdure; so all the expressiveness of a sinewy pugilist cannot make up for his deprivation of general morale.—All the muscles, which gymnastic & other collateral exercises of body develop, must be appropriated by manly motives & courses of life, or they do not form the physique of a proper &, thence, truly & fully beautiful, man. (J, XIX, 319)

December 7, 1868

There is something soothing to the nerves in oysters, especially

---

[22] Newcomb used similar arguments to rationalise his insertion of his "Songs of Love" in his *Journals*.

[23] Newcomb was not present in this group, but joined several people who were peering through a fence at a drunken party.

raw, which suggested the discovery of a narcotic element in them. (J, XIX, 344)

December 12, 1868

The man who labors for wages, gets work as well as wages. The man who lives on an income, gets wages without work. Wages & work normally belong to each other in a kind & degree that is not generally conceded & considered. And work & virtue intrinsically belong to each other more than is even generally suspected. Few laborers duly consider that, in some collateral respects, work is a privilege & a pleasure in itself, as in main respects, it is such in its ends. (J, XX, 3)

December 19, 1868

A man, who deals in moral principles is quick, & subtle, & suggestive, in the finding of illustrations for them in what he sees, hears, & reads, &, above all, enacts.—One advantage of carrying some choice excerpts from authors, as from Shakspear, in the memory, &, thence, of occasional recitation of them, is the inevitable tallying of them with prominent thoughts concerning principles which are operative in the general consciousness & conduct. I continually find illustrations of truths in the passages which I recite although the passages neither directly suggested the truths to me, nor, until I had carried the truth to them, operatively indicated them to me. (J, XX, 27)

.   .   .

The exquisitely irregular, but graceful & effective, markings out, interlineations, & groupings of the trachea of some little insect, which I saw, in a microscope, yesterday, palpably demonstrated the inefficiency, deformity, monotony, & arbitrariness of the angular, formal, & equal lines which most architects use in ceilings, frescoes, & pavements. It was a model of suggestive, & morally symmetrical, inventiveness. It was a study of variousness & of general expression, which furnished continually ample occupation & relief to the eye, instead of, like the vaulting of many pretentious edifices, a . . . stiff uniformity of lines which the eye takes in at a glance, & which it does not need or wish to look at but once. (J, XX, 27-28)

December 23, 1868

People influence each other, more or less, especially where there is more positiveness in one party than in another, by means of conscious presence as well as of conscious performance. Forthputting & interaction are involuntary as well as voluntary in their tenure & operation. Every person has a pervasive effect on society & in nature, through his mere principle & power of life. . . . (J, XX, 41)

January 2, 1869

If a hale & hearty old man . . . —which every old man should be— an aged youth, is not regarded & met at either his own virtue or valuation, he must be duly content, under proper conditions & exceptions, to pass as a youth in disguise who does not, in that plight, expect to be fully recognised & fellowshipped as what he is. . . . (J, XX, 97)

January 4, 1869

I, yesterday, commenced the third committing of the Psalms to memory, having finished the second course, on the last Sunday of the last year, which I begun with the beginning of 1864. I felt that the good of my general morale, as well as of my memory, would not allow me to give [up] a practice which has been, on the whole, of great use to me. (J, XX, 103)

January 6, 1869

If matter had intelligence & activity in, & of, itself, it would be manlikely intelligent & active apart from man. The stuff that forms the eye of man would see in trees as well as in men; & it would see through beasts as it sees through men. Humanity could be engrafted on stones through human blood; & the constituents of the blood would, irrespective of their previous connection with men, serve whatever animate or inanimate object they are in, as they serve men. If matter makes man, all matter would be man. The fact that circumstances alter cases does not effect the essential point, in its own place, of this proposition. Different proportions & conditions of the same elementary matter make different objects in nature: as—so much oxygen & hydrogen form water—so much forms earth—so much forms air—& so on; but there is nothing of the integral & positive difference between matter in one natural object & in another, as there is between matter itself & man himself, & as there is between matter in itself & in man. (J, XX, 116)

January 19, 1869

Form is to humanity, what conduct is to morality.—In some sense, form may be said to be invisible conduct; & conduct, to be invisible form. (J, XX, 171)

February 9, 1869

The unnaturalness, risk, & discomfort of foreign travel, &, especially, the abnormal life which it requires in its ministers, as sailors, & firemen, makes one seriously ponder whether he has any moral right to go over the sea. Temporary nomadism in travellers, &, far worse, professional nomadism in mariners, are issues in the question.—It is something to say in justification of using established methods of foreign travel that they support sailors, as well as society, & give them action, poor as it is, which is better than no action: that they bring emigrants from an old & overstocked, to a new & ample country, & introduce the nations of misgovernment to a government of men.—It is manly, because, moral, to duly consider such questions. It does not imply fanaticism & morbidness to be exact regarders of the social constitution, just as it does not to be steadfastly true to marriage during abode amongst polygamists & savages as well as amongst monogamists[24]. . . . (J, XX, 243)

February 12, 1869

Soreness is the result of extreme sensitiveness of sense. Sensitiveness of sense is the result of extreme sensation of sense. Accordingly, an over-worked brain is an overwrought brain, &, as such, is, in one, very sore & very sensitive. Extraordinary excessive, concentrated

[24] Three years later Newcomb fulfilled his youthful dream of going to Europe.

& aggravated thought & feeling, sentiment & emotionalism, induces exaggerated & morbidly entertained consciousness & conviction. The ecstasies of anger, & of the passions in general, are similar in tenure & operation, so far as nervousness, hallucination, & perversion are concerned, to the ecstacies of the sentiments. The phenomena of a sore head are similar, other things being equal, to those of a sore heart. In the temper of mind, as of metal, loss of condition is loss of caliber. (J, XX, 250)

March 23 1869

Old age is far more a matter of custom & of conventionalism than of condition. After a certain time of life, people are expected to put on senility, just as in certain places they are expected to put on solemnity. Moreover, few or no people, train themselves for old age, & so do not easily take to it. They are not versed in the habit of it. As children are trained for early manhood, early manhood should be trained for late manhood.—Old persons are expected to restrain, to deny, to forclose, to alter, & to pervert themselves. Though they are vivacious & frolicksome, they are mocked if they do not seem grave & listless; though they are strong, they are jeered at if they show strength; though they love color in dress, they are ridiculed if they do not attire in mourning; though their appetite is as ardent as it is apprehensive, they are slandered if they do not abstain. The remedy is in their hands. They must be positive. They must combine, & support each other. They must be true to themselves & to their age. They must make themselves respected because of their life. They must look to action, not to approbativeness, for resource & re-gard. Their force will become their fame. . . . (J, XXI, 3)

March 31, 1869

Many persons heedlessly & moodily reproach one another for affecting manners. They do not consider that the putting on of man-ners is the putting on of morals. Most people are everything human that they are, almost wholly because of what much, or of what little, of manners they have. A common & silly fault is practiced in the accrediting of manners, with the evils of the men who doff & don them. If a person is gruff at home who is genial abroad, the uselessness of manners, instead of the inconstancy, &, thence, the manner-lessness, of the person, is generally commemorated & stigmatised. But for manners, the person would be gruff everywhere: with manners, he would be genial everywhere. . . . (J, XXI, 34)

April 16, 1869

Science should seek some substitute for fire in the culinary department. The grass supports powerful bulls, happy sheep, & nomadic buffaloes, but it is not boiled, or baked grass. The water which stews vegetables acts as a sort of gastric juice upon them, before they get into the stomach of man, &, so, extracts, like it, but without it, the most nourishing portions of them. (J, XXI, 71)

April 22, 1869

Manly apperance for the sake of scope, not of show, is the ambition of a man. Many men affect something of manly manner in the ends of approbativeness, not of action. They are proud of their mien, or mood, or gait, not because of the possession & performance of strong power as men in life, but of the sensation of sentimental consciousness as men in semblance. The superficial tenure of much prevalent manner & culture in society is attested in the aversion of many, so called, first class people to any demonstration of manner in other classes, which is like their own. If they took to manners as to morals, they would rejoice in the prevalence of good manners as much as in that of good morals.—A man's respect for positiveness in himself & in others is commensurate. . . . (J, XXI, 82-83)

April 27, 1869

Culture is consecutive & consistent. It is homogeneous. As between two clubs of ball-players, I always expect the most genteel of the two, other things being equal, to win the game. The end of culture is excellence in character & conduct. Where refined men fail in competition with coarse men, it is for want of the power which comes through practice; they have more of the power which comes through principle, so far as principle can be predicted without due . . . practice. The Princeton Students played an admirable game of ball with the Athletics here the other day, & virtually beat them. I left before the last inning, when there was a tie; & at the end of their last inning the collegians made five, &, it is said—being, probably, sure of the game—allowed the Athletics to make six, though excitement & wildness of play. Excitement is, in itself, wildness, as fear is, in itself, frenzy, unless it is firmly suborned to strength. It is the vice of imaginary & nervous temperaments & is common to all classes. I saw that the Princetonians were getting unsteady in the gusto & eagerness of their, otherwise, manly ambition.—They beat the Athletics, last year, & gave early challenges before they disband in May, through graduation. The Athletics accepted; the meaner Atlantics & Mutuals of New York, declined on the score of want of practice—a resolute excuse in a momentous cause, but a pretence, or other selfishness, in a passing game of prowess. However, the collegians were doubtless in incessant practice.—I detail this as a memorandum in the ends of general manly training. Mind & muscle are made for each other . . . The best man is the man of both mind & muscle. . . . (J, XXI, 94-95)

May 4, 1869

The misjudged woman-rights movement is based on the false & abnormal predication that a woman must have, apart from a man, all the prerogatives & privileges of a man; whereas the very ordination of marriage, & this very constitution of the sexes, presupposes & requires a division of prerogative & privilege, as of person & of performance. The men & the women do separate things, but they do them conjointly. The wife works & votes through her husband; the husband keeps house through his wife. The husband & the wife being, morally, one person, one person would have two votes, if each voted. The woman has no more right to be a voter, than to be a warrior. Widows & spinsters must take the misfortune of deprivation in politics as they take it in every thing else. . . . (J, XXI, 114)

May 8, 1869

It does a man service to know who & what his ancestors were. If they were of the right mould, he gains secret self-respect, confidence, purpose of confirmation, & self-identification. If they were deficient, he is specially reminded wherein to be vigilant, cautious,

& active.—Although a man who knows himself will know his ancestors, & although a man who determines to be a man will be a man, whether, or no, his ancestors were manly; yet, his knowledge of them may assist him to take heed against the presumption that he has such and such human traits & tendencies in the background & base of his constitution, merely because he is, apparently, a man in descent . . . for, if his ancestors were unmanlike in any respects, he is put on his guard against trust in imaginary capital, & if they were manlike, he is inspirited by the addition of ancestral piety to personal piety & of filial self-respect to personal self respect.—Genealogy favors moral self-scrutiny. (J, XXI, 126)

May 15, 1869

Men & women will never come in collision & competition on grounds which are common . . . unless they are unsexual in their standpoints. . . . I was reminded of this by standing awhile, yesterday af^n between a fine looking matron, & a pretty girl, whom I took to be the mother & sister of one of the stalwart players at a game of base-ball. The young woman talked rather slangy as well as masculinely, but not intentionally. Feminine women sometimes borrow phrases from men, because they like men, & forget that phraseology is, as men are, in some measure, as sexual, or so allotted, as is dress. I thought it hard that she should talk so; but I did not lose sight of her real femininity, such as it was. . . . (J, XXI, 149-150)

May 26, 1869

Vice seeks beauty, as the worm seeks the flower, to slay it, not to serve it.—On the terms that vice is no novelty to vice, anything which vice has identified with itself is no longer fair & fresh in its regard. The beauty of virtue is piquant & provocative to the lust of vice; but beauty once vitiated is no longer beauty to vice, for vice knows how to pluck, not how to produce, beauty. (J, XXI, 187)

June 24, 1869

There is no morality but marriage.[25] (J, XXI, 267)

[25] Most of Newcomb's philosophy is constructed around this axiom.

July 9, 1869

The bare-footed boys, who trip along the streets, little thinks that their feet are the admiration, the joy, the envy, & the pride of manly observers. They do not see that men of genius gaze at them with delight, & that artists look at them as at models of beauty. . . . It should be remembered, moreover, that dirt is cleansing, &, probably, otherwise hygienical, so that getting dirt on the feet—which can be timely washed—is a good not an evil.—Providence dresses as well as feeds man; & not only morbid, but excessive, care about raiment as about nourishment, is as unnecessary as it is untrustful. It may be doubted whether all close fitting dress is not—beyond all contrary in summer—baneful in respect of excluding the air from the pores of the skin. . . . A long loose robe, loosely belted at the waiste, like a tunic, would serve much normal purposes much better than the present style. It would give better ventillation to the skin. The blanket, as worn by Indians, makes a better over-coat than the French make. . . . (J, XXI, 303-304)

August 4, 1869

It was formerly the saying that walls have ears; yet this was true in a sense which was not thought of, &, hence, not applied to persons as well as to houses. A man's presence proclaims his principles & his opinions. No ambitious thinker can hide his thoughts from his fellows, unless he hides himself; & there is no complete hiding place in the wide universe. Plagiarism is predicable through presence, as well as through publication, so far as plagiarism is predicable at all. (J, XXII, 17-18)

August 12, 1869

He who flees from the world which is evil, despite good in it, flees from the world which is good, despite evil in it. Men are as irrational & insane in attempting to live in solitude, because the world is wrong in many of its practices, as they would be in attempting to live in water because the land around them is not so fertile as it should be. (J, XXII, 44)

August 14, 1869

Yesterday, coming up Broadway, I passed a man, who turned round to eye a woman—who was going into a hall before which he was standing—with the stolid earnestness, on much of the same plane, that I saw the male monkey at Central Park frequently eye the female.[26]—It was the business of lechery, not of love, which sobered his face, & which steadied his form. The monkey's love was not a man's love; but this man's love was a monkey's love. (J, XXII, 48)

August 20, 1869

The good in the evil of drink is not merely cheerfulness but child-likeness, such as each are under that condition. Middle-aged & old men frolic, abandon themselves, take refuge & resource in pleasure & play, & so on, during the incitement of liquor as they would not, being what they, as yet, are, in other states. . . . As drink shows men something of what they should be without drink, in respect of kindliness & animation, so it shows them what they should be, without drink, in respect of innocence & youthfulness. (J, XXII, 61)

September 7, 1869

The dissatisfaction of ill-mated husbands & wives with each other affords a proof of the truth & the good of marriage, inasmuch as it serves to prove that they expected to be, that they expect to be, & that they ought to be, well-mated & happy in marriage. . . . Domestic infelicity is no more argument against wedlock, than dyspepsia is against food. (J, XXII, 97)

September 15, 1869

Sin conspires with solitude, in that it makes a man sole arbiter, in himself, apart from principle, of character & conduct. Its end is as its origin, in self. It induces morbid & excessive thought which, of itself, tends to make a man sullen, apathetic, & cold. It tends to passive reserve, through its hold of voluminous, clueless & labyrinthian speculation. . . . (J, XXII, 114)

---

[26] Newcomb spent some time in New York at Central Park observing the sexual life of the animals.

September 17, 1869

Action is the all of art. Athletes, as it were, awake statues out of stony sleep &, in one, vitalise & mobilise them on the play ground whence they were monumentally reproduced. A brawny fellow, big as Hercules, played statuary as well as cricket to me, the other day, at Camden; & lither & finer forms moved about the wickets, like reanimated Antinouses.[27]—But, as the athlete's action of his person in the arena is far beyond the action of his statue in the gallery; so action as a whole man in the world, is far beyond his action as a mere athlete in the arena. Broad shoulders, sinewy legs, & capacious chests, are for something else than play in the field, just as they are for something else than show in the gallery. It is much to be a beautiful athlete, just as it is much to be a beautiful statue; but a beautiful man of life is the all in all of athletism & of statuary. The end of manly force & beauty is favored, not attained, in gymnastics. The power of man as a lover is the full significance & scope of his power[28] as an athlete, & of his beauty as a show. (J, XXII, 121)

September 22, 1869

A sensual man separates & spoils what should be a manly act, by doing some part of it merely because it feels good to him; a sensuous man saves the full masculinity of his morale by feeling good because, also, he is doing a fully manly act. (J, XXII, 146)

October 3, 1869

Compromising virtue[29] proposes that brothels are the almshouses of benighted love, the hospitals of sick celibacy, & the training-schools of otherwise idle & submerged virility; that, like poor-houses & asylums they are unsightly but, as the world goes, necessary, inasmuch as, amongst previously stated reasons, unmarried women are driven out of their homes, under the modern system of society if they indulge in otherwise wholly unmet & unrequited passion, & saving the fact

[27] Antinoüs was a page of the Emperor Hadrian and was famous for his beauty.
[28] This idea seems to be the foundation of most of Newcomb's praise of "action," "full manly scope," and similar virtues.
[29] At this period Newcomb wrote down several dialogues between "Compromising Virtue" and "Uncompromising Virtue." The latter always had the last word in the debates. They are clearly representative of Newcomb's own inner struggles.

that better arrangements, as in the case of kept mistresses, might be made which would supersede brothels by more convenient & less unnatural methods of housekeeping for courtesans somewhat as, on other terms, almshouses could be superseded by the allotment of paupers to families; that nature had better & rather be abused by illicitness than altered by abstinence . . . that man has the rights & duties of mere nature, like monkies, horses, bulls, & birds, until he has the rights & duties of fully normal nature, or, of grace . . . that cohabitation is a natural, & marriage is an artificial, rite; & so on. *Uncompromising virtue* rejoins that brothels are, indeed, almshouses so far as almshouses are monuments of inert, unmanly, idle, & wretched men, & that they are asylums, so far as asylums are houses of morbid pathology & disease; that every young man & old man can find a mate if he is virtuously & vigorously predisposed & predetermined to do so . . . that arguments for illicitness in case of privation are arguments for cannibalism in cases of starvation . . . that marriage is no more artificial than kindness, industry, cleanliness, temperance, & every other virtue & that it is the central & consummative, whole virtue of all partial virtues. . . . (J, XXII, 185-188)

Everything that man does is in the series & shape, however remote & subordinate, of marriage. Thus, his relations to the earth are somewhat similar to his relations to a woman. He gets from & goes to, the earth. He reaps & plants, plants & reaps. His very discharge of digested food is a sort of impregnative return to the earth. (J, XXII, 190)

November 5, 1869

Out of whatever men delight in, they soon invent a dogma. . . . Corsetism is now openly advocated & recommended in print as doing no harm, & as beneficial to the figure & to corpulency. Some dilettanti of dress wish to wear corsets, or some bloated person wishes to become reduced in plethora, & he presents in a periodical, the doctrine of corsetism, just as some dilettanti of sectarianism wishes to be a ritualist &, accordingly, pleads the doctrine of transubstantiation & of mariolatry. . . . (J, XXII, 321)

November 20, 1869

The facts that nothing exists but through cause & for cause; & that cause is absolute, thorough, & eternal; serve to show the immortality & the general providences of man. If it were worth [while] to create a man, it is worth while to keep him created. Not only, is what is done, done; but also, what is done, is a plane & a pledge of what is to be done. Every living person may reasonably assure himself that, once provided for, he will never be left unprovided for. A playwright can, at will, erase personages out of his dramatic plots; but providence can never dismiss its personages out of its plan of life. Undoing is a sign & a need of crudity, not of completeness. Even a dramatist sees to it, if he has sufficient wit & character, that every one of his personages are maintained in place & performance, on far grander, goodlier, & normaller terms, than once a peer, always a peer —once a man, always a man. (J, XXIII, 36)

November 28, 1869

By ecstasy I always mean, in my disparagement of it, a state of pietistical abstraction & emotionalism. What may be called, by some, ecstatical, in the better sense of the word, is another affair. A life, a chronic condition, a flighty mood, &, in general, a plane of unbalanced, onesided, headlong, encyphelical, infatuous & visionary emotionalism, rapture, quietism, sentimentalism, fanaticism, & sensationalism, & all that sort of thing, is the evil which I designate. (J, XXIII, 79)

January 6, 1870

. . . On the steps of the Academy of Music, last night,[30] awaiting the opening of the doors, beside me, in a little crowd of interesting young, Americanised, Germans & others, stood a dirty, & rather soft looking young man, whose attire made me wonder that he could think of, or afford, going to an opera. The others rather coldly treated him. I did not talk to him, but I resolutely included him[31] in

[30] He heard *William Tell.*
[31] Newcomb's inclusion of the young man seems to have been highly "Transcendental."

the company & gave him some share of notice. This was a good beginning of the pleasant evening within. . . . (J, XXIII, 209)

January 16, 1870

The traditionalising mythologist is less reasonable than rationalising mythologists, in that he expects & desires signs & wonders as proofs of moral truths; but he is more reasonable, in that he expects & desires some sort of unquestionable authority for the extraordinary propositions, plans, relations, & general conduct of mythologism, & abstract pietism. Many, so called, rationalists in sects—as some of the Unitarians—are more sentimental & arbitrary than their more thaumaturgising & literalising brethren, in that they assume, of their own accord & action so called truth & facts, which the common sense of the world confesses & alledges to be beyond the natural & normal cognisance, or assurance of the human mind. . . . (J, XXIII, 237)

January 25, 1870

It is not unlikely that women may have the right of suffrage conferred on them, in some places . . . but, I doubt if the innovation will be maintained, & if it . . . will not fall down of itself. (J, XXIII, 271)

January 27, 1870

These are the rights of women: to have such occupations as will most thoroughly womanise them, & to reciprocate with mates who have been thoroughly masculinised by manly occupations. Men should get most what men can; & women should get most what women can; & each sex should give to the other what each can get. The, so called, strong minded, women should learn with shame the lesson which every group of two trees presents in every landscape—each tree, in order to form a strong & graceful whole, lopping off something which, if retained, would interfere with the scope & semblance of the suited pair. (J, XXIII, 276)

.   .   .

Part of the sweet significances of childhood is its suggestion of natural & normal trust. It takes its dependence on parentalism, & on all providence, easily & contentedly. It asks, seeks, & expects to receive, what it wants. It knows neither, vexation or worriment of care. Its cheerful & active condition is a constant reproach to the morbid distrustful & corrodingly anxious adultism, as well as a constant reminder to all persons of general innocence. (J, XXIII, 277)

March 4, 1870

Men, who know most about a given subject, are generally briefest in discourse about it, because of their tendency to give conclusions, results, & applications, instead of, like others, the processes through which they came to, & are yet on the way to, them; also, because of their correlative preoccupation with the mastery & action of other things, as well as with masterly action of that thing. (J, XXIV, 59)

March 16, 1870

The conflicts of pettiness in penuriousness & in pride could be as graphically as coarsely delineated in the representation of a man going along the street, with a dirty nose, which he was afraid to wipe, when anybody passed him, because he would then betray his possession of a ragged & unwashed handkerchief, & which he did not care to wipe, when nobody passed him, because, then, the condition of his nose would not be seen. (J, XXIV, 111)

April 14, 1870

One of the methods for making strong men, is to make strong women. . . . There was much true cunning in the Indian custom of making porters & laborers of women; for, though the untutored males saw no farther than the keeping of himself strong, for hunting & fighting, they therein . . . procured young men strong, through the active & able constitutions of both parents. A man is far more complacent at meeting young women with heavy bundles of wood on their heads, or with heavy baskets of coal & of meat on their arms, than at seeing, already spoilt, pampered, oversized women riding in carriages, or waddling along fashionable promenades in fashionable swaddling-clothes.—Yesterday af^n, I met two little girls with baskets of coal, resting on the railway-side, one of whom, with some humor, however seriously, asked me to carry her coal for her up to the street.

I saw she was not distressed, & I refused to mar her exercise, telling her it would do her good. (J, XXIV, 212)

April 17, 1870

The theory that the human family is a lineal development & descendant of the animal family, is additionally refuted by the patent fact that the monkeys, apes, & other alledged progenitors of mankind exist to this day, & show no sign of ending their kinds in the shapes & souls of men & women. A series in the forms of creation, is another affair from a series in the ancestries of creation. As a Caucassian is above an African, so an African is above a monkey; but the African no more comes out of the monkey, than the Caucassian comes out of the African. (J, XXIV, 226)

April 22, 1870

The sphere is part of the scope of a mourning man,[32] & he must keep to it. Badly off as he may seem to be on the best plane & in the best place that he sees, or thinks, he can get, he must abide there, or he will lose what prospect & chance he has. . . . (J, XXIV, 242)

April 26, 1870

The greater happiness of horses under african riders is always notable. Both of them are nearer nature than are white men. (J, XXIV, 258)

May 12, 1870

As the appropriation of food feeds man by means of his organs of digestion, so the attainment of it feeds him by means of his organs of mobility. Before the eating of his harvested crops make blood for the farmer in autumn, the planting, hoeing, & reaping of them have made muscle for him, throughout spring & summer. . . . (J, XXIV, 320)

July 10, 1870

During the Kyrie Eleison, at the Cathedral, today, while pre-

[32] Mourning, that is, for his lack of a wife and home. It is in this sense that Newcomb ordinarily uses the word.

postured for the special imprecation of mercy, the fact that, in some respects, ceremonial worship was an art, & was an artificial affair, was suggested to me by my sense that all the mercy which could be mine was already at my disposal, & that all this ritualistical pomp, poetry, music, rhetoric, was an extra performance like an operatical drama, a stage performance, an allegorical masquerade, & a symbolical spectacle.—This did not impair its relative truth & use, such as it was, any more than etiquette in society, & ceremony in war, impairs sociality, & soldiership. (J, XXV, 195)

October 6, 1870

Firmness is essential to force; but it is a poor force which depends on firmness, only or chiefly, for general condition & conduct. Many a old man, & even many a young man finds himself palpably feeble as well as flat, the instant that he merely relaxes his firmness, because he has previously relied too much upon it for action & appearance. Factitious stiffness will uphold an unsubstantial man, in some sort, somewhat as starch will give seeming consistency & strength to a flimsy & frail piece of cloth; but in the one case, as in the other, the first searching occasion betrays the adventitious secret to everybody who has not known it before.—I know a young man,[33] in whom I am much interested, who, against all my protestation, warning, & exculpation, has set himself down to excessive & extra labor as a book-keeper, through his determined ambition to become a head & master. I tell him that rank & that money are nothing, without manhood & honor; that drudgery is dishonorable & unmanly. . . . Excessive toil is virtual & moral miserliness, in that over-workers sacrifice pleasure, power & practiveness to abstract ambition, as misers sacrifice it to abstract covetousness; the former err with labor, as the latter err with money.—Men, indeed, must so far conform to the world as to keep in it, & as to be of it; but they must, as they can, so conform as not to lose completely manly ends & condition.— Wise love for others will insure wise life with others; & wise love of manhood will insure wise manliness of life. (J, XXVI, 34-35)

[33] This young man is almost the only friend Newcomb mentions in the later part of his sojourn in Philadelphia.

October 13, 1870

Many a man gets to be fifty years old, before he learns the splendid lesson, so as to believe in it, & to ply it at heart, that, through manly faith & action, manly vigor makes manly virtue a most practical blessing—& some men never learn it.—Resolution is one of the preconditions of vital resource. To be, & to do, a man's most is, indeed, a recipe of great account.—When a man determinately puts his foot down, & says,—knowing what he says & what he designs,—"I will, henceforth, & now, be cautious & energetic in all manly strength & scope," he gives promise of a most incrementative plane & performance. He cannot be, thereafter, whatever he has been, morbid, passive, & ineffective. (J, XXVI, 50-51)

October 26, 1870

The fact that love lives by means of giving, & that it gives by giving essentially of itself, is attested in the fact that the beauty of a man is, palpably, his masculinity & reproductiveness. All regard of his sturdy & splendid shape, by women, &, even, by men, is a regard of its virile power & purpose. No regard, however abstract, of any athlete is so abstract as to exclude all admiration of his morale as a male. The beauty of woman is, also, palpably, in the eyes of men, & even of women, her sexual symmetry & significance. (J, XXVI, 84)

November 4, 1870

. . . Kepler kept his eye on fact, & threw away hypothesis after hypothesis, as so much fiction, when it could not stand the test of fact. After sixteen years of intense toil he had on hand an hypothesis which accorded with fact, but which he had nearly thrown aside, because of a blunder merely in his reckoning. He perseveringly applied himself to it over again, &, finding his mistake, found it to be the true one. Before he found out his laws, he had faith in the existence of laws. Sixteen years' strain could not but have fetched a true germ of thought.—But the stars studded the skies in vain to astronomers so far as they gave up their lives to the mere study of them; for they fulfilled their ends, whether or no the secret of their piane & procedure was known by man. (J, XXVI, 100)

APPENDIX

A List of Books in which Newcomb Is Mentioned

BROOKS, VAN WYCK. *The Flowering of New England, 1815-1865.* New York, 1936.
———. *The Life of Emerson.* New York, 1932.
BROWN UNIVERSITY. *The Historical Catalogue of Brown University, 1764-1934.* Providence, 1936.
BROWN UNIVERSITY. Registrar. *Record of Standing, Absences, and Term Marks of Students.* 1827-1907.
BROWN UNIVERSITY. United Brothers' Society. *Constitution and Records for 1811-1865.* (Newcomb's name occurs in the pages covering the meetings which took place in 1833-1837.)
BROWNSON, O. A. *The Spirit-Rapper, an Autobiography.* Boston, 1854.
BURRAGE, HENRY S., comp. *Brown University in the Civil War.* Providence, 1868.
BURTON, KATHERINE. *Paradise Planters.* London, 1939.
CODMAN, J. T. *Brook Farm: Historic and Personal Memoir.* Boston, 1894.
COOKE, GEORGE W. "Brook Farm," in *New England Magazine,* n.s. vol. XXVII (1897), p. 391-407.
———. *An Historical and Biographical Introduction to Accompany the Dial.* Cleveland, 1902.
CURTIS, G. W. *Early Letter of George Wm. Curtis to John S. Dwight,* ed. by G. W. Cooke. New York, 1898.
EMERSON, RALPH WALDO. "Brook Farm."
———. *Journals,* ed. by E. W. Emerson and W. E. Forbes. Boston, 1909-1914.
———. *The Letters,* ed. by Ralph L. Rusk. New York, 1939.
HARASZTI, ZOLTÁN. *The Idyll of Brook Farm as Revealed by Unpublished Letters in the Boston Public Library.* Boston, 1937.
HAWTHORNE, NATHANIEL. *The American Notebooks,* ed. by Randall Stewart. New Haven, 1932.
[KIRBY, GEORGIANNA BRUCE] "Reminiscences of Brook Farm," in *Old and New,* vols. III (1871), p. 175-185, 425-438; IV (1871), p. 347-358; V (1872), p. 517-530.
KUNITZ, STANLEY J., and HAYCRAFT, HOWARD. *American Authors, 1600-1900.* New York, 1938.
LATHROP, ROSE H. *Memories of Hawthorne.* Boston, 1898.
ORVIS, MARIANNE (DWIGHT). *Letters from Brook Farm, 1844-1847,* ed. by Amy L. Reed. Poughkeepsie, 1928.
OSSOLI, SARAH MARGARET (FULLER). *Memoirs.* Boston, 1852.

SEARS, JOHN VAN DER ZEE. *My Friends at Brook Farm.* New York, [c1912].

SCHLESINGER, ARTHUR M. *Orestes A. Brownson, a Pilgrim's Progress.* Boston, 1939.

SEDGWICK, ORA (GANNETT). "A Girl of Sixteen at Brook Farm," in *Atlantic Monthly,* vol. LXXXV (1900), p. 394-404.

SPICER, WILLIAM A. *History of the Ninth and Tenth Regiments Rhode Island Volunteers.* Providence, 1892.

STERN, MADELEINE B. *The Life of Margaret Fuller.* New York, 1942.

SWIFT, LINDSAY. *Brook Farm: Its Members, Scholars and Visitors.* New York, 1900.

THOREAU, H. D. *The Writings . . . Journal,* ed. by Bradford Torrey. Boston, 1906. Vol. VII.

WADE, MASON. *Margaret Fuller, Whetstone of Genius.* New York 1940.

INDEX OF NAMES

in

Selections from the Journals of Charles King Newcomb